PRAISE FOR HANDLE YOUR PURPOSE

"It's not just about the finish line. It's the journey that gives it meaning. When you see each challenge as part of that journey, you'll discover the strength to keep going."

— NORDINE ZOUAREG, 2X Mr. Universe, Mr. World, and Mr. Europe, bodybuilding champion, best-selling author of InnerFitness, and host of the No-Limits Life iHeartRadio podcast.

"Jonathan challenges us to stop waiting for the 'perfect' time and start making every moment count, one intentional step at a time."

— DR. DELPHINA JOYCE AVILA, Founder & CEO of Journey Options YouChoose© and national inspirational speaker.

"By focusing on the time we have and taking purposeful steps toward our goals, we can face even the toughest setbacks with a confident mindset, one that empowers us to overcome challenges and reach new milestones."

— DONALD OSTHEIMER, President of Test Solutions & Asset Consulting LLC.

Paperback: 978-1-951475-46-8
Hardcover: 978-1-951475-47-5
Ebook: 978-1-951475-48-2

Library of Congress Control Number: 2025919898
First paperback edition February 2026

Any references to historical events, real people, or real places are used fictitiously. Names, characters, and places are products of the author's imagination.

Cover Art and Interior by Amanda Blake Design

Arrow Press Publishing
Charleston, SC
www.arrowpresspublishing.com
info@arrowpresspublishing.com

HANDLE YOUR PURPOSE

How Purpose Revealed Through Small Choices Changes Everything

JONATHAN MATEI

To Karena Kilcoyne

Knowing you as a friend and witnessing the strength it took to overcome your childhood fears and anxiety has motivated me to reach milestones in my own life.

—

To Roy Hurly Lukens

Your friendship, influence, and example, as a retired U.S. Navy veteran and successful entrepreneur, has opened doors to incredible people and led to a life-changing Bible study we now share. When you invited me to that business seminar in February 2023, the idea behind this book was born.

CONTENTS

Preface   9

Foreword   13

Introduction: Where It Started   17

One Box at a Time   31

Commitment Brings Results   53

Handle Your Thoughts Before
Distractions Divide Your Attention   79

How Deep Breathing Can
Help You Regain Mental Focus   133

A Simple Decision That Creates Momentum   147

Lost Time   161

Turning Uncertainty Into Results   209

Take Charge of Your Time   241

The Power of Showing Up Each Day   257

Pruning Dead Branches   283

A Lonely Dream   305

Efficient Time with God   321

One Conversation at a Time   349

Conclusion   361

Notes and reliable sources   365

PREFACE

As the author, I want to clear up any confusion that might come up for readers along the way. This book is not solely about my experience as a package delivery driver, although many of the insights and principles were shaped during my time there. I also draw on earlier life experiences and examples from others. My time as a delivery driver played a big role in shaping this book, so expect other topics and lessons to show up throughout these pages as it continues.

I've always been the kind of person who looks beyond what's in front of me. Over the years, I've watched the people around me, friends and coworkers, live believing that tomorrow isn't possible. Not in the sense of survival, but in the sense of achieving something greater, something beyond themselves. I've seen people settle, not because they weren't capable, but because they believed they weren't. That's where this book was born.

I first started writing as an author on April 18th, 2019, and from the very beginning, the ones who doubted me weren't strangers. They were the people who knew me best, the ones who loved me, the ones who wanted to protect me. They've seen your strengths, your struggles, your habits, and your patterns. Their wisdom comes from experience, and their caution often comes from a place of love.

Just as a tree is rooted in the ground, its branches still reach toward the sky. That's where things get difficult. Sometimes, the people who know you best can also be the ones who hold you back, not because they don't believe in you, but because they think they already know your limits. They see you as an extension of themselves, of what's familiar, of what's been done before. When you try to step into something bigger, something beyond what meets their eye, their first instinct is to pull you back to safety.

That's not a bad thing. Wisdom and caution are valuable. There comes a time when you must decide for yourself. You must handle your purpose, not in defiance, not in rebellion, but in responsibility. Your future is yours to build. It's not about proving anyone wrong; it's about proving to yourself that you can go further.

This isn't just a book about chasing goals or accomplishing dreams. It's about you. It's about stepping outside the limitations that have been placed on you by your surroundings, by tradition, by the voices that say, this is just how life is.

That's what culture is: it's your version of normal.

Culture is just a mindset that has seen the way things have been done for so long that they start to feel normal, good or bad. It is often influenced by the people you choose to surround yourself with. You don't have to inherit their doubts. You don't have to carry their fears. You don't have to repeat their patterns.

It's often said that you're born looking like your parents, but you die looking like your decisions. Every choice you make shapes the person you become. If you want more for your life, it starts with choosing differently. It starts with creating a new culture for yourself.

For me, choosing differently meant stepping into something bigger than myself. In doing so, I lost people. Not because I wanted to, but because they couldn't come with me. The higher you climb, the more parts of the journey fall away. Much like a rocket launching into space, the higher it goes, the more pieces detach, because they weren't built for that altitude.

Some people in your life aren't meant to go where you're going, and that's okay because some will leave on their own, others you'll have to let go, but the journey will always be worth it.

This book is here to serve you. I know I share a lot of personal experiences, but this isn't just about me. It's about showing you that your future is possible, that your purpose is now, and that your potential is greater than you realize.

If you feel stuck, if you feel like you're surrounded by people who don't believe in what you're trying to do, if you feel like your dreams are too big for the life you were born into, then this book is for you. The truth is, you are capable of more than you think. It's time to step into it.

FOREWORD

In a world that constantly urges us to hustle harder, plan further ahead, and chase after what's next, *Handle Your Purpose* invites us to do something radically different: pause, take a breath, and return with peace.

When Jonathan first shared the heart of this manuscript with me, I was immediately moved, not just by the stories within it, but by the mindset behind them. As someone who has worked across education, leadership, and emotional wellness, I've seen firsthand how powerful it can be when people begin to live deliberately, not reactively. This book doesn't offer surface-level motivation. It delivers something deeper: a grounded framework for living with intention, no matter where you come from or what season you're in.

Jonathan's story begins with the ordinary rhythm of packages in, packages out. As you'll soon discover, it's within this rhythm that he finds something extraordinary. He learns to see the value in what most of us overlook: the moment in front of us. Whether you're a student, a parent, a leader, or a delivery driver, the invitation remains the same. Handle your moments with care, because they shape your life.

I deeply relate to this message. As a cancer survivor, former executive leader, and now founder of Journey Options YouChoose™ (JOY), my life has been a series of unexpected turns. In each pivot, I've discovered the same truth Jonathan describes: your power is in the present. The future may be uncertain, but the next moment is yours to steward.

JOY means journey options you choose. It is rooted in your free will, which means your ability to choose your path, even in the face of challenge. JOY begins with mindset. Get your mind in order, and all else will follow.

What makes this book different is its practicality. Jonathan teaches readers how to move from doubt to discipline, from scattered thoughts to focused presence. His "What if it does work?" mindset flips fear on its head. His use of high-performance habits, like the five-minute rule and micro-decisions, makes productivity feel possible. His insight on worry vs. concern is worth the read. He helps us understand how worry divides our attention and weakens our steps, while concern strengthens our focus and positions us to act with wisdom.

Each chapter feels like a conversation with a trusted friend. Jonathan's voice is authentic. He speaks from the trenches of real life, where purpose and pressure collide. That's what makes this book so relatable. It's not about chasing perfection. It's about reclaiming peace in the chaos, choosing purpose over distraction, and learning how to lead your own life, one choice at a time.

In my work, I train leaders in what I call the JOY Mindset: a framework centered around wholistic wellness, resilience, values-driven action, and self-leadership. Reading this manuscript, I recognized a kindred message. Jonathan doesn't just talk about growth; he walks it out, moment by moment. He reminds us that the biggest shifts don't come from grand gestures, but rather from small, consistent, intentional choices.

If you're holding this book in your hands, consider it a sign. You don't have to wait for a "better" time to change your life. You don't need perfect conditions to move forward. Everything you need is already here, in this moment, in your mindset, and in the choices you make today. Jonathan's story will show you how.

May this book become a trusted guide on your journey. May it give you the peace to stop drifting, the courage to start choosing, and the wisdom to recognize that your greatest power is found in the now.

With Gratitude and JOY,

Dr. Delphina Joyce Avila
Messenger of JOY
Founder & CEO, Journey Options YouChoose™(JOY)
Author, Speaker, Leadership Trainer

www.JOYOptions.org
@JOYOptionsYouChoose | @MessengerofJOY

INTRODUCTION: WHERE IT STARTED

IN 2007, seventh grade at Marley Park Elementary School in Surprise, Arizona, was the year I could never forget. Mr. Gregovich was my math teacher, and one thing that always stands out when I think about that time is the old TV mounted in the top-left corner of the classroom. It was a bulky television sitting on a platform attached to the wall, where the school's morning announcements played.

I'm sure a lot of people my age—millennials—remember those TVs in classrooms. Back then, students were selected on a rotating basis to make announcements and read daily updates for the entire campus. These students were often members of the student council, a group of elected representatives responsible for organizing events, voicing student concerns, and fostering school spirit. Being chosen to do the morning announcements was a small but significant role, giving students a sense of responsibility and a chance to develop public speaking skills.

Every morning, we'd start by standing up, placing our right hand over our heart, and reciting the Pledge of Allegiance. Then we'd sit down and listen to the students on the screen go over school events, reminders, and anything else on the schedule.

What really made Mr. Gregovich's class memorable wasn't just the TV; it was the giant stuffed SpongeBob SquarePants toy sitting right next to it. It was such a strange contrast. Here was this strict, no-nonsense educator, a man in his mid-forties with a master's degree in mathematics who carried himself with authority, yet he had this huge SpongeBob plush sitting right there in the classroom. It almost didn't fit his personality.

Mr. Gregovich was the kind of teacher students were a little afraid of. He was serious about his subject, expected discipline, and didn't tolerate nonsense. Then there was SpongeBob. It was almost like two completely different sides of him coexisted, namely the disciplined mathematician and the guy who secretly loved cartoons.

Another thing I remember about him was his right eye. It wasn't aligned with the other one; it bulged slightly, making it noticeable. My friend Logan Murphy and I would sometimes whisper about it in class, making silly comments like immature kids do, until Mr. Gregovich would catch us and shoot us a look that shut us up really quickly.

School was always difficult for me. It felt impossible to keep up. No matter how hard I tried, I just couldn't grasp math. It wasn't just one subject; I was failing nearly everything, especially reading and writing. My grades were always low, and no matter how often I told myself I'd do better, I never seemed to get there.

Logan, on the other hand, was smart and naturally confident in class. He picked up on things quickly, always ahead of the game, while I sat there drowning in confusion. It felt like I was stuck in this cycle, always behind, always the kid who didn't get it.

Parent-teacher conferences were the worst. Nothing terrified me more than sitting in a near-empty classroom in the evening, just me, my parents, and my teacher, while they discussed how badly I was doing. I can still hear Mr. Gregovich telling my dad that I wasn't paying attention, that my grades were low, that I just wasn't present.

I remember the way my dad reacted, extremely frustrated and disappointed, making it clear that I wasn't living up to his expectations. Those nights stuck with me. The feeling of walking into that room, knowing I had failed, with the sense that my dad would be upset and physically punish me when I got home, was a weight that never left.

Then high school came around, and I told myself, *this is my chance.* It was 2009 and I had just started at Valley Vista High School in Surprise, Arizona. It felt like an opportunity to hit the reset button, and to finally take things seriously. I was older now, and I figured this was the time to step up, to get my act together. I chose to believe that this was the moment everything would change, and that somehow, I could shake off my past struggles and start fresh. Maybe, just maybe, I could do well this time.

I remember walking into my first math class in high school, and just like that, yet again...another math class. I don't know what it was about math, but those classes always seemed to have the strictest teachers, the kind who were most intense, demanding, and always the hardest on me. No other subject gave me as much anxiety as math, and this time was no different.

My teacher, Mr. Benjamin, was a retired Air Force veteran who drove a silver 1997 Corvette, and the moment I saw him, I knew this was going to be rough. He reminded me so much of Mr. Gregovich from two years earlier, which was terrible. Just like Gregovich, he carried himself with a sense of authority that made him intimidating. He had this habit of pounding on the newly integrated electronic whiteboard, the kind that had recently replaced the old overhead projectors, as he wrote. He was a fast writer, almost aggressive with the interactive marker, with numbers and formulas appearing out of nowhere at a speed I couldn't keep up with. Sometimes he would talk while writing on the board so fast that nothing would show up at first, it looked like he was writing on air until the white screen finally caught up and everything appeared a second later.

Unlike Gregovich, he didn't have a bulging eye. Instead, he was deaf in one ear. After working around fighter jet engines for over twenty years, he had lost part of his hearing.

Everything about that class was a nightmare for me. I was the quietest person in the room, sitting in the back, just trying to survive. I never spoke unless I had to. I never raised my hand. My entire goal was to blend in and not be noticed.

Of course, that's not how things work, because students in the back typically get picked on more than those in the front row.

One day, during a very long lecture on solving linear equations, Mr. Benjamin went on about math problems, writing equations on the board, breaking down formulas, and explaining concepts that, to me, sounded like a foreign language. I looked at the board, but I wasn't really listening. The words, the numbers, and the explanations all blurred together into nothing. The audio felt muffled, like the indistinct chatter of a conversation I wasn't part of. I'd space out, lost in my own thoughts, barely aware of what was happening in the room. I just wasn't paying attention. Honestly, deep down, I didn't care.

Then, out of nowhere, what got my attention was when he stopped talking.

Mr. Benjamin started pacing the room slowly, with his arms crossed, one hand on his chin, looking down at the floor, deep in thought. He wasn't just picking someone at random; he was hunting. His eyes scanned the room, his steps slow and deliberate.

"Alright," he finally said. "I'm going to call on someone I don't usually call on."

I froze. My body heated up instantly. I could feel my pulse pounding in my ears. I knew exactly who he was going to call on. I was the quietest person in the room and had somehow dodged his attention for months, and now it was my turn.

He paused for a moment, almost dragging it out for dramatic effect. Then, in a loud, sharp voice, he said, "Jon."

It felt like my blood froze the second I heard my name. My face turned red-hot, my breath caught in my throat, and my blood pressure spiked so high I thought I might pass out. To make it even worse, everyone in the room turned to look at me, their heads shifting back like dominoes. Then came the moment I dreaded the most, the question. He pointed at the whiteboard and asked me to solve some kind of Japanese math problem, one I had absolutely no clue how to answer. I stared at it, my mind completely blank. The heat rose in my face, my hands started sweating, and my throat tightened. The students kept looking at me, waiting for my answer, which only made it worse.

I replied with my answer, and it was, "Uh... well... I mean... um..."

That was all I could get out. It was humiliating. I had nothing to say. I could hear a few people snickering. My ears were ringing. My mind was racing, searching for anything—anything at all—that I could say to make it seem like I had some kind of clue, but I didn't, and I was stuck. Mr. Benjamin sighed, nodded slightly, and moved on to someone else. Once I was off the hook and the attention shifted away, my entire body turned cold, like a rush of freezing air had saturated me. The damage was done, and I sat there, feeling completely exposed. I hated math, I hated this class, and I hated the way it made me feel.

Then, something completely unexpected happened later that year. It was near the end of the school year, and a buzz had started in the classroom. A conversation in the back caught my attention. Alfonso was the guy who sat behind me, one of the cool kids and laid-back type, was talking about arm wrestling. A couple of guys—John Spoonmore (the football player) and Nick—were also laughing, tossing jokes around, but the moment I heard the words, I perked up.

I had always loved arm wrestling. It was one of the few things I was good at. So, I turned around and said, "Hey, I can arm wrestle you."

Alfonso looked at me, surprised, but then grinned. "Alright, sure."

Just like that, word started spreading. People started paying attention. Suddenly, this random conversation had turned into a class-wide scene. The same class where I had spent the entire year embarrassed, failing, and quiet was now buzzing with excitement. Then, the craziest thing happened. Mr. Benjamin, the teacher whom I feared the most, the one who had humiliated me earlier in the year, actually stepped in to lead the match. He walked over, placed his hands over ours, and made sure we were appropriately positioned.

Then he counted down.

"Three... two... one... go!" I slammed Alfonso's hand down instantly. The class erupted. People laughed, cheered, even pulled out their phones. Then, I noticed something, and because I was facing the back of the room, I had a clear view of the door. The classroom door had a window, and through it, I saw someone watching. It was a girl, standing just outside, maybe Alfonso's girlfriend, waiting for him. She had just witnessed me beat him. It was only minutes before class let out, so maybe that's why she was there. Some classes ended a little earlier than others. That was the funniest part of all.

Alfonso groaned, shook his head, and said, "Alright, one more time! I wasn't ready."

So, we reset. Once again, Mr. Benjamin positioned our hands and counted down. "Three... two... one... go!" Right away, I could tell he was only relying on his arm for strength. His shoulders were tense, but the leverage from his torso wasn't there, and that's when I began to gain control. Once again, I won, and the class went wild with laughter, and it turned into one of the funniest memories from that year. I had spent the entire year struggling, failing, and feeling out of place, but for once, I finally felt like the cool kid in class. Just as the excitement settled, the bell rang, and reality hit again. I packed up my stuff and went off to my next class... where I would struggle all over again. At first, everything about high school felt refreshing. There was more flexibility, more freedom, and it felt like I was stepping into new ground, but something deep inside of me didn't feel right. It felt like I was lacking purpose.

I began to think that maybe this was just my reality. Maybe I was destined to be the guy who never figured it out. I imagined myself at thirty, forty, even fifty years old. Still failing, still stuck, and still lost. I was convinced that my struggles in school meant I would struggle in life. That's just how it felt; like I wasn't only bad at math, I was failing at everything, until something finally changed.

It took years, well beyond high school and even beyond college, but something finally clicked. The turning point came in 2020, when I started working as a residential delivery driver. That job, which on the surface seemed like nothing more than handling boxes all day, ended up being where I learned one of the biggest lessons of my life. I began to understand something about disappointment and expectation. For so long, I had been setting expectations for myself without even realizing it. Every time I tried to achieve something, whether it was studying for a test, turning in an assignment, or any other task, I was expecting to succeed. I believed that if I put in the effort, I would get the result I wanted.

Missing those expectations repeatedly made me feel like a constant failure. I set mental deadlines, convincing myself that I had to accomplish something by a certain point. When I missed that invisible target, the disappointment hit me like a ton of bricks. Then, I asked myself a simple, unexpected question that would completely change my life: *What if I reversed it?*

What if I expected challenges ahead of me instead of just hoping to be good at something? What if I started factoring in obstacles from the beginning? Instead of assuming everything would go smoothly, what if I acknowledged that setbacks were part of the process? That way, when difficulties came, when I struggled, got confused, or hit roadblocks along the way, I wouldn't be devastated. I would be ready. I had already anticipated it. I wasn't disappointed when it happened; I knew it was approaching.

When you expect challenges in advance, your expectations remain intact, and disappointment becomes nearly impossible. This mindset doesn't just prevent frustration; it keeps you focused and moving forward without getting sidetracked. That shift in mindset changed everything for me. It didn't mean I was filling my mind with negativity. I was simply being mindful, acknowledging the potential challenges while still reaching for something meaningful. It was like living on two spectrums at once: trying to be good at something and accomplish it, while also recognizing the challenges that were going to come.

In a way, those two forces fueled each other. Knowing the roadblocks ahead didn't make me negative; it pushed me to ask: *How far am I willing to go despite them?* I started approaching life differently. I didn't just aim for goals; I learned to anticipate the struggles that would come with them. Most importantly, I began to understand that every single moment I had was mine to claim. Every moment, good or bad, belonged to me.

For years, I let moments slip away, failing to recognize their value. I believed the moment didn't belong to me simply because I wasn't winning, but that wasn't true. Even the struggles and failures belonged to me; the only difference was whether I chose to handle them. That's what this book is about. It's about understanding that every single moment is yours. It's not just *a* moment and it's not just *the* moment; it's *your* own, to invest in, and to build something life-changing, something you can personalize and shape into a reflection of who you are and the future you're creating with every moment that passes. Whether it's a season of struggle or a season of achievement, it belongs to you. The key is learning how to own it. How to embrace both the wins and the losses. How to shift your mindset so that even the obstacles become part of your journey forward.

Looking back, I never would have imagined that the kid who struggled through school and failed repeatedly would grow into someone capable of running multiple businesses, saving money, and mentoring others. Yet, here I am, now in my thirties, with even people older than myself turning to me for guidance. Some of those people include teachers, entrepreneurs, and business owners—the very people I once feared—now come to me for advice.

It's incredible to see how what once felt like my greatest weakness has become my greatest strength. I used to think my struggles defined me. Now, I see that they shaped me, because I renewed my perspective. I believe the same is true for you. Wherever you are in life, and whatever challenges you're facing, I hope this book helps you see that you're not alone. That your struggles aren't the end of your story, but instead it's a sign that you're choosing not to procrastinate, making the most of your time by valuing each second and minute instead of waiting on perfect days to come.

A MESSAGE JUST FOR YOU

Life has a way of piling up on us, with responsibilities, deadlines, and daily tasks stacking higher and higher until it feels like we're drowning in them. No matter how well we plan or how organized we try to be, the sheer weight of everything at once can feel overwhelming. I've been there. I remember standing in the back of my delivery truck, staring at hundreds of packages stacked from floor to ceiling. No matter how carefully I planned my route, the sight of it was always overwhelming.

The second I focused on the sheer number of stops, the weight of the bigger boxes, and the ones that had tumbled off the shelves, I felt stuck. It seemed impossible to get through. When I stopped looking at the mass of boxes in front of me and instead focused on just one at a time, everything changed. Delivering one package, then moving on to the next, made the entire process faster. It turned an overwhelming task into something simple and manageable.

No matter who you are or what you do, life can feel like a large truck overwhelmed with packages, a never-ending list of tasks, people to care for, and responsibilities pulling you in a hundred different directions. When you learn how to focus on just one moment at a time, everything becomes clearer, the stress becomes more manageable, and you find your rhythm. Instead of feeling stuck, you start moving forward. This message is about helping you do exactly that.

WHY THIS MATTERS TO YOU

We're all given the same amount of time every day, which is 24 hours, 1,440 minutes, or 86,400 seconds. Most of those seconds slip away unnoticed because we're too busy rushing from one thing to the next. It often feels like there's never enough time. The pressure to keep up can leave us feeling exhausted and drained, hoping to make it to the weekend. What if the time you need is already there? What if you just haven't been seeing it?

When you start handling your moment and taking control of how you move through your day, something shifts. Instead of feeling like time is against you, you start working with it. You stop getting lost in the big picture and begin focusing on the moments that matter most. Here's the truth: small moments only lead to big change if you claim them intentionally.

We often think that the only way to feel in control is to clear our schedule, finish every task on our to-do list, or build the perfect system. The real key is learning to use the time you already have, but differently and better. This isn't about getting rid of responsibilities. It's about reclaiming the moments in between.

- The seconds waiting in line at the store
- The quiet moments right after waking up
- The urge to scroll endlessly on your phone

Those seconds are already there. You don't need more time. You just need to see the time that's slipping by unnoticed and take it back.

HOW THIS BOOK WILL HELP

The ideas in this book aren't just theories. They're practical shifts you can make today through small, simple adjustments that create a real impact on your daily life. When you start living one moment at a time, you'll notice five big changes:

1. **You'll Feel More in Control**
   When you feel overwhelmed, it's usually because you're trying to juggle everything at once. When you shift your focus to what's in front of you, you regain a sense of control. Instead of reacting to life, you start choosing how to move through it.

2. **You'll Feel Less Rushed (Without Changing Your Schedule)**
   Most of us think we don't have enough time. The truth is, we miss out on countless unnoticed minutes every day by worrying about things we can't control.
   When you slow down just enough to *notice* these moments, your entire day starts to feel less chaotic, less rushed, and more intentional, even if your schedule stays the same.

3. **You'll Start Noticing What Actually Matters**

   The problem with living on autopilot is that we miss the small things, like the things that make life meaningful. When you start handling your moments, every day becomes more alive. A simple conversation becomes something you actually *listen* to. A quiet pause between tasks becomes a chance to breathe. Even the busiest days feel more balanced and fulfilling.

4. **You'll Stop Feeling Stuck**

   We've all been there at one point, where we are facing so much at once that we don't even know where to begin. The way to get through it isn't by thinking about everything at once. It's by choosing one thing, one task, one moment, and one small action. When you stop focusing on the whole mountain and start taking it one step at a time, everything becomes easier.

5. **You'll Feel Like You're Living, Not Just Surviving**

   When you reclaim your moments, you stop feeling like you're just getting through the day. Instead, you begin to experience it.

The goal isn't to do more, but instead it's to live with more intention. That's exactly why this book was written. Whether you're balancing a job, raising a family, working toward a goal, or just trying to find a better rhythm in life, you deserve to feel present, in control, and at peace with your time. You don't need to change your whole life overnight. You don't need more hours in the day. You just need to start claiming the time that's already yours. One moment at a time. Every second that passes is an opportunity that can expand into something greater than you ever imagined.

What will you do with the time that's already yours?

ONE BOX AT A TIME

*Great things are not done by impulse, but by a
series of small things brought together.*

— VINCENT VAN GOGH

CHAOS ERUPTED in my residential delivery truck, packages tumbling like an avalanche. Boxes fell off the shelves, cluttering what little aisle space remained. I could barely move.

Would I make it home on time for my family's Christmas Eve party after working all day?

I wasn't so sure.

As I drove across a street cross-pan, another box came tumbling off the shelves, adding to the chaos. I glanced back at my cargo, and it was a total disaster. This was after I had sorted the boxes and made sure to drive slowly to avoid exactly this kind of mess. It was almost 4 p.m., and I thought to myself, *I'll never get through all these boxes in time,* especially the large furniture boxes stacked in the back of the 18-foot-bed P1000 aluminum step van. I made it to my next residential stop, thankful to subtract one package from this disastrous cargo mess. I approached the 2500 section, a designated shelf area near the front of the cargo space inside the truck to locate the package with the 2518LP, which was a large package identified by the SID logistics sticker code on the box, but I couldn't find it. Everything became even more overwhelming.

After nearly ten minutes of searching, the package still eluded me. The PackageRoute computer map indicated it was a giant floor box, yet it was nowhere in sight. On this Christmas Eve, racing through my sleigh, I frantically searched for that one crucial delivery, fearing that if I didn't find it, I might shatter a child's holiday joy. I couldn't let that happen. Not this year. Climbing over a mountain of boxes back to the driver's seat, I told myself, *Maybe I'll find it later and get it delivered before 8 p.m.* Just as I reached the front cabin, the resident's garage door opened. A man stepped outside and started walking toward my truck as he expected his delivery. *How do I explain that I can't find it?*

He approached with a smile and asked, "How are you, sir?"

"Living the dream, well, more like a nightmare dream. But hey, I've got my sense of humor as my survival kit for the day," I replied. The man laughed. I didn't. I couldn't leave now; the man was standing right beside my door, watching and waiting for his package. I had hoped he wouldn't show up at the wrong time, because honestly, delivery driving can be a stressful job. Especially when you're doing it alone. Sometimes, when frustration builds up, you just need to let it out. Maybe even shout a little. I really didn't want to do that with him standing there—listening.

My mind couldn't stop stressing about the hundreds of boxes still in front of me. There was no way I could finish everything today. After more searching, my foot caught between two heavy boxes as I walked back toward the front of the cargo area, and I fell, hard onto the cold metal floor.

The man peeked his head through the side door. "Are you okay?"

"No," I replied. Lying there, I looked up, and there it was. The package I'd been searching for all along: a mini electric Jeep for kids. What a surprise. It had been right in front of me the entire time. In that moment, it felt like the box had won, not just the battle, but the entire war. After all the searching, the falling, and frustration, I finally found it. Now, I had to hand it over like a defeated soldier surrendering his weapon. I wanted to pound that box into the ground, to settle things once and for all. With the customer watching, all I could do was pass it over with a forced nod, knowing full well...

This fight wasn't finished.

How in the world did I not see that box? It had been sitting right there in plain sight the entire time, mocking me while I tore through the truck like a maniac—literally wasting my time on purpose—all while the customer stood there waiting, probably wondering what was taking so long. He was probably also wondering to whom I was talking. Maybe he thought there was another worker in the truck, helping me search. After all, some delivery trucks have two people working together. Nope, it was just me with no helper, basically *One Man and a Truck*. I was having a full-blown argument with a box. If anything, it must've sounded like a chaotic team effort, except it was just me, battling cardboard like it had a personal vendetta against me.

As if that weren't enough, working a job like this isn't just about battling the workload. It's about battling the road, the people, and their problems, too. It's like you're carrying not just the weight of the boxes, but also the weight of every impatient driver around you.

Sometimes, it feels like everyone's stress gets dumped onto you the moment you hit the streets. I figured I might be better off driving a garbage truck. At least then I'd be picking up junk on purpose. Like fifteen stops earlier, before I even got to the one where I tripped, fell, and almost broke my nose, I had a run-in with someone's bad mood. One moment stood out more than the rest. I was waiting in the northbound left-turn lane on N Cotton Ln, waiting for the green arrow at the traffic light. The moment it turned green, I began making a smooth left onto W Greenway Rd heading west. As I curved through the intersection, passing the opposing left-turn lane, a man in his 50s with a long white beard, wearing a green Mountain Dew T-shirt, driving a 2011 tan Toyota Avalon, in the opposite left-turn lane, still at least ten feet away from me, laid on his horn. It wasn't just a quick tap; it was a full, drawn-out, aggressive honk that screamed, *Yeah, I'm pissed off, and I want you to know it.*

I wasn't even close to him. He was still slowing down, not even reaching the white line yet, but somehow, my mere existence must have ruined his day. You can tell a lot about a person's mood by the way they honk. A short honk doesn't always mean much; maybe it's just a quick reaction or a moment of impatience that fades fast. Then there's the kind of honk that drags on, loud, deliberate, and impossible to ignore. That kind of honk feels like it's loaded with all the frustration they've been holding in, like they've already had a bad day and now they've decided to dump it all on you.

In that second, you become their target for reasons that have nothing to do with you. It makes you ask yourself what they're even trying to accomplish. Holding the horn for five full seconds doesn't solve anything. It just makes everything worse. It's not only aggressive and obnoxious; it's embarrassing, not just for them but for me, too.

Everyone around can hear it, and some people even stop what they're doing to glance over, wondering what just happened or who the honk was aimed at. It's loud, childish, and dramatic. If anything, it makes them look more unstable than in control, like they're spiraling over something small while the rest of us are just trying to get through the day.

I was extremely heated, but I decided to just drive off, shake my head, and tell myself to just let it go. *It's fine,* I thought. *I'll just mention him in my book.* That's the cool thing about being a writer; people don't realize they might end up as material. Honk at me all you want, buddy. Congratulations, you just made it into my next book.

Fifteen stops later, I was still thinking about it as I climbed through my truck, searching for that box. I was already frustrated, extremely exhausted, and then I tripped. When I saw that large box for a mini electric Jeep box, literally right in front of me, like it had been there all along, mocking me, it felt like the whole day had come full circle.

Still feeling worked up and trying hard not to argue with that silent box, I jumped up and stuck my messy hair out the door. I spotted the recipient and forced a smile, then said, "Guess what? There's your box! It was like it was playing hide-and-seek or something!" The man gazed at me for a couple of seconds in silence, his eyes filled with unease, clearly puzzled about what had just occurred.

"Great," he said with a smile. "I'll get my hand truck." "No need for that, sir, I've got my convertible hand truck," I replied with a smile. The man looked intently at me with concern written on his face, and said, "I don't have all day for you to hunt for your hand truck this time. I'm getting mine." Embarrassment washed over me. "Um...alright then," I said quietly. *Ouch,* I thought to myself. *That was embarrassing.*

Honestly, he wasn't wrong, my hand truck was buried somewhere underneath an ocean of boxes.

After an embarrassing amount of time later, I dropped off the package, I climbed into the driver's seat, strapped in, pulled away, and sighed. *Here we go again.* It had been tough finding what I needed just now, and I knew I'd be doing the same thing all over again at the next stop. As the day went by, I continually asked myself:

Why is this so hard? Why do I struggle to manage the load in my truck? Why do the other drivers seem faster and more efficient? What am I doing wrong?

I tried hard to maintain thirty stops per hour, which was the pace my manager expected from every driver. Falling below that too often usually raises concerns about whether I could handle the route.

This wasn't just something I struggled with as a delivery driver. I had felt the same pressure at many of my previous jobs. The last ten years taught me nothing about how to save time and work fast. They just told me to show up, work, and go home. While working here, I've started learning it for myself by becoming aware of a perspective on time that most people overlook, one step outside the busy routine and makes room for what matters. Maybe I'm not meant to work for someone else's time.

After wrapping up a long, exhausting day, I drove home that night under a dark sky. The streets were nearly empty, and the time was approaching closer to 9 p.m. I made the quiet drive through my neighborhood, imagining the house full of light and laughter, with people still talking in the kitchen and music playing in the background. I pictured my family gathered around the table, maybe a few guests still over, and leftovers waiting on the counter. In my mind, it didn't feel too late. But when I stepped inside, the lights were off, the house was quiet, the food had been put away, and everyone had already gone to bed.

It was disappointing having to work on Christmas Eve in the first place. At least the next day would be Christmas Day, and I had it off to sleep in, be with my family, and finally get a break from all those boxes. I just hoped the wrapped gifts around the tree wouldn't trigger any leftover PTSD from all the boxes I had to carry the day before.

THE DAY IT STARTED MAKING SENSE

Sometime later in the week, while we were organizing our trucks in the morning, I approached one of my co-workers in the warehouse dispatch zone. He was the fastest guy on his route, consistently outpacing every other driver and often hitting over forty stops per hour. "Tyler," I asked, "how do you finish so fast? You're always the first one back, with over two hundred stops in your truck every day. Why is it so easy for you?"

"I get here much earlier than you do, Jonathan," he said with a grin. "More than that, I focus on one box at a time. It's not about the mass of boxes in the truck. It's about *that one box,* the one that matters right now."

That explained a lot, that really surprised me. As simple as it was, I don't know why I hadn't thought of it before. I had been working here for a few years now, and for some reason, it wasn't clicking to me. Honestly, how true is that for life, too? Most of us focus too much on multitasking and stressing ourselves. I remember thinking, *wow, something so small can be that profound and life changing.* That helped me realize one of the biggest things I had been doing wrong. I kept showing up later than most. This makes sense now because every day I arrived late and almost everyone had already organized their trucks and started to leave the warehouse. So, I took Tyler's advice and figured I'd try it his way.

The next morning, I showed up early to work. My manager Fred glanced up, shot me a double take, then immediately looked at his watch with a raised eyebrow, like he was silently asking himself, *"what is he doing here so early?"* I went to my designated station and took extra time to organize my truck more securely than usual, just to see how the day would go. As I began my next route, I kept thinking about what Tyler said: "One box at a time." My mind couldn't process two hundred boxes at once, especially when they were stuffed tightly on the shelves and falling all over the place. So, I made a deliberate choice: I'd try it his way. At my first stop, I ignored everything else in the cargo. I focused on the one package I needed, SID 1020, which was the tracking sticker code on the box, according to the computer. I found it, delivered it, moved on to the next stop, I repeated the process, and kept going. Without staring into the dark, bottomless abyss of packages stacked to the ceiling, I just kept going, one box at a time.

As I was going through my day, making my stops, and driving on, I clicked the setting on the top right corner of my tablet to open the PackageRoute performance screen. I couldn't believe it, I was so happy, I saw that I had already completed 92 stops out of 229, and it wasn't even 12 o'clock yet. Then I just sat there for a second, in complete disbelief, like one of those quiet moments where you look up, blink slowly, and think, no way, was it really this simple all along? It was such a shock, and I felt genuinely excited to see how the rest of the day would go. Part of me hoped that my manager saw the numbers on their phone, too. Maybe this time I'd soon get off their radar.

I continued practicing this method for about a month, until my brain fully recalibrated to think *one box at a time.* I became much faster and less overwhelmed by the mountain of packages filling my truck almost every day. It became a habit. On my next day of work, I returned with a simplified mindset, focusing on one step at a time without overthinking or panicking, just completing one delivery after the other. My route suddenly felt lighter, more manageable. I didn't think about how many stops I had left or what my cargo looked like. I focused only on the one package that needed to be delivered, and that was enough. Now that the habit is solid, I seldom even see the large stacks of boxes and dozens of bags on the shelves. My brain knows how to locate the package I need. I don't have to worry about the whole load, just the next step.

When I finished my route that day, I returned to the warehouse, parked my truck, closed out the day in my scanner, and stood next to the driver's seat, facing the windshield. Turning around, I looked through the bulkhead door into the cargo space. It was completely empty, the entire area was clear, and I stood there for a moment, truly amazed by what I was seeing. Earlier that same day, hundreds of boxes were stacked up to the ceiling with no room to walk through. Now it's nothing but open space. As I stood there in silence, I started to wonder to myself: *What if I could imagine this empty cargo space tomorrow morning before my route? What if I could start the day already visualizing the end, and knowing that step by step, I'd get there?* That simple thought was enough to motivate me to keep going.

Well, the next morning I did just that. I walked in and saw the cargo space packed full, with boxes scattered all over the floor and nothing in order. The package handlers who work the conveyor belt had loaded my truck the night before, but they were clearly in a rush to get home and get out of there, so it was not organized at all. I wasn't worried, nor was I overwhelmed. I had already developed the mindset of focusing on one moment, one package at a time, and keeping the end in mind. Before organizing a single box, I stood there, looked at the mess, and remembered what I had seen and told myself the day before. I said, today this truck is going to be empty again, one package at a time. That thought gave me the motivation I needed. After much organizing, I began heading out to drive to my assigned ZIP code.

As I maneuvered through my deliveries, a thought struck me: *this is like living life in slow motion, like working with tiny frames of time instead of rushing through the whole picture.* Every moment felt deliberate, and I was fully present in each one. Reflecting on my progress, I realized how much I had improved since adopting this new habit. Just a month ago, I was overwhelmed by the sheer number of boxes in my truck. The pressure stretched my delivery times and drained my motivation.

Granted, this job is still stressful, but I feel more at ease now. It's like my mind finally has space to breathe, and I'm finally gaining control and thinking clearly again.

Later during my route that day, I glanced at my truck cargo, and I saw an entire shelf empty. The 8500 SID logistic shelf that was once packed with bags and hidden packages was now bare. Just forty minutes earlier, that shelf had been my biggest worry. Now, without even realizing it, I had emptied it by simply working with one box at a time. It reminded me of something simple but true: It's like staring at a clock. When you focus on time, it crawls. On the contrary, when you're engaged in something else, it flies.

Time passed, and before I knew it, I was three-quarters through my route. By that point, the truck had cleared out, and I could finally walk through the aisle.

"That was easy," I thought.

It wasn't about the number of boxes, and it never was. It was about delivering one package at a time. After all, I was paid to deliver each package, not to fret over the whole load. I finished the route, parked my truck in the warehouse, and headed home. As I drove, I reflected on the past two weeks, and the new mindset I'd developed. This approach wasn't just for work. It applied to life. Too often, I fixated on my current circumstances and stressed about solving them all at once. I worried that I wasn't where I wanted to be in life. I tried to force my future into the present. The truth is most of us have long-term dreams and goals. My dream is to become an entrepreneur, a pastor, and a paid motivational speaker to fund my church.

A few years ago, I was discouraged and disappointed, mostly because I was too focused on my long-term goals and the person I wanted to be twenty years from now. I kept comparing myself to others who seemed to be succeeding, and it left me feeling overwhelmed and frustrated. There was a chasm, so to speak, between who I was and who I wanted to be. Maybe you can relate, especially when it comes to your own dreams. I often wondered how to reach my long-term goals quickly and effectively. The lesson learned through my delivery job, or *One Man and a Truck,* as I like to call it, was this: focus on one small thing at a time, just like those packages.

By concentrating on one task at a time, I finished faster and felt more accomplished. This mindset shift was powerful. It wasn't about the mountain of boxes, or the grand life goals. It was about taking small, intentional steps. Each step brought me closer to my goals; the journey became manageable and rewarding. That was the lesson I learned, and it changed everything.

FROM DELIVERY TO DISCIPLINE:
How the Job Taught Me Intentionality and Inspired This Book

Working as a delivery driver wasn't just about delivering packages; it was a life lesson. It was a long season that I had to endure and grow through. It became an experience that shaped the way I view life, work, and the importance of being intentional with every moment. When you're in a job that demands so much of your time, energy, and focus, you begin to see things differently. You realize that it's not just about the big goals or dramatic moments. It's about what you choose to do in the smallest ones. Those small moments have the biggest impact on your overall journey.

At first, the job as a driver felt overwhelming, as many jobs often do when you're starting out. The truck would be packed with countless boxes, and every morning, I'd face that sea of packages, wondering how I'd ever get through them all so fast. It felt like an impossible task. Over time, I began to see that handling packages wasn't just about moving boxes from point A to point B; it was teaching me a bigger lesson about life. I realized that if I tried to tackle everything at once, I'd be consumed by stress and frustration. Instead, I needed to approach each delivery with intention, focusing on *one box at a time.*

When I first started as a delivery driver in Arizona, they told us to move fast and just run it. No matter how hard I tried, I couldn't keep up with the other fast drivers out there. Everything changed when I stopped trying to rush and started focusing on one box at a time. This cleared my mind, slowed my thoughts, and surprisingly helped me finish faster by teaching me to think clearly instead of just moving quickly.

Some of the other drivers who always finished first and rushed through their routes were the same ones who ended up getting injured. In the long run, it didn't turn out so well. They had to go home, miss work without pay, and some had kids to feed and a wife waiting at home. They used to call me the slowest one out there, and from time to time they would even pick on me or question me, asking over and over, "Why are you so slow?" or "How come you don't move faster?" The thing is, they were the ones who kept getting hurt while I kept showing up, day after day. Believe it or not, after all those years on the job, I was never severely injured, not even once, because I've always been focused on the long run. Granted, I've had minor injuries that required some attention, but nothing serious enough to take off work. The only way to stay healthy, consistent, and have longevity in this kind of job is by being mindful of the time I have right now and how I choose to use it.

One time during the heat of the summer, my other manager, Andrew, texted me while I was on route, asking me, "Hey, are you at a restaurant?" and my first thought was honestly a bit offensive, *No, I'm out here in the heat, reorganizing my entire truck to create an aisle.* He followed up with, "Are you okay? You've been stopped for a while." The truth is, I was working the whole time, just not the way they could see. That kind of thing is a big pet peeve of mine at work.

I've got a close coworker who started working at this job at the same time I did back in early 2020, He is 29 years old, and now he has to work part-time because his legs just can't take it anymore. He spent years running nonstop trying to impress the managers, but in the end, it didn't work out the way he thought it would. All around me, it felt like everyone was rushing to beat the clock, but I had to find a different way.

My approach to work changed, but even more than that, my mindset shifted. Every box became an opportunity: a chance to be present, to work with what was right in front of me, without getting lost in the mountain of tasks still waiting. By breaking down what seemed like an enormous challenge into smaller, manageable pieces, I discovered something unexpected: I was not only more productive, but I was also more at peace. This was a lesson that followed me into every aspect of my life.

You see, life is much like that truck full of packages. We often look at the big picture, everything we can see right in front of us, and we become overwhelmed. What if we shifted our focus? What if, instead of fixating on the entire journey, we simply concentrated on the step that's right in front of us? That realization changed everything for me. Instead of feeling defeated by the sheer volume of work ahead, I learned to take things one task, one step, one moment at a time. In doing so, I discovered something important: life's big goals and dreams aren't achieved in one giant leap. They're built slowly, one small, intentional action at a time.

Working with packages helped me develop a mindset centered on intentionality, specifically focusing on what matters right now. When I stopped worrying about all the boxes that were waiting behind me and started paying attention to the *one* I was delivering, I found a sense of peace and purpose. It was like a switch flipped, and suddenly, everything became more manageable. I wasn't constantly battling the overwhelming question, *"How am I going to finish this?"* Instead, I asked, *"What's the next step I can take?"* That's where the power of this mindset really comes into play. By narrowing my focus to what was right in front of me, I discovered that I could handle more than I thought possible. It's that approach of taking small steps with full intention that allowed me to make steady, meaningful progress. Not just at work, but in every aspect of my life.

This is why I felt compelled to write this book. It's not just about my time as a driver or the challenges I faced; it's about sharing the mindset that I developed during that journey. I want others to understand that the key to achieving big goals is to start small, to be intentional with every step, and to focus on what you can do *right now*. The time you have *now* is all you have. We all have a tendency to get caught up in the big picture, to feel overwhelmed by everything we need to accomplish. The truth is the most effective way to move forward is by working with the small things before moving on to the bigger things.

There were days when the boxes in my truck seemed endless, when I felt like I'd never reach the end. By choosing to focus on one box at a time, I realized that I was making progress, not because I could see it or feel it, but because I believed it. It was my mindset that kept me moving forward. Isn't that how life works? We move forward not by leaps and bounds but by taking one step after another. When we concentrate on the task at hand and give it our best effort, we slowly but surely get closer to where we want to be. In due time, I realized I was saving so much time, because once my mind cleared up, it didn't wander anymore. It just moved straight to the point. I wasn't overthinking anymore, and I wasn't stuck in procrastination like so many of us can be. It was simple, just one small step at a time, and honestly, anyone can take a small step.

This experience taught me that intentionality is not just about doing one thing at a time, it's about being fully present in that moment. It's about giving your all to whatever you're doing and trusting that each small effort is building something greater than you can see right now.

SMALL STEPS, BIG WINS:
How Being Intentional Pays Off

My friend Paul owns a fulfillment company in Arizona, and he's incredibly skilled at what he does. He sells a wide range of high-quality computer accessories like SteelSeries gaming headphones, keyboards, mouse pads, and more, all on behalf of other businesses that pay to store their products in his warehouses across Arizona. His team handles the storage and shipping each time a customer places an order online. Funny enough, I became good friends with him because I used to deliver to his company when I worked as a delivery driver. I'd back my truck up to the dock and do regular pickups for almost a year, loading up pallets of SteelSeries headphones, keyboards, and mouse pads. Over time, I kept hearing the warehouse guys talk about the owner who rides a Ducati, drives a Porsche, and even a McLaren. Sure enough, when I finally met him, he just casually said "hi," and seemed like a down-to-earth guy, which surprised me because I didn't expect someone that wealthy to be so humble or to choose a field like sales.

I always wondered how he managed to succeed in an area where so many people struggle, especially with sales calls, since most people love to buy stuff, but they hate being sold to, let alone over the phone. People will gladly go shopping and even rack up debt buying things they love, but the moment someone approaches them to sell something directly, like a solicitor, it becomes a big problem. I mean, who wants to pick up a cold call from a salesperson?

I wouldn't.

One morning, when I was off from work, I went to Paul's office for a meeting to go over a car drawing he had commissioned from me. It was for his 2020 Porsche 911 Carrera S convertible. His car was a deep blue model with sleek black wheels, red brake calipers, and a soft top that made it look like something straight out of a luxury car ad. We made our final decisions on the picture dimensions, 17" x 34" in landscape orientation, and the type of materials used, which was colored pencils at the time. I had asked for $2,000 weeks earlier over the phone, but I already knew I'd settle lower. After two minutes of negotiating, we settled on $1,000, for what became my very first commissioned drawing, which we were both happy with. It didn't take too long because I already had a clear plan in mind before walking into his office. That art piece is still on his wall, and we continue working together, even today.

After that meeting, Paul invited me to observe him during a call with a prospect, and that's when I realized there was real art in what he was doing. We were sitting in his office, a space decked out with paintings, sports memorabilia, and a cool personal touch. Paul had this calm, confident presence about him. He leaned back in his comfy black reclining swivel office chair, took a sip of his coffee, and gently swayed side to side on his chair. He had the call on speaker as the ring-back tone sounded, and we waited for the prospect to pick up. Holding his phone out in front of him horizontally with the screen facing up, then glanced up toward the ceiling and said, "I'm about to make a live sales call. Just watch how this works." I nodded, curious but not entirely convinced. As I stood there, I didn't think he'd be able to get the person on the other end to listen, let alone engage in a real conversation, especially one that could lead to a sale.

There was a moment of suspense, and then someone answered.

"Hello?" they said, sounding a bit distracted. What Paul did next was fascinating. Instead of launching straight into a sales pitch, he introduced himself calmly.

"Hi, this is Paul from Axle on Demand. I hope I'm not catching you at a bad time. Could you spare just 30 seconds?" That was it, just 30 seconds.

This approach was brilliant because asking for thirty seconds isn't a huge ask. Most people can spare that time without feeling pressured or overwhelmed. The prospect on the other end agreed, likely thinking it wouldn't hurt to listen for just a moment. Within those thirty seconds, Paul didn't push a sale. Instead, he mentioned something relevant and valuable to that individual, something he'd learned from researching their business ahead of time. He acknowledged their work, demonstrating that he understood who they were and what they cared about.

Then, Paul took it a step further. He said, "I understand this may not be the best time for a longer chat. Is there a better time tomorrow when we could connect for just one minute?" The person paused for a few seconds and then agreed, setting up another touchpoint. It was a simple, respectful approach that didn't feel pushy or scripted, and that's when I started to see the genius behind it.

The next day, Paul told me that he called the prospect back for that promised one-minute conversation. This time, they were more receptive and more willing to engage. Still, Paul didn't push the sale. Instead, he subtly hinted at how he could offer something of real value to their business, referencing specific challenges he'd identified through careful research. By the end of that short call, he had secured a fifteen-minute Zoom meeting for later that week. Again, it wasn't about forcing a decision. It was about building trust and showing genuine interest.

As the Zoom call approached, Paul prepared thoroughly. He came armed with insights, tailored solutions, and a deep understanding of the prospect's business needs. When they finally connected for that fifteen-minute call, Paul delivered his message with confidence and intention by focusing entirely on how he could help that *individual* succeed. By the end of that meeting, they weren't just interested. They were invested.

They scheduled another follow-up, and about a month later, Paul closed the deal, securing a long-term fulfillment contract with a new client. What stood out to me most was how Paul took the prospect on a simple, gradual journey, one that didn't feel like a big obligation. He didn't try to rush the process or push for a quick sale. Instead, he focused on each phase, treating every interaction as its own important step. He didn't jump ahead or overwhelm the person with information.

That experience taught me an important lesson: achieving something isn't about forcing things to happen all at once. It's about acting with purpose, taking things step by step, and staying present in the moment. Paul's approach wasn't just about selling. It was about building trust, understanding the person on the other end of the call, and offering genuine value every step of the way.

I began to realize that Paul's method isn't just applicable to sales; it's a mindset that can be used in every area of life. We often feel overwhelmed by the big goals we set for ourselves or the massive projects we take on. Just like Paul, we can break these challenges down into smaller, manageable steps. By focusing on what's right in front of us, we can move forward with clarity and purpose.

This approach of taking one step at a time is exactly why I felt compelled to write this book. I wanted to share the lessons I learned from observing Paul, working with packages, and from countless other experiences that taught me the power of taking mindful actions.

Many of those experiences are ones I'll begin unpacking in the next chapter and continue exploring throughout this book.

When we focus on one thing at a time, we're not just making progress. We're building a solid foundation for future achievement. It's about putting your energy into the task at hand, doing it well, and trusting that each step will lead you to where you want to go. Paul's method was a clear idea that people respond to authenticity and genuine interest. No one likes to be rushed, pressured, or sold to. They want to feel understood, respected, and valued. By thoughtfully approaching each situation with those values in mind, Paul built something stronger than a sale: he built trust.

This experience was more than just a lesson in sales; it was yet another life lesson. It reminded me that every big accomplishment starts with a single step. When we focus on what's directly in front of us, we avoid feeling overwhelmed. We become more effective, more thoughtful, and more capable of handling whatever comes our way.

Looking back, I realized something important: life always moves one step at a time, whether we notice it or not. Every decision, every task, every small moment builds on the next. The more we focus on what's right in front of us, the easier it becomes to handle whatever comes next.

What happens when doubtful thoughts enter the picture? Even when we break things down into manageable steps, questions like *"Am I doing the right thing?"* and *"What if this doesn't work?"* creep in. Sometimes, those doubts don't just come from within. They come from the people around us, those who can't always see beyond what's right in front of them. Those who make us second-guess ourselves, despite their best intentions.

I had to face that reality when I first started writing. Not everyone understood why I was doing it, and some doubted whether it was worth the effort. Instead of asking, *"What if this doesn't work?"* I asked, *"What if I could go farther than I ever imagined?"* That shift in thinking changed everything.

Maybe it could change everything for you, too.

FINAL THOUGHTS
How to Use This Every Day

→ **Treat Every Moment Like a Fragile Package**

Each moment is a delivery. Handle one at a time. Stay focused and handle it with care, and don't worry about the rest until it's time, lest the fragile opportunity pass you by without you even noticing.

→ **Slow Down to Speed Up**

Rushing creates mistakes. Focus on what's in front of you. When you handle the small moments well, everything flows more smoothly.

→ **Plan Without Overthinking**

Think ahead, but don't let distress take control. Set your direction, then work step-by-step. The future is built in the moments you manage today.

2

COMMITMENT BRINGS RESULTS

"You don't have to be extreme, just consistent."

— UNKNOWN

WHEN I first took the step toward becoming an author, it wasn't strangers who doubted me and tried to stop me. It was people I had spent much time around while growing in my career and reaching for ventures greater than myself. Some thought they were protecting me from what they feared for my future. Others believed they knew me inside and out. It was as though my own inner critic had been duplicated in them.

They'd say things like, *"Don't do it, your writing style doesn't flow consistently,"* or *"You have to be famous to become an author."* Others would scoff, "*No one will take you seriously unless you already have a household name,*" or remind me, "*It takes years, why even try?*"

They weren't wrong in what they said, because it genuinely took many years to reach where I am now. Seven long years, to be exact, years filled with doubts, small wins, and steady growth. Rather than letting their words discourage me or cause me to stop altogether, I chose to keep moving forward, building momentum, gaining experience, and proving through consistent effort that time itself was never the real barrier. It was a process that shaped me more than I could have predicted at the start. Am I alone in this, or can anyone else relate?

If you don't think it's going to happen, it won't. It's that simple, no overcomplications, no excuses, just reality. If you tell yourself it's impossible, you've already lost. You've already closed the door before it even had a chance to open. If you believe, even just *a little bit,* you give yourself a fighting chance.

NOW WHAT IF?

That's what most people ask themselves. They hesitate, they doubt, and they let fear creep in. I never asked that. I never let doubt take control. Instead, I asked the *optimistic* kind of what-if: What if this could go even further? What if I push a little harder? What if I take just one more risk?

Think of yourself as a thermostat. A thermostat doesn't just react to the temperature; it sets the temperature. You have the power to decide and say to yourself: *I want this to happen.* You can turn the dial up or down, making the choice to adjust, recalibrate, push forward, or even hold yourself back by allowing hesitation, fear, or uncertainty to take control of your life. It all starts with the words you tell yourself:

"This is going to work."
"I can do this."
"I will make this happen."
Or...
"This will never happen."
"It's too hard."
"I'll never be good enough."

What you say becomes what you see, and what you believe becomes your reality. If you keep telling yourself it won't happen, then it won't. That's not an opinion, but it's a fact. You can't expect something to manifest in your life if you've already decided in your mind that it won't. Your words and your beliefs set the tone, just like a thermostat sets the temperature. If you don't believe it's possible, you've already shut the door on it.

OTHER PEOPLE'S OPINIONS ARE NOT YOUR REALITY

People will tell you:
"It's not possible."
"It's too hard."
"It'll take too long."
"Someone like you can't do something like that."

Their opinion, their experience, and their mindset were all formed by the path they've walked, the challenges they've faced, and the beliefs they've chosen to accept along the way. Everything they think or say is a reflection of their own life, not yours. What they carry belongs entirely to them, and no matter how loud their voice may sound or how confident they seem, their perspective does not determine your identity, your value, or what you are capable of achieving. What didn't work for them might work for you. Their fears don't have to be yours, their doubts don't belong to you, and their limits aren't yours to accept. The only person who gets to decide what is possible is you.

WORK WITH WHAT YOU HAVE RIGHT NOW.

We often get caught up in the next thing, the next step, the next hour, the next milestone. What if, instead, you simply focused on this moment? The truth is that the next hour is not even promised. All you really have is now, this minute, this small window of time right in front of you, and that alone is enough.

You don't need to know exactly how it will all work out, and you don't need a perfect plan. What matters is that you take what you have, use it, and move forward with it. If you can stay intentional with just one moment, you can begin to build something far greater than you ever imagined. Progress often begins quietly, through one moment at a time, one small decision that builds on the last, and one simple what-if, the kind that has the power to open a door to something far greater than you imagined.

This moment is all you'll ever have, so give yourself the positive what-ifs, for the moment you're in right now.

20/80 VISION:
Seeing What Eyes Can't

Do you know how people say, *there's more than meets the eye?* Well, that phrase holds a lot of truth especially when it comes to life, faith, and the future.

Right now, the reality of what is right in front of you is only about twenty percent of the bigger picture. It's the part that's visible, the part that makes sense in the moment. The other eighty percent is the part you *can't* see yet. That's where God's promises, plans, and everything He has in store for you exist. It's already set aside for you with your name on it; you just haven't reached it yet.

The problem is that most people only focus on the twenty percent. They live based on what they see, what they can measure, and what feels real to them in the present moment. If you're a practical person or a realist, it's easy to get stuck there, and to believe that what's right in front of you is all there is.

Jesus said, *"Seek first the kingdom of God, and all these things will be added to you."* In other words, if you focus on what really matters, like your faith, your relationship with God, then the rest will follow. Your job isn't to figure out every detail of the eighty percent. Your job is to handle the twenty percent that's in front of you right now and trust that God is taking care of the rest.

Think about it this way: Jesus also said not to worry about tomorrow, because today has enough trouble of its own. That doesn't mean you shouldn't plan for the future, but it does mean you shouldn't let worry or doubt take over just because you can't see how everything will work out. If you only make decisions based on what's visible in the twenty percent, you'll always feel limited. You'll second-guess yourself and feel like you're not enough, like you're going to let people down, like your dreams are too big. The truth is that what you see now isn't the full story.

The key is to use what's in your hands right now, which represents the twenty percent that's visible, as a way to stay connected to what's ahead. It's about moving forward in faith, even when you can't see the full picture. God has already placed the eighty percent in your future, and if you keep walking, you'll get there

When you share your plans, goals, and ideas with someone, too soon, out of pure excitement, you might expect them to understand what's stirring inside of you. The vision is so clear, it almost feels tangible. It's intensely vivid and alive, so much so that it seems real, even though it hasn't happened yet. In fact, it feels so authentic that you begin living as though it already exists. Some may not understand what you're talking about. They might get confused, shut you down, or simply not take you seriously. The reason they don't understand is that they weren't shown what you were shown. God revealed something to you that was tailored specifically for your life, something big that belongs in the future.

Many stay on a path shaped by a familiar mindset they've accepted as their norm. They didn't see what you saw, which is why they won't always recognize what you're preparing for. It's as if you're looking up into the sky and watching the clouds part, only to find God appearing there, holding a large, heavy box that carries weight and purpose. Before dropping it, He helps you anticipate the fall. He tells you to get ready, to grab your gloves, prepare your hand truck, review your map, and even check your scanner. He gives you the passion to carry it, the skill to assemble it, and the direction to handle it when it comes. In reality, the preparation is happening now. That's what today is about. Most will never notice that part, because it hasn't yet come close enough to meet their eye or solidify into something they can finally see for themselves. This preparation positions you to leave behind what's familiar and step into something better that will soon become reality.

That's why you should not force your vision into places where it isn't welcome. Sharing it too early can be as though tossing a heavy package toward someone who has no idea it's coming. They aren't prepared to carry what you're already strong enough to hold. It's often better to build quietly until the result becomes real enough for others to see for themselves.

There's a saying that warns not to hand your pearls to pigs, meaning you shouldn't offer something valuable to those who won't recognize its worth. That's not to call anyone a pig, but rather to acknowledge that some simply have no interest in what you're building, and that's okay.

SMALL MOMENTS SHAPE EVERYTHING OVER TIME

I was getting ready for this worship hour at Zion City Church in Tucson, Arizona. It was something that happened every day for the EDGE college students, and it was a time set aside for worship and prayer before they went off to lunch. This particular session was in 2018, and by then, I had been involved in the worship team for a few years. I was comfortable behind the drum set and had become familiar with the natural flow of worship sets, including when to slow down, when to build up, and how to follow the worship leader's cues.

That morning, I showed up early, around 10 a.m., to get everything set up in the prayer room. It was an acoustic set, so instead of a full drum kit, I was playing the cajón. It's a portable wooden box drum you sit on and play by stroking the front surface with your palms for deeper tones and your fingers for lighter, sharper sounds. I liked the simplicity of it, because the raw sound fit perfectly with the intimate vibe of that space. I checked the mic levels, settled in, and waited for the worship leader, Nestor, and our guitarist, Treigh, to arrive. We were getting ready to play

No Longer Slaves by Jonathan and Melissa Helser. It's a long, flowing song, and as a drummer, it's my job to feel out the dynamics, build when it's needed, and ease off when it's time to let the vocals carry.

The students slowly filled the room, some already deep in thought, some quietly chatting. Nestor led us into the first chords, and I followed along, tapping into the steady rhythm, and everything felt good as the room began to settle into worship. I was in the zone, as always, and simply feeling the energy and the flow.

The energy of the song had started to come down, as the band eased into a quieter moment. I didn't notice it then, but during a softer part of the song, which was a space meant to breathe and pause, I kept playing. It wasn't anything wild, but I kept stroking the cajón with my palms, and it was enough to stand out. It was enough to disrupt that delicate stillness. I didn't realize it in the moment. I thought I was following the flow, feeling it out like I usually did.

After about an hour, the session ended, the students filtered out to lunch, and I started packing up my cajón, sliding it into the carry bag.

That's when Nestor approached me.

"Hey, man," he said casually, but there was something in his tone. "That one part where it slowed down? You should've stopped on that one part. It felt awkward; everyone was wondering why you were still playing. Even Cameron, who's completely tone-deaf and doesn't know a thing about music stopped praying and looked at you like, 'What is this guy doing?'"

I felt a bit offended as I paused. My hands were still on the zipper of the bag.

"What do you mean?" I asked, feeling my face heat up. I wasn't trying to be defensive, but it caught me off guard. I thought I was flowing with the music.

"That part right after the third 'I am a child of God,' you were supposed to pull back," he said. "The piano takes over from there, and the whole song drops into this quiet space. It's meant to breathe, not stay heavy. You kept playing hard all the way through, and it clashed with the flow. When the lead singer comes in with 'I am surrounded by songs of deliverance,' that's where the drums are supposed to come in gently. Then, after he says, 'let us sing our freedom,' that's when you build up and come in strong. It's supposed to rise gradually, but you came in too soon."

"Yeah, it's just... that moment needed space, you know? Maybe check out Bethel's drummer on YouTube, watch how he follows the flow. Might help."

That was it. I nodded, but inside, I was frustrated. Not even angry, just confused and a little embarrassed. I mean, I'd been doing this for years. I knew the songs, the flow, and how to read cues. So why did I mess this up?

It brought up something I thought I had outgrown, a familiar and uncomfortable feeling of being misunderstood. Growing up with five sisters, I was the only boy in the household. It always felt like I was speaking a different language, like my thoughts didn't always land how I intended. Now here I was again, feeling like I was doing everything right, but somehow still off.

I didn't say much more to Nestor as I packed up my gear and left the church campus for the day. My mind was spinning the entire drive home, unsure of what to think or how badly I had messed up. Did I really mess up that badly? Was it that noticeable?

Honestly, I was so frustrated that I drove straight to Freddy's Steakburgers. I figured if I was going to feel like this, I might as well drown it in a burger, fries, and a massive Signature Turtle sundae.

Over the next few days, I did what Nestor suggested. I went on YouTube, searched Bethel's worship sets, and watched their drummer. I watched video after video, but honestly, nothing stood out. I didn't see what I was missing. I kept thinking, *I'm already doing this. What else am I supposed to learn here?*

Something told me to keep going, and out of quiet curiosity, I did.

Instead of watching the whole performance, I started focusing on the little things, like the way the drummer used ghost notes on the snare, the timing of his pauses, and how he let silence speak louder than sound.

I went back to practicing, but this time, I wasn't just running through entire songs, I broke things down. I focused on the tiniest details, like how I transitioned from verse to chorus, and how I controlled the soft taps on the cajón.

It wasn't easy; in fact, the process felt slow and, at times, almost pointless, but I kept showing up day after day, not just physically, but mentally, too. I wasn't just hitting drums; I was studying them, listening to them, understanding how every sound had weight. Then, gradually, something began to shift, I started noticing a difference in the way I approached each practice session, with more patience and purpose. It wasn't immediate; I didn't wake up one day suddenly flawless. Little by little, I noticed my approach becoming more intentional as I was adapting, watching intently to the worship leader's cues, and observing the fragile atmosphere of the room.

One of the biggest things I've learned during these practice sessions is that being a good drummer isn't just about locking in on my own drum set or trying to perfectly play what I practiced; it's about staying connected with the whole band and being flexible. Before Nestor gave me feedback, I was mainly focused on what I had practiced at home, trying to memorize every part and play everything exactly like the studio versions from Bethel or Elevation Worship. However, playing live on stage is completely different. Things change instantly and spontaneously. Maybe the worship leader decides to repeat a section, or the energy in the room shifts, and I have to be ready for that.

Nestor told me that while it's important to be one hundred percent prepared, I also need to be one hundred percent ready to adjust and improvise when things don't go exactly as planned. That really stuck with me for such a long time, and I used that advice later on when I joined a worship support network and played drums for churches all across the Phoenix area.

Now, instead of keeping my head down and only focusing on the drums, I'm always looking around, watching the worship leader, the keyboardist, the guitarist, even the bass player, just staying super aware of what's happening. As the drummer, I've realized I help lead the dynamics and direction of the song, so I need to stay connected to the whole team. The more I became present in the room, like paying attention to every little detail and engaging with focused effort in how I played, the more everything came alive. I wasn't just trying to get through the songs anymore; I was fully engaged, making sure even the smallest things were right because I knew they mattered.

That level of focus took a lot of time and effort, but it was so worth it, not just for me, but for the congregation, too. I was intentional and sensitive to every part of the worship set; it helped create an atmosphere where people could focus on worship and fully engage.

When everything flows together so well, it allows the Holy Spirit to move freely in the room, which impacts hearts and changes lives. As a drummer, the way I play and how sensitive I am to the flow of the music can either open the door for the Holy Spirit to move or unintentionally hold things back.

When I'm fully in tune with the team and the moment, it creates space for the Holy Spirit to work powerfully. People in the congregation aren't just attending another service; they're having real encounters with God. When they leave those doors, they leave changed. Their time at work, at home, and in their relationships are different because of only one experience.

All of this was made possible because I made small tweaks and tightened some bolts in my mindset. This method isn't just for me as a drummer; it's something every musician on stage carries. We all have to be intentional and sensitive to the things that shape the direction and dynamics of the music. When the whole team leads with the same heart, it creates a powerful atmosphere that impacts people's lives

Hopefully, this gives you a sense of how powerful the ripple effect can be from something as simple as this, not just in your own growth, but in how it impacts the people around you when you show up, stay mentally engaged, and stay committed time and time again. Sometimes, you won't even realize you're making an impact in other people's lives, and that's the cool part.

So, anyway, weeks passed, I played more worship sets, and I could tell things were clicking. I felt more connected, more in sync. It wasn't just about playing notes anymore; it was about creating moments. Then, after one session, Nestor came up to me again, only this time, his tone was different

"Hey, Jon," he said, smiling, "you sounded great today—seriously, the way you followed the flow was powerful. I can tell the Holy Spirit was flowing through you on stage, it was solid." Those were his exact words, and I couldn't have been prouder of myself. I was excited when

I heard it, and I walked off feeling proud of myself, like all the quiet effort I'd been putting in was finally in the light. That was it, no long speech, no critique, just acknowledgment. It didn't mean anything to him, but it meant everything to me.

I can't explain how good that felt; not just because he noticed, but because I knew how much work I had put in. The long hours of focusing on the little things, showing up even when I didn't see progress all paid off. Looking back, I realized it wasn't just about the drums. It was about learning how to stay committed. To keep showing up, even when things didn't make sense. Even when I felt misunderstood. I started thinking about how often we assume that "showing up" just means being physically present. It's more than that; it's about showing up with focus, determination, and willingness to break things down and start small.

I remember walking into church the following week with a renewed approach. I wasn't just there to play; I was there to *listen, to feel,* and to notice things I hadn't before. It felt like a fresh start, even though nothing on the outside had changed. The room was the same, same faces, same instruments, same setting, but something inside me had shifted.

We were getting ready for another worship set. Nestor was there, tuning his guitar, and Treigh was adjusting his amp. The room started filling with the soft hum of conversations and the quiet strumming of guitars. I sat down on the cajón, running my hands over the wood surface, just taking it all in. This time, though, I wasn't rushing into the rhythm. I was patient, waiting and watching. We started playing a different song this time, it was something slower and more intimate. The kind of song that pulls you in if you let it. I kept my playing light, leaving space where it was needed. I could feel the music breathe, and for the first time in a long time, I was breathing with it.

Then something unexpected happened.

Midway through the set, Nestor signaled a cue for a spontaneous moment, it was one of those hand gestures our band uses when it's time to shift on the fly. He always did it in a subtle way, so the congregation wouldn't even notice. Only the band could really tell what was happening. For example, when we're ending a song, he will life up the neck of his guitar toward the ceiling while still strumming, and that's our signal to wrap it up very strong. Those subtle cues were not just about transitioning to another song. They often prepared us for something deeper, like the moment when he wanted the room to sit in silence and become more sensitive to the Holy Spirit. I caught the cue instantly, and I stopped with no hesitation; the silence wasn't empty, it was *full*. It was in that stillness that I realized how important those quiet moments are. It's not about constantly filling the space with sound. Sometimes it's about stepping back and letting the moment speak for itself. After the set, Nestor gave me a nod, nothing more, but that small gesture said everything. It wasn't about perfection. It was about growth.

A few days later, Nestor asked me if I could join a special worship night happening the following week. It wasn't the usual small prayer room session; it was a full worship night in the main sanctuary that can accommodate over a thousand people.

I agreed, but deep down, I felt that old nervous energy creeping back in. This wasn't the acoustic set I was used to; this was different. The night of the event came, and the sanctuary was already buzzing with people. The lights were dimmed, and the stage was set. I wasn't on the cajón this time, they had me back on the full drum kit. The stakes felt higher, and every sound I made would echo through the entire room. I sat behind the kit, hands gripping the sticks tighter than usual. The first few songs went smoothly, but I could still feel the tension building inside as I sat behind the kit, overthinking every fill and every beat. I was so focused on avoiding mistakes that I lost sight of the music itself and the purpose behind why I was playing.

Then came the song, Nestor leaned over and quietly said, "Let's let this one breathe a bit." I nodded, but inside, I wasn't sure what that meant for a full drum kit. On the cajón, it made sense, but on a full drum set it felt like more pressure, more room to make mistakes. The song started slow, and I eased into it. I tried to stay relaxed, but halfway through, the music built up, and I got caught up in it. I added a few extra fills on the toms, nothing crazy, but enough to break that space Nestor had wanted. Eventually, after some time, the song ended, and the crowd responded, but I knew I had missed it.

Afterward, as we were packing up, Nestor came over.

"You did good," he said, "but remember what we talked about, sometimes less is more." It hit me harder than I expected. I thought I had already learned that lesson. Here I was, still wrestling with it. On the drive home, I couldn't shake the feeling. It was like I had taken a step forward, only to slide a little back. Maybe that's how it works most of the time; progress isn't always a straight line. Sometimes it's two steps forward, one step back. So, I went back to practicing, but this time, it wasn't just about the drums. It was about understanding my role by knowing when to lead and when to follow.

Weeks turned into months; worship sets came and went, and slowly, I noticed something. I wasn't thinking so hard anymore, I wasn't second-guessing every move, I was just playing with purpose. Then came one particular set. A night when everything just *clicked*. We were deep into worship, and I could feel the room leaning into the music. Nestor signaled for the band to drop out, leaving only the vocals. I caught the cue instantly, and I let my hands hover, not touching a single drum surface. The silence filled the room like a wave, and it was powerful and raw.

When the music picked up again, I came in softly, just enough to support, not overpowering anyone, it felt effortless and natural. After that set, Nestor didn't need to say anything. I could tell the whole team looked at me, we were in sync and fully connected.

That worship set marked a turning point in how I approached more than just music. It showed me the impact of being fully engaged in small, present moments. From that experience forward, I began to pay closer attention to how small decisions shape the way we grow, respond, and move forward. It opened my eyes to how much our choices, especially the ones we think are small, carry the power to shape everything that follows.

In life, we all have a role to play, no matter how big or small it may seem. It doesn't matter if you're a single mother juggling two jobs, a student working through assignments, or someone managing multiple responsibilities at work. What matters is how you show up.

Are you playing your role with intention? There's a big difference between doing something just to get it done and doing it well. When you focus on the task at hand, no matter how small, you're paving the way for tomorrow.

It's really in the small moments that we often overlook where the most meaningful progress happens. We tend to underestimate the impact of a few minutes here or there, thinking they're too insignificant to matter. Those small slices of time are precious opportunities slipping by, there are moments that could be used to take one more step forward, reflect, or simply breathe and reset. It's easy to believe that only big actions lead to progress. It's the steady, intentional use of those fleeting moments that truly prepares us for what's ahead.

Sometimes we're so focused on the future that we fail to recognize how the present is shaping it. Every choice we make is like planting a seed. Over time, with consistent care and attention, those seeds grow into something meaningful. Whether it's spending five extra minutes refining a project, reaching out to encourage someone, or pausing to reflect on our goals, these simple actions quietly build the foundation for the future we envision.

Time moves forward whether we use it wisely or not. It's often in the unnoticed moments where preparation quietly takes root. By recognizing the value in these brief windows of time and engaging with them fully, we begin paving the way for the life we want. It's a slow but powerful process, one that reminds us that progress isn't about massive leaps, but about steady, intentional steps.

I often sit down to relax in my living room or to read a book, and by the end of it, I realize how much time has passed. It's easy to get caught up in the moment without noticing how quickly time slips away, especially when we're constantly multitasking or distracted. What if we could make the most of that time by being fully present in whatever we're doing?

I came across something interesting. There's research out there showing that when we're intentional and focused on one task at a time, our productivity and emotional well-being can significantly improve. This idea isn't just something that *sounds* good, it's backed by years of solid research.

One of the most well-known experts in this field is Dr. Ellen Langer, a Harvard psychologist who has spent decades studying mindfulness, specifically the practice of being fully engaged in the present moment. Her studies have shown time and time again that people who approach their daily activities with mindfulness and intention not only get more done but also find greater meaning and satisfaction in both their work and personal lives.

THE SCIENCE BEHIND BEING PRESENT

Her research offers a fascinating look at the power of being present. What she's found is simple but powerful: when people focus on what they're doing in the moment, they experience improved concentration and greater fulfillment.

For example, in one of her well-known studies, participants who approached their daily tasks mindfully reported feeling more satisfied with their work even when those tasks were routine or mundane. Just being fully engaged in what they were doing gave them a deeper sense of purpose. Dr. Langer's work on mindfulness highlights how powerful it is to be fully present in the moment, and I've realized how true that is in my own life.

I remember one afternoon having lunch in Scottsdale, enjoying a pastrami sandwich. As I was sitting there, I started thinking about how, in a couple of hours, I had set aside some time to review this manuscript you're reading right now and make a few finishing touches. I knew I had planned about thirty minutes to work on it, but I also knew there were times when I wouldn't follow through with that plan. I'd get distracted or convince myself to push it off for later. What stood out to me was how I caught myself in that exact moment, already thinking about skipping the task. That awareness alone was a moment of mindfulness. It made me realize that being present isn't just about slowing down or staying calm, it's about catching yourself in those moments when you're tempted to avoid something important.

It's like developing a mental muscle, a skill that helps you notice when you're slipping away from what you intended to do. It becomes an opportunity to pause and think, *"Okay, I'm already thinking about not doing this, but that thought itself is a chance to shift."*

In that moment, I thought, *"I'm already sitting here thinking about it. Why not just follow through?"*

It wasn't about forcing myself to do something I didn't want to do. It was about recognizing the opportunity and leaning into it. So, I decided that when the time came, I'd sit down and commit just twenty or thirty minutes to working on the manuscript. I didn't need to overwhelm myself with the idea of finishing everything. I just needed to be intentional with the time I had. That practice of catching myself in the moment became a small but powerful habit. The more I noticed those moments, the more I trained my mind to respond with *action* rather than *hesitation*.

That's the heart of being present: staying conscious of what's happening in real-time and making intentional choices. It's a skill that develops over time by helping you stay engaged and purposeful, even when your first instinct is to put things off. When I leaned into that self-awareness, progress started to come naturally. I didn't need to feel motivated every single time; I just needed to be attentive to the opportunity in front of me. Whether it was writing, studying, or handling small tasks, recognizing those moments and choosing to engage with them made all the difference.

That kind of mental awareness helped me realize that even when I *don't* feel like doing something, the very *thought* of avoiding it can be a signal and an invitation to pause, reset, and lean in. That small shift in thinking creates real progress over time. Honestly, I thought that was really cool, the fact that I had developed this kind of skill. Being able to catch myself in the exact moment when I wanted to check out or avoid something? That was incredible.

That hesitation, that quick moment of "maybe later," is a moment in itself. Being able to recognize it, to shift my mindset right then and there? That's a skill I'm truly grateful to have discovered. The awesome thing is that the benefits don't stop there. Dr. Langer's research shows that practicing mindfulness can have a positive impact on our health, too.

In one of her landmark studies, elderly participants who were encouraged to be mindful about their daily activities showed remarkable improvements in their overall well-being. They felt more energized, more involved in life, and even demonstrated better physical health, such as increased mobility and improved memory. The reason for this is straightforward: when we're fully aware, we reduce distress levels. When our bodies aren't stuck in a constant state of "fight or flight," we function better mentally, emotionally, and physically.

Lowering distress levels through simple awareness is one of the reasons why it's so beneficial, not just for getting more done, but also for staying healthy in the long run.

I read a book called *InnerFitness*, authored by my friend, Nordine Zouareg. His incredible work offers five simple steps to overcome fear and anxiety while building your self-worth. I enjoyed it and felt encouraged by everything he shared. My main takeaway from his book was his explanation of the two kinds of stress. *Distress* is the harmful kind that weighs you down and makes you feel overwhelmed and unstable. *Eustress* is the beneficial kind that helps you stay sharp and focused. Understanding the difference will allow you to regroup through tough situations with a clear mind.

Reading *InnerFitness* helped me see stress in a new light and provided a better understanding of how to navigate difficult moments. I highly recommend checking it out for yourself.

THE PROBLEM WITH MULTITASKING

Now, you may be thinking, *"But I have so much to do, how can I focus on just one thing at a time?"* It's a common thought, especially in today's fast-paced world. We often feel like the more we juggle, the more productive we'll be, but research tells a different story.

A study from Stanford University found that people who frequently multitask are less efficient than those who focus on one task at a time. In fact, multitaskers have more trouble filtering out distractions and are slower at switching between tasks. This means that multitasking doesn't just slow you down, it can also reduce the quality of your work. That's why being intentional with only one thing is so important. When we make the choice to focus on a single task, we're able to give it our full attention, which usually leads to better results. It's not about doing *more;* it's about doing things *better.*

Whether you're tackling a big project, spending time with family, or simply cooking dinner, being fully present allows you to engage more deeply with the task at hand, and that leads to more meaningful, productive outcomes.

SMALL STEPS, BIG IMPACT

You don't need to make huge changes to start seeing the benefits of making conscious choices. In fact, small shifts in how you approach your day can lead to big improvements over time.

You could start by dedicating just fifteen to thirty minutes each day to one task, completely free from distractions. Maybe it's reading a book, writing, or working on a specific project. Whatever it is, give it your full attention for that short period of time. You'll be surprised at how much you can accomplish when you're truly focused.

For example, as an author, I've learned that it's not about how much time I spend writing each day, it's about being *consistent*. When I started writing years ago, I used to think I needed to sit down for hours at a time to make real progress on my books, but that only led to burnout and frustration.

Now, I usually dedicate no more than thirty to forty minutes a day to writing, and that's on a good day. Some days, it's just twenty minutes. I might spend that time brainstorming ideas, jotting down notes, or writing parts of my manuscript. It's not always a huge, impressive effort, but it's consistent, and that consistency is what really makes the difference over time.

There are days when I feel like I didn't accomplish much, but I've learned to be okay with that. I remind myself that even a little bit of progress is still progress. What matters is showing up every day, even if it's only for a short time. Over the course of a year, all those small steps add up, eventually, the book was done. It didn't happen overnight, but it happened because I stayed steady and didn't overwhelm myself.

Even the smallest preparation, done consistently over time, will eventually meet the right moment, and that's what matters. I believe God has already orchestrated specific moments in life that are meant to align with our preparation, and when that steady effort finally connects with the timing He set apart, it creates an impact that no last-minute effort could ever produce. It all depends on the person, which is why you must study your journey, get to know your path, understand your limits, and pay attention to how your mindset and performance grow along the way. I've found that keeping things simple makes the process so much easier. When I take on too much at once my mind gets cluttered and I lose focus. When I break it down into smaller, more manageable pieces, it feels lighter. I can focus better, and honestly, I enjoy writing that way. I learned a lot about this mindset from watching an interview with Jeff Bezos. He talked about how Amazon started small, and how he enjoyed the process of slow, steady progress.

One thing he said that really stuck with me was, *"Big things start small."* That helped open my eyes to the fact that anything is possible; it's so true. It's easy to look at accomplished people or finished projects and assume they happened overnight, but they didn't. They started with small, purposeful steps, just like anything else.

I've taken that mindset into my writing, and even into running my web development agency. Some days I'll spend time writing, then shift gears and focus on client work or other responsibilities. I've learned to keep it simple, stay consistent, and trust the process.

That's the thing about small steps, they don't always feel big in the moment, but they're powerful. Over time, they build into something you can see. Whether it's writing a book, building a business, or working toward any goal, it's about taking those small, steady, intentional steps each day. Honestly, that approach makes the journey a lot more enjoyable. You'll find that not only are you getting more done, but the quality of your work improves, and the process itself becomes more enjoyable.

THE EMOTIONAL BENEFITS OF BEING PRESENT

Aside from boosting productivity, practicing purposeful presence has a major impact on our emotional well-being. When we're constantly pulled in different directions, it's easy to feel overwhelmed and anxious. When we focus on one task at a time, we create space to fully experience the moment, and that can be incredibly grounding.

Studies have shown that people who practice purposeful presence tend to have lower levels of anxiety and depression. That makes sense, when we're fully present, we're less likely to worry about what's next or dwell on the past.

Dr. Langer, whom I mentioned earlier, highlights how a purposeful mind can lead to emotional resilience. By being just a little more aware, we're better able to manage our emotions and make thoughtful, intentional decisions. This brings peace to the mind, calms the nervous system, and helps your emotions settle by quieting the brain's stress response. The sympathetic branch, a network of nerves, which gets the body ready for fight-or-flight, also plays a role in how emotions rise and react under pressure.

A SIMPLE SOLUTION TO GET STARTED

So, how can you live out the purpose that's already in you?

The good news is it doesn't have to be complicated; start small. Choose just one step each day to approach with your full focus. Maybe it's spending twenty minutes with your children without checking your phone or taking a walk without distractions.

The goal is to train your mind to be fully present in whatever you're doing. Over time, this practice will become more obvious, and you'll start to notice that you're not only more productive, but more connected to the moment itself. You'll be living it, not just letting it pass by. Although this will also become a habit, that's not entirely the whole idea of this book. Habits, if you're not careful, can sometimes make you slip into autopilot, and it becomes normal. I'm not saying you should avoid habits. They matter. However, when something stays obvious, you have a sense of purpose in every little thing. Just as Dr. Langer's research has shown, the seeds you plant today through intentional actions will grow into the breakthrough you see tomorrow.

In the end, the key to progress isn't about doing more, it's about being fully engaged in what you're doing *right now*. When you focus on one task at a time and stay present, you set yourself up for both productivity and peace of mind.

That's where real growth begins.

FINAL THOUGHTS

Set the temperature.

The "what if" you choose to believe matters more than you think.

→ **What you tell yourself shapes what you expect, and what you expect slowly becomes what you experience.**

→ **When you focus on one thing at a time and make small, intentional choices each day, you begin to see steady progress that lasts.**

HANDLE YOUR THOUGHTS BEFORE DISTRACTIONS DIVIDE YOUR ATTENTION

"Where the mind goes, the man follows."

— JOYCE MEYER

HAVE YOU ever wondered where your thoughts go when you're not paying close attention? Based on what many researchers have summarized from findings reported by Anne Craig in the Queen's University Gazette, we have, give or take depending on the person and their situation, 6,000 thoughts running through our minds every single day, but believe it or not. Only a small portion of that qualifies as rational thinking. The rest of our thoughts are mostly just noise and mental loops. It's our minds circling around what happened yesterday or jumping ahead to what might happen tomorrow. That means only a small fraction of our mental activity is real thinking, but the good news is, there's a way to start gaining control over those scattered, high-energy thoughts before they shoot off in every direction. It starts when you surrender your mind to the Lord, because He gives you the peace that surpasses all understanding, and it's only through that kind of peace that your thoughts begin to settle, like waves slowly calming after a storm, and become easier to guide.

There's a devotional blog I've been reading by Heart Treasure that reminded me how simple prayer can be, especially when you're overwhelmed or don't know what to say. In this blog, they highlighted that a characteristic of a person who has little experience of peace is prayerlessness. Prayer is very simple; it means to talk to God with humility, the One who created you and hears you every day. All you need to do is be as simple and honest as you possibly can. I understand that prayer can feel difficult for some people, especially when thoughts are scattered, almost like fast-moving lasers that shoot off in every direction before we even get a chance to slow them down or think twice.

A lot of people assume prayer has to sound perfect, almost like reading a script or preparing the right words in advance, but the truth is that prayer isn't about how you say it, it's about how you approach God and how you position your heart before Him. All it takes is humility, the willingness to be available, and the decision to come as you are, because when you make yourself available to God with a genuine heart, the words tend to follow naturally.

Prayer is powerful and necessary, and it brings the peace we need to reset our focus. At the same time, God has also given us wisdom and practical insight to help us stay grounded and navigate the day with intention. There are simple techniques and choices we can apply that make a real difference in how we manage our thoughts.

When you stop and sit with that, it's kind of shocking, because it means that out of all the mental capacity we're given each day, only a tiny fraction of it is being used to focus on what matters right now. Only a small amount is what we're left with to solve our world's problems, to focus on what's right in front of us, and to make rational decisions. That small amount is all we have to build something real with our lives. We try to build a future for ourselves, navigate relationships, raise kids, chase dreams, and heal old wounds. For most people, we're doing all of that while running on just scraps of clear thinking. The craziest part is that most of us are choosing to live that way without even knowing it.

What if we didn't have to live that way, and what if there really was another option. I remember sitting in math class many years ago, learning about reciprocals, where Mr. Gregovich explained that if you want to flip a fraction around, you just invert it by turning it upside down. You take what's on the bottom and move it to the top. Mr. Gregovich used to drill that into us so much that it still pops into my head sometimes when I'm not even trying. Now, all these years later, I realize it's not just a math trick; it's a life principle, too. If the majority of our thinking right now is out of our control, and we're mostly remembering yesterday or worrying about tomorrow without ever living intentionally, then what would happen if we flipped it? What if we made most of our thoughts about living today, thinking clearly, solving what's in front of us, and being present in our lives instead of drifting through them half-asleep?

Wouldn't it be nice if most of your thoughts were working for you instead of out of control? What would it feel like to tackle your world's problems with focused clarity instead of scattered attention? Picture being present with your family, not just in the room, but fully engaged, emotionally alive, and mentally sharp. Think about stepping into your workplace, your dreams, and your calling. Imagine having a strong, clear mind, one that isn't knotted up in old regrets or hijacked by worst-case scenarios. Envision the lightness of a life where your thoughts are finally free to move and flow, no longer stuck in a traffic jam of yesterday's baggage or tomorrow's fears.

When your mind gets trapped in that endless loop of remembering and worrying, it creates a kind of mental instability. You end up replaying old regrets, rethinking past conversations, and reliving scenarios that no longer exist, all while trying to brace yourself for whatever might go wrong in the future. Your thoughts jump back and forth so often that you lose track of the present moment entirely.

You can think of it like mental cholesterol, where too many thoughts are bouncing around at once, blocking the flow of new ideas and making it harder for any single thought to move forward without getting tangled. Your thinking starts to feel heavy and slow, like there's no open path for a useful thought to pass through clearly. That kind of buildup doesn't just stay in your head. It begins to weigh down your focus, affect your mood, and shape how you respond to everything around you. Eventually, you stop noticing the simple decisions you need to make today, because your attention is caught between yesterday and tomorrow. The result is a constant sense of pressure that clouds your ability to move forward and makes everything feel more overwhelming than it is.

This is why worrying is so dangerous: it divides the mind by acting like a track switch, guiding your thoughts onto separate paths that pull in opposite directions as you try to focus on today and tomorrow at the same time, even though your mind can't fully deal with both days at once. That's why it fractures the way it does, because the mind isn't built to carry two days at the same time.

Out of the 6,000 thoughts your mind is capable of generating each day, worry cuts them in half, slashing them down to about 3,000 thoughts that may be heading in the right direction. They still aren't clear or focused enough to create real momentum. Here's the sobering part: even after that split, as I have mentioned earlier, only a small portion of what's left is purposeful thinking, which means you're down to somewhere in the neighborhood of about 400 clear thoughts a day.

How is it even possible that God could have more thoughts about you than all the grains of sand on the seashores? Not just one seashore, and not just a single coastline, but every seashore spread throughout the earth, all the beaches you've ever stood on, and every shoreline you've never even known existed, and every stretch of shoreline that runs quietly along the edges of lands you may never step foot on. It doesn't stop there, because when God speaks of sand, it goes beyond what we see along the coast; most people don't realize that deserts around the world are filled with even more sand, especially in vast and dry places where dunes rise and fall with the wind, where no buildings stand, and where the land rolls on for miles, layered with fine, dust-like grains.

Think of the Sahara, the Mojave, the Arabian Desert, the Australian Great Victoria and Great Sandy deserts. These are endless regions of sand where human footprints rarely last more than a few minutes. Yet even with all of that, we still haven't reached the end, because what many people never think to consider, and I'm sure this may not have crossed your mind either, is that beneath the deep dark oceans lies even more sand, hidden under unknown water, mixed with mud and rock, resting in complete darkness where no one sees it or touches it, but it's still there.

These forgotten layers, buried and untouched, are also part of the picture God was describing when he said his thoughts toward you outnumber every grain of sand. Most people might respond by saying, "Well, he's God," and while that is true, there's something more personal when you grasp that you were made in his image, which means you were created to think, reflect, and carry thoughts in a way that mirrors his nature. God's mind is never split or tangled by fear or anxiety, and every thought he has is intentional, whole, and filled with purpose. Just like the verse out of Jeremiah 29:11, where it says, "For I know the plans that I have for you." That verse is one of the most quoted lines in the Bible, and you've likely heard it many times. What many people don't realize, though some may, is that nearly every modern Bible translation uses the word *plans* when quoting that passage. It's familiar, widely accepted, and often repeated.

Here's a fun fact that adds more depth to the verse and is worth noting. Out of all the modern translations in print today, only a small number of them choose a more personal word, one that is intended to speak directly to you and only for you. My favorite is the King James Version, and it says, "For I know the *thoughts* that I think toward you." That single word, *thoughts*, adds something more personal and more intentional. It reminds us that God is not only making plans for our lives, but He is also thinking about us every second.

Isn't it amazing that God wants to walk with you every day, to watch you grow, to be part of your life, and to stay involved in everything that matters to you? That kind of steady presence is exactly what helps you take ownership of your choices and live with confidence, even when life feels noisy or uncertain.

With all of this in mind, it really comes down to something so simple but so powerful: choices create your life. What you make of your life, the path you carve through your days, the way you show up for the people and dreams that matter to you, all of it is built on nothing more and nothing less than choices. Those choices don't come out of nowhere. They grow out of the small, unseen cogs that keep your life turning, the thoughts that run through your mind every single day. Those tiny, almost invisible choices you make in your thinking are what build the gears that drive everything else. Every decision you make, every emotion you feel, every step you take, it all starts with what you're allowing yourself to think about.

If you intend to change your life, you must move away from the noise of constantly rehearsing old regrets and future fears and begin living with peace. It's not about flipping some magic switch overnight. It's about learning a skill called cognitive defusion. Cognitive defusion is exactly what it sounds like: you're not arguing with a thought but learning how to separate yourself from the thoughts that try to hijack your mind; it's about choosing. It's about standing back, noticing a thought like worry or fear when it shows up, marking it for what it is, and saying, "No, I'm not giving you space to run my day." It's about stepping back into the driver's seat of your mind and filtering what you allow to stay. Cognitive defusion is how you get most of your control back.

The whole idea of cognitive defusion is this practice of filtering your thoughts, not by fighting them, but by using discernment to recognize harmful thoughts and becoming aware of them. Essentially, you're refusing to let the wrong ones stay, it's not something that modern psychology invented. It's rooted in the Bible.

In 2 Corinthians 10:5, it says, "We destroy every proud obstacle that keeps people from knowing God. We take captive every rebellious thought and bring it to obedience to Christ." That's the original blueprint. God has been telling us from the beginning that our minds need to be guarded, that our thoughts need to be captured, that we are not called to let just anything run loose inside our heads. Cognitive defusion is just a new way of describing what Scripture has already taught, that freedom begins by choosing which thoughts you allow to stay and which ones you refuse to entertain.

The best way to remember cognitive defusion is to break down the word itself. The first three letters of cognitive—cog—can be a simple way to picture gears, kind of like a mnemonic trick to help the word make more sense. Have you ever noticed how wind-up toys and wristwatches have all those little wheel components inside, spinning and locking together? Those delicate wheel components are called cogs. That's why those illustrations of cogs moving in someone's brain, like you often see in cartoon shows or artistic visuals, are meant to depict the mind in motion, with tiny gears spinning as thoughts form.

I know this might seem like a rabbit trail, but this reminds me of the SpongeBob SquarePants episode called Patrick SmartPants. Patrick, who is known to be the dumbest character on the show, falls off a cliff and lands on brain coral fields, where one of the coral cones ends up replacing the top of his head, making him an overnight genius. The very next scene shows rusty, unused cogs in his head forcing themselves to spin, the rust and cobwebs fall away, and it is like his brain is finally starting up. Go ahead and judge me for being a SpongeBob fan, I'm fine with it. I'll take the hit, because this scene is one of the best ways to unpack what the word cognitive means.

Your brain works the same way. I'm not saying you have Patrick's brain or calling you dumb by any means. I used that scene to unpack the meaning of a word for you. That's why we call it cognitive functioning, because everything you think, feel, and decide is running through a network of these mental gears. When you practice cognitive defusion, you're choosing which gears you want to keep spinning and which ones you want to let go. You're diffusing the wrong thoughts, like the worrying, the regret, the rehearsing, and you're keeping the right gears turning.

Jimmy Evans, author of Marriage on the Rock and founder of XO Marriage, once said something that has stuck with me for a long time: bondage simply means a house of thought. When you let thoughts go unintended, when you allow them to live unchecked inside your mind, they don't stay harmless. They begin materializing and building a house. They begin setting up walls. Without your consent, they begin taking charge of the way you see yourself, the way you feel, and the way you live. Before long, those thoughts aren't just passing ideas, they are running your life. That's what bondage is. It's exactly why so many people are living with only a small portion of their lives being free, because most of their mind has been surrendered to the past or hijacked by fear about the future. They aren't living free. They are stuck. They are trapped inside a house of thought they never meant to build.

Your life is made up of thoughts and choices. Bondage, at its core, is just the result of the wrong thoughts being allowed to stay too long. So, the question becomes simple: which one are you going to choose? Are you going to continue letting most of your mind live in the past, or in the endless loop of what you think tomorrow will look like? Or are you going to tear down the old walls, capture the wrong thoughts, and start living today with one thought, one choice, one cog at a time?

As Jesus said in Matthew 6:34, *"Therefore do not worry about tomorrow, for tomorrow will worry about itself. Each day has enough trouble of its own."* I love how simple and practical this teaching is. It reminds us to focus on what's right in front of us instead of getting overwhelmed by what *might* happen in the future.

Jesus isn't saying not to plan or prepare. Of course, we need to be responsible, but He *is* reminding us to trust God with what we can't control and to put our energy into today. Think about it: if you're so worried about tomorrow, how can you give your best to the role you're meant to play right now? Once you've done your part, played your role, and done it well, you can move forward without carrying unnecessary burdens.

Life is about taking it piece by piece, step by step, and as Desmond Tutu once said, you must eat the elephant one bite at a time, because real growth happens slowly and intentionally. That kind of approach matters, especially when it comes to how we face the pressures of daily life.

So, ask yourself if you're truly present in your role today, or if fear and worry have been quietly holding you back. Think about how much could begin to change in your mindset if you released that weight for just one day and gave your full focus to the moment right in front of you.

Today is the only power you have to make a change and to move forward. You can't edit tomorrow because it hasn't happened yet, and you can't rewrite yesterday because it's already done. All you have is today, this very moment, and how you choose to spend it matters.

God has given you this day as a gift. A chance to create, grow, and to take your next step forward. So, why waste it on worrying about things you can't control? Focus on what's in your hands right now and let God handle the rest. The way I see it, you can only be in one place at a time. You can't teleport or suddenly switch to working on something else you think is more important. You're human, and all you have is the present moment right in front of you.

So instead of overthinking or stressing about everything else you *could* be doing, it's better to focus on where you are and what you have right now. That's all within your control. When you accept that, it becomes easier to get things done. You realize, *"Okay, this is the time I have, and this is where I'm at."* Whether you're at your desk, in a meeting, or just brainstorming ideas, that's your moment to make progress. It's that simple.

This applies to everyday things, too. If you're doing homework, give it your full attention instead of thinking about what's next. If you're cleaning the house, focus on one room at a time instead of getting overwhelmed by everything.

By staying present and working with what's in front of you, things start to feel more manageable, and you get more done.

BEING WORRISOME CAN LEAD TO MENTAL INSTABILITY

When my thoughts are fixated on tomorrow's worries, I notice how easy it is to let today's opportunities slip away. It's like I'm caught in this subtle dance where worrying about the future stops me from grabbing the chances right in front of me. I've seen how the fear of what's next becomes a barrier to living in the moment, sidelining the very opportunities that tomorrow might bring. The danger of divided attention becomes so obvious in the form of a mental tug-of-war between what I need to handle right now and the weight of the "what ifs" about tomorrow.

I've experienced how this feels firsthand, especially in times when my mind is split between the urgency of what's happening now and the worries of tomorrow. I know it's easy to take the reality of what you see right now and associate it with the future, thinking that's how it's going to be, but that's not necessarily the truth. It could be the bills that need paying, stress about work, or the hurt left behind by a tough conversation with someone close to me. That kind of internal division sows seeds of confusion. It stops us from being fully present. Honestly, the mind becomes like a battlefield, where the present moment is constantly fighting against the uncertainty of the future.

If you're too caught up in tomorrow, you'll miss today's opportunities. If you miss today, you'll end up pushing aside tomorrow's possibilities, too. You can't expect anyone to hand you a future that's already solidified; something fully built and added up. It's something you have to be real with yourself about, something that only happens when you put serious weight behind your mindset and fully lean into it.

During my studies at Bible college, I learned that the word *worry* comes from an ancient Greek term, *merimnáō*. It comes from a root word that carries the idea of division, with *merízō,* meaning "to divide." In Greek, *nous* means "mind," but *merimnáō* isn't built from that word; the point is that worry splits your attention. When I really thought about it, it made perfect sense, because worry represents a divided mind that pulls your mental focus in separate directions and makes it harder to stay fully present.

Without taking intentional steps to address the things that worry us, we can easily fall into what James describes in the Bible as being *double-minded,* unstable in all we do. Worry creates that kind of mental instability through a constant shifting of focus between now and later, between faith and fear.

James 1:8 warns us about this exact thing, explaining how double mindedness leads to unfocused thoughts and unsteady decision-making. I've also realized there's a big difference between *worry* and *concern*. Worry traps you overnight in a loop that never ends, and it paralyzes you. It tears your focus apart and makes you anxious for no real reason. It keeps you stuck in fear, caught in endless cycles of "what ifs" and "maybes."

I've been there, feeling completely frozen and unable to move forward because the anxiety was just too much. Worry doesn't help you solve anything because it drains your energy and feeds your imagination with worst-case scenarios. All your strength goes into *fearing* the future instead of *facing* it. Concern, on the other hand, is something entirely different. It's like a productive form of worry. Concern acknowledges there's an issue, but it chooses not to be overwhelmed by it. It's about making a conscious decision to *deal* with the problem rather than letting it deal with you. This kind of mindset remains controlled and focused. It doesn't scatter your thoughts the way worry does, instead, it channels them toward real solutions.

I've noticed that when I'm concerned, not worried, I can stay calm and think clearly. Concern pushes me toward *action*, not despair. It helps me focus on the steps I *can* take, instead of getting lost in fear over what might happen. This reminds me of the Apostle Paul and what he told the Corinthian church. He urged them not to be divided, but to be of one mind. He was addressing the same kind of division about which I've been talking. Paul emphasized that only Jesus—the Prince of Peace—can bring reconciliation to divided thoughts.

I think about how often this happens in marriages, too. So many couples struggle because their minds aren't unified. Their interests are different, their goals don't align, and that leads to conflict and confusion. Paul's words, *"the two will become one flesh,"* have always stood out to me. When he says *"flesh,"* I believe he's also talking about the mind. He's saying the two will become of one mind.

When that unity is missing, it causes trouble. When couples are united in mind and spirit, God can help them reconcile the worries of today and tomorrow. That unity creates space to focus on the present and to intentionally build a better future together.

I also think about John C. Maxwell's "Law of Intentionality." He talks about how growth doesn't happen by accident; you have to be deliberate about it. That applies here, too. Focusing on what you can control right now, especially where you place your focus and energy, is what truly makes all the difference.

Being of one mind, whether it's with yourself, your spouse, or even your faith, is something I believe you can only achieve with the help of the Holy Spirit. That kind of unity doesn't just happen on its own. It's something you have to work toward, pray for, and choose to live out every day.

When you think about the time you have from this perspective, everything starts to make sense as you begin to see how worry paralyzes, blinds, and divides your mind from the things that matter most, trapping you in fear and indecision. Concern, unity of mind, intentional problem solving, and focused living are God's way of setting us free. By choosing to focus on today and refusing to let our minds be pulled in different directions, we position ourselves to create a better tomorrow. It's a mindset shift that takes effort, but it brings with it a peace and purpose that can transform how we live.

TURNING LIFE'S PRESSURE INTO PURPOSE

I watched a memorable 1979 interview with Billy Graham not too long ago on YouTube. The interviewer brought up a common perception that despite his unwavering faith, Graham must have still felt worried about life's pressures, especially with his incredibly tight schedule, constantly traveling the world, and flying in-and-out of airports. People wondered how he managed to balance everything with so little time for himself.

Graham's response was profound. He clarified that he wasn't worried; rather, he was *concerned*. His concern came with a proactive mindset. Rather than letting it overwhelm him, he used it to guide his decisions and solve problems, which kept him sharp. Despite the challenges of flying around the world for speaking engagements and crusades, Graham's concern led him to strategize intentionally, ensuring he could fulfill his commitments without being consumed by them.

Worry could have easily consumed Graham, leaving him frazzled and ineffective. Instead, his positive concern allowed him to approach his responsibilities with a clear mind and a strategic plan. He was able to think rationally, addressing the issues at hand without succumbing to the paralyzing effects of worry.

Concern is the *good type* of worry; it's an acknowledgment of problems paired with a willingness to solve them. It applies just enough mental pressure to keep us aware and engaged without tipping us into the chaos of a divided mind. While worry scatters and leaves you unstable, concern focuses and motivates. It's a balanced approach that enables us to navigate life's challenges with clarity and purpose. Concern works best in circumstances when you approach the situation from a different angle.

I want to show you what kind of angle I'm referring to, because it offers one of the most effective ways to face whatever challenge you're dealing with. The word circumstance can be divided into two parts: *circum* and *stance*. *Circum* brings to mind the word circumference, which refers to your surroundings, not just the pressure, stress, or environment around you, but also the internal space within your mind. It includes the thoughts you rehearse, the things you're carrying from yesterday, the weight of today, or the uncertainty of tomorrow.

Stance is the position you take within those surroundings, the mindset you choose, and the way you respond to what's happening. Concern begins when you stop spinning inside that negative circle of worry and decide to take a stand, asking yourself what needs to be done and how you're going to move forward. That's why, when using this kind of idea, what once felt like panic became poise and what used to be chaos started to look like composure.

Worry steals your peace away, and that's exactly what the enemy wants. The adversary, the devil, wants your mind anxious and distracted. He wants your peace to be taken away, but God wants you to have peace of mind.

How Worry Affects Focus:

- Anxiety causes you to pay more attention to threats or negative things.
- This makes it hard to concentrate on what's happening right now.
- Instead of being present, you're stuck thinking about future problems that *might* happen later.

Impact on Peace of Mind:

- Constant worrying means you're always preparing for the worst.
- This prevents you from enjoying positive moments today.
- You miss out on being at peace because your mind is focused on potential future issues

Why This Matters:

- Focusing on the future all the time, without a solid plan, can make you feel unsettled.
- It creates a cycle where you're always anxious about what's next.
- To find peace, it's important to break this cycle and focus on the present.

Worry robs you of the ability to be in the moment. It only makes you focus on problems you have no control over, making it hard to relax and enjoy life as it's happening. This insight supports the idea that worry can prevent you from experiencing peace and contentment today. It aligns with the belief that the devil wants to steal your peace, while God desires you to have a peaceful mind and heart.

We can all agree that life is short, but often, life feels short because we don't make the most of it. Worry drains the life from your days and, in turn, shifts your focus to counting the days in your life. It pulls your attention away from the present and pushes it toward anxiety about what lies ahead. This constant state of worry takes the vibrancy of your current moments and causes you to dwell on the uncertainties of tomorrow.

THE BATTLE FOR YOUR ATTENTION

During the cold winter of 1944, in the thick of World War II, a clever operation called *Operation Greif* was set in motion. Led by the infamous German commando Otto Skorzeny, this plan aimed to create chaos and confusion among the Allied forces during the Battle of the Bulge. It was bold and cunning: German soldiers, who spoke fluent English and wore American uniforms would infiltrate the Allied lines. Their mission was to spread false information, sabotage equipment, and stir up deep distrust and paranoia among the troops.

As the operation began, its impact was immediate. American troops, already exhausted from the relentless German offensive, now faced a new and sneaky threat. Rumors quickly spread of unknown figures tampering with vehicles, cutting communication lines, and giving false orders. The unity and sense of purpose that had driven the Allied forces began to crumble under the weight of suspicion and fear.

This mental division had real consequences on the battlefield. Soldiers became wary of each other, unsure if the person next to them was a friend or an enemy. Checkpoints were set up where troops were intensely questioned, often causing delays and confusion. Precious time and resources were spent trying to find these infiltrators, which ended up diverting focus from the crucial task of stopping the German advance.

In full reality, the Allies were being cognitively robbed. The distractions created by Operation Greif caused them to miss crucial opportunities to strengthen their positions and launch counterattacks. Instead of focusing on their immediate goals, they were consumed by fear of the unknown, which left their minds divided between the present threat and potential dangers. The psychological toll of this operation serves as a powerful analogy for our daily lives.

When we allow ourselves to be distracted by worries about tomorrow, we lose sight of the opportunities and responsibilities of today. Just as the Allied soldiers were hindered by the fear of hidden enemies, we too can be paralyzed by anxieties about the future, making us ineffective in the present. Today's challenges are enough to handle on their own. The question is: will you tackle the problems right in front of you, or let anxiety and fear of the future hold you back?

Planning for the future is vital, but it's how you handle the interruptions and issues of today that minimize tomorrow's worries.

Imagine a writer who dreams of publishing a bestseller but constantly worries about how it will be received. This worry distracts the author from the act of writing, causing the writer to procrastinate and miss daily writing goals. Much like the Allied forces during Operation Greif, their mind is divided and their productivity suffers.

The lesson from Operation Greif is clear: worry and distraction can be just as dangerous as any tangible threat. By letting fear and uncertainty dominate our thoughts, we sabotage our ability to act decisively and effectively in the present. To overcome this, we must train our minds to focus on today, embracing each moment and opportunity with clarity and purpose.

The psychological warfare used by Skorzeny's operatives during World War II highlights a timeless truth: distraction and worry can derail even the strongest forces. They divert focus and weaken their resolve. By recognizing and fighting these mental diversions, we can ensure that we are not robbed of the precious moments and opportunities that today offers. Just as the Allies eventually overcame the chaos of Operation Greif, we too can triumph over the distractions that threaten to divide our minds and impede our progress. The key to a more enriched and stable existence lies in untangling the web of divided thoughts. Redirecting the focus towards the present unravels the mental divide and opens the door to a fuller engagement with life's opportunities, allowing us to live unencumbered by the weight of tomorrow's uncertainties.

James 1:8 serves as a poignant reminder: *A double-minded man is unstable in all his ways.* In contrast, a singular, unwavering focus on the task at hand fosters stability and completeness, both in our daily endeavors and spiritual lives.

As we navigate the balance between today and tomorrow, the art of undivided attention emerges as a powerful ally, guiding us toward a more balanced and fulfilling life.

NAVIGATING DISTRACTIONS:
Finding Focus Amidst Chaos and Social Media

One day, I received an unexpected call from my cousin Darius. He excitedly asked if I wanted to join him at a car show in a cool warehouse near downtown Phoenix. Being a car enthusiast, I couldn't resist, so I quickly agreed and told him I'd be on my way. I drove up to his house, and we enjoyed a quick coffee before hitting the road. We took the I-10 freeway towards downtown, engaged in some casual conversations. It was a good time, filled with a moment to catch up and talk about everything under the sun.

Little did we know, something unexpected was about to happen.

As we cruised along the freeway, I decided to change lanes to catch the next exit. I glanced at the side mirror, checked my blind spot, and did a quick shoulder check. There it was, a speeding car in the lane I wanted to switch to. I figured I'd wait for it to pass before making my move.

The car sped up beside us, and I noticed it was a minivan. Now, you wouldn't expect anything unusual from a minivan, right? As I looked closer, I saw something that left me utterly speechless.

Inside the minivan was a dad, casually driving over 70 mph, with his wife beside him and kids in the back. What really caught my attention was that this dad was holding a bright yellow book *right in front of his face, literally at face level*!

Yes, you read that right.

He was literally reading while driving. His wife in the passenger seat didn't seem to mind at all, just staring straight ahead at the road, head tilted and half-asleep. The kids were in the backseat playing, just doing what kids do. Everything about that minivan seemed completely normal, just so routine and ordinary, except for one thing that made it hard to believe: the dad was actually reading a book.

I couldn't believe my eyes. I nudged Darius and said, "Are you seeing this? That driver is reading a book while driving!" Darius glanced over and burst out laughing, unable to comprehend why someone would risk their entire family's safety... for a book.

It was both hilarious and terrifying at the same time.

Darius, unable to believe his eyes, quickly pulled out his phone. He wanted to get a close-up of the book title because let's be honest, it must be a No. 1 New York Times Best Seller book if this guy was willing to risk it all to read it. As the minivan sped ahead, it was tough to get a clear shot because it kept accelerating, and we had to keep catching up. I was driving my brand-new car, and even with that, I found myself pushing just to stay close enough. Eventually after two solid minutes, Darius managed to snap a clear photo. When he showed me the image, I couldn't help but laugh out loud.

The book was titled *The Power of Discipline: How to Use Self-Control and Mental Toughness to Achieve Your Goals by Daniel Walter*. The irony was just too much to handle. Here was a man reading about *self-control* while demonstrating a complete lack of it, as he was literally reading while driving!

We continued to follow the minivan for a bit, amazed at what we were witnessing. The dad held the book so close to his face that it seemed like he was more interested in the pages than the road ahead. For a full minute, he was completely engrossed and totally oblivious to the dangers around him. It was like watching a surreal scene from a comedy movie, except this was real life, involving real people, and serious consequences. I couldn't wrap my head around why the father, the one responsible for leading and protecting his family, would make such a reckless decision, especially one that put their safety at risk for the sake of reading a book. Hadn't he ever heard of an audiobook? Probably not, I'm assuming.

Eventually, the minivan exited the freeway, and we lost sight of it. Even as we made our way to the car show, we couldn't stop talking about the bizarre incident. Surrounded by beautiful cars and the hum of engines, we were fully immersed in the event, and yet, we still couldn't shake off the absurdity of what we had seen.

We laughed about it, sure, but beneath the humor was an underlying concern. Why are people so distracted nowadays? It's one thing to glance at your phone while driving, which is already dangerous enough, but to sit behind the wheel, with the effort of trying to read a best seller book? That was a whole new level of distraction.

As we walked around the car show, admiring the sleek designs and powerful engines, the topic kept coming back up. Darius and I pondered why people seem so inclined to distract themselves, even in dangerous situations like driving. It's like we're always looking for something to occupy our minds, even at the risk of our own safety.

I couldn't help but think about how deeply our culture's obsession with multitasking and constant stimulation plays into this. We live in a fast-paced world where everything is about convenience and speed, but somewhere along the way, it's led us to make some irrational choices.

These distractions, whether it's binge-watching TV, procrastinating or constantly checking your phone, can prevent us from focusing on what's important. It's akin to a driver reading a book. You may not physically endanger anyone, but you're still allowing distractions to pull your focus away from your goals.

INTENTIONALITY DEMANDS BOLD CHOICES

I'm sure you're already aware that nothing in life happens by accident; everything unfolds for a reason, even if the meaning isn't clear right away. You must be intentional and mindful of the choices, actively taking steps forward toward what could become your future.

Time is the one resource we can never get back, making each moment a powerful opportunity to shape our lives. Instead of simply going through the motions or filling the day with distractions, consider this: every small decision you make, like what you prioritize or how you spend your hours, can create a ripple effect that influences your future in ways you may not even see yet.

Think of your time like planting seeds. Each choice, whether it's dedicating an hour to learning a new skill, calling a loved one, or intentionally taking time to rest, will grow into something bigger over time. It's not about giving up what you enjoy, but about balancing leisure with actions that move you closer to who you want to become and what you want to accomplish.

The habits you build today are silently building the foundation of your future, like your career, your relationships, and even your sense of purpose. Just one choice can lead to a series of others that ultimately define our entire path.

In an article published on Forbes, senior contributor Toni Fitzgerald reported that Americans spend more than three hours per day watching television, making it the most time-consuming leisure activity. This is not even including your phone screen time or anything else, it's kind of insane if you ask me. This adds up to about 1,000 hours a year, time that could be used more productively.

Forbes mentioned that rising prices, like groceries and other daily costs, made some people change how they watch TV. It didn't stop them from watching, but it got their attention just enough to shift their habits a little. Some stopped paying for cable and started using cheaper options like Amazon Prime instead, which shows how the distraction didn't fully go away, but it started to change. It's interesting how something as simple as a price increase can interrupt a routine that once felt automatic. Sometimes all it takes is a small shift to make people notice what they've been doing without thinking. It just goes to show that even constant distractions and daily routines can be interrupted when change forces people to pay attention.

Imagine redirecting just a fraction of that time toward activities that matter, like advancing your career, building a business, or strengthening relationships with loved ones. The results could be transformative. Being intentional with your time also means making intentional choices in your daily life. For parents, this could involve choosing to engage with your children through meaningful activities rather than passive ones like watching TV without keeping track of time.

Now, I'm not saying watching TV is completely bad. I mean, keeping up with the news when necessary is fine. It becomes an issue when you lose track of time and spend your days passively unengaged and unproductive. As long as you're not letting it take over and drain your energy daily, it's okay to enjoy it in moderation. The focus should be on making sure it doesn't overshadow the things that matter in your life.

If you start paying attention to how you're spending each second, it can completely change the way you approach your goals. It's not just about hours or minutes; it's about recognizing the value of every moment.

When you become aware of the seconds within an hour, your entire approach to time would change. You'd start working differently by thinking and acting more efficiently because you're no longer just focused on minutes or hours. Instead, you recognize the value of each passing second, making you more mindful of how your time is truly being spent.

Worry is the enemy of being intentional.

It adds a heavy weight to your mind while stealing your peace. It sneaks in, making you think you're just being cautious or preparing for something, but instead, it keeps you stuck. When you're caught up in worry, your thoughts are all over the place, and it's so much harder to focus on what matters. You end up spending so much time thinking about "what if" scenarios that you completely miss the opportunities right in front of you. Worry slows you down and steals the opportunities you could have used to grow, connect, or move forward.

When you let worry take over, it's like hitting a pause button on your ability to be intentional. You're so wrapped up in worst case scenarios that you forget to focus on what's right in front of you. You worry because you think no one else will carry the weight of your situation, so it feels like you're addressing the matter, but that doesn't help; it only makes the problem feel bigger than it is. If you can start focusing on what you can control and let go of the rest, you'll notice a big shift. It's about making small, simple choices like being present, taking action, and trusting that things will work out. That's how you take back your time, your peace, and your purpose; it's not easy, but it's worth it.

THE EFFECTS OF ADD AND SOCIAL MEDIA

You know, distractions are something we all deal with, whether we have Attention Deficit Disorder or not. For people with ADD, staying focused can be a real struggle, but honestly, I feel like it's hard for everyone these days. Apps like TikTok and constant notifications are always pulling at us, making it tough to stay on track with what really matters.

TikTok is so good at grabbing attention with quick, entertaining videos that only last a few seconds. This constant stream of short clips trains the brain to crave instant bursts of information, making it harder to focus on one thing for an extended time. It's interesting how people are drawn to those brief, bite-sized videos, but often miss out on the little meaningful moments happening in real life—unless you're using it for business purposes.

I see no issue with creating content but consuming it just to kill time can become a major problem if you don't manage your screen time carefully. It is the responsibility of the consumer to set a screen time limit, not so much the content creator.

This obsession with short content chips away at patience and even the ability to appreciate what truly matters. Even for those who don't have ADD, shorter attention spans are becoming more common, making it tough to dive deeply into tasks that require focus.

Personally, I haven't engaged much with TikTok in the typical scrolling way. I've mostly used it for business, mainly to post and create, but not consume. My mind hasn't picked up the habit of craving those quick, dopamine-packed videos like many other people have. I can definitely see how easy it would be to fall into that cycle, where every swipe trains the brain to chase the next burst of instant entertainment.

Life can feel overwhelming, with so many notifications, emails, and responsibilities competing for our attention every day. It's like being stuck in a loop of "continuous partial attention," which means you're physically present, but your mind is scattered, jumping from one thing to another without being in the moment.

There are ways to regain focus, even in the middle of all these distractions. Breaking tasks into smaller steps can make them feel less daunting, and setting specific times to check social media can stop it from taking over the day. Practicing mindfulness is like a workout for the brain. Even something as simple as listening during a conversation or asking thoughtful questions can help train the mind to stay present. By incorporating small habits like these, sharper focus and a calmer mindset become much more achievable.

Based on my personal methods and way of living, simply taking a short minute to stop everything I'm doing, regroup, slow my thoughts, and take some deep breaths has been one of the best tools for helping me slow down. It's not just about staying mentally aware; it's about connecting with that deep sense of presence you feel in your core.

Modern conveniences, like cars and highways, make it easy to believe rushing through life will help manage time better. Procrastination often sneaks in with thoughts like, "There's still time to speed to work or soccer practice at the last minute." Rushing creates mental urgency, leaving people feeling frazzled and overwhelmed. Combined with the fast-paced nature of social media, it's no wonder focus feels harder to maintain.

Hundreds of years ago, people had to travel for days to reach their destinations, which made them more aware of time. Today, with our efficient transportation and instant access to information, time feels faster, leaving us in a constant state of hurry. To slow down, we have to learn to be present in the moment, not just mentally, but with our entire being.

When we turn our attention to the living presence of Jesus Christ through the power of the Holy Spirit, something begins to happen deep within us. A bubbling spring of living water starts to flow from our inner being, located in the belly or core of the torso; that flow brings eternal life and peace. It is in that place that we can slow down, think more clearly, make better choices every day, and ease the mental pressure that life throws at us.

While ADD can pose unique challenges to maintaining focus, many people experience similar struggles due to today's fast-paced, digital world. Understanding these challenges and actively working on strategies to improve focus can help anyone stay present and make the most of their time. This not only boosts productivity but also enhances the quality of life, allowing for a deeper connection to the present moment.

The rise of platforms like TikTok has dramatically changed how we consume content, affecting our attention spans and mental health. Studies show that the quick, engaging videos on TikTok, often less than sixty seconds long, have led to a noticeable decrease in attention spans. I'm sure you've heard of this before, the average attention span has dropped from twelve seconds in 2000 to just eight seconds, even shorter than that of a goldfish.

This decline in focus is closely linked to the constant stream of short-form content that keeps users engaged through rapid, entertaining visuals. TikTok's "For You" page, powered by advanced algorithms, delivers videos matching viewers' interests. This customization keeps people hooked, activating the brain's reward centers and releasing extra dopamine, which is a chemical that makes us feel good.

However, this process can lead to a cycle of addiction, where we constantly seek more content to maintain that dopamine high. When the videos stop, your dopamine levels quickly return to their normal state. This can leave you wanting to keep watching because your brain is looking for the next bit of stimulation. Over time, heavy, compulsive use is connected with higher rates of anxiety and depressive symptoms, especially in younger users. The instant gratification offered by platforms like TikTok has also made us more impatient. We're used to getting quick rewards, which makes it harder to focus on activities that require more time and effort, like reading or working on a project.

This is especially concerning for younger users, whose brains are still developing. They might find it harder to control their screen time and focus on other things.

This shift affects more than just our ability to pay attention. The endless flow of information can overwhelm us, leading to "information overload," which makes it hard to concentrate, affects memory and increases stress levels. The American Psychological Association points out that this constant barrage of ads and information makes it challenging to stay focused on one task for long. Social media's design also encourages multitasking, which can lead to lower-quality work and higher stress, which is a big deal for both school and work performance. While TikTok offers entertainment and connection, they can also distract us from being fully tuned in. By constantly seeking quick, fleeting pleasures, we lose sight of the importance of using our time wisely. Time is a powerful and flexible tool that, when used wisely, can help us create more time for the future.

Interestingly, kids in China do not use TikTok the same way it's used in the United States, where the app is mostly filled with trends, dances, and fast entertainment. Their TikTok version, called Douyin, is designed with structure and purpose, including a 40-minute daily limit for users under fourteen, along with restrictions at night to help protect rest and focus. Most of what they see on the app is meant to teach them something meaningful, like how to play an instrument, understand science, or learn new skills that help them grow day by day. Meanwhile, many users here in America scroll for hours watching influencers teach dances, follow trends, or show people how to twerk, often without realizing how much time they're giving away to things that may feel fun but leave the mind empty.

Aynne Kokas, a professor of media studies at the University of Virginia and author of Trafficking Data, explained that China has very different laws when it comes to how companies can target children. In China, kids under the age of eighteen are only allowed two hours of smartphone screen time each day, which is part of their effort to keep kids from getting addicted to their devices. That kind of limit shows how much more control they have over how young people use technology compared to what we see here in the United States. I'm not someone who believes in conspiracy theories but based on everything I've seen and what's happening around the world, it really seems like there's a silent war going on where China is building up the minds of their kids, while over here, we're shortening our attention span because of all the entertainment.

Having healthy limits might feel uncomfortable at first, especially for kids who have never been taught how to manage their screen time or how to step away from a screen when it's no longer serving them well. It may seem unusual or even frustrating to be told when to stop watching videos or when it's time to pause and take a break, especially in a world where phones are often treated as something you can use at any given moment, for as long as you like, without a second thought.

However, when those limits are established with consistency and care, something deeper begins to develop within those boundaries. Kids begin to fall into a steady rhythm that helps them become more aware of how their time is spent. Even though they may not realize it right away, they start to develop quiet habits that help them think more clearly and make better decisions over time. They begin to notice how too much screen time can make them feel drained, and instead of always chasing the next video or trend, they learn to look around and pay attention to what really matters during the day. These types of limits are not just rules that stop things from happening; they are simple practices that make room for focus, clarity, rest, and growth.

When clear boundaries are put in place, the result is not restriction, but a deeper kind of freedom that allows people to move through life with more peace and direction. A nation surrounded by strong and protective borders does not experience confinement or limitation; it experiences stability, because the people within those walls are free to live, grow, and thrive without the constant fear of unexpected threats or outside harm. That same idea applies on a personal level, especially when it comes to how we interact with our phones or how we guide the habits of our children. When time limits are introduced with intention and care, they do not take something important away; they give something back that often goes unnoticed, like stillness, mental space, and the ability to focus without interruption. These kinds of boundaries become steady anchors that show us time is valuable, that rest matters, and that it is possible to live without being pulled in every direction by a screen.

In essence, social media can rob us of the ability to harness time's potential, preventing us from being fully present and intentional in our daily lives. Yet, we often miss out on this opportunity because so much of our time is spent soaking in content rather than creating something for our future. To make tomorrow a reality, we need to minimize screen time, focus on the present, and use our time to build a better future instead of getting lost in the endless scroll of today.

This reminds me of something Kim John Payne often talks about, how slowing down can help us reconnect with what really matters. He is a strong advocate for mindfulness and intentional living. He is also the author of *The Soul of Discipline*. Kim believes that in a society constantly pushing for activity and productivity, it's crucial to make a deliberate effort to slow down. The goal is not only to take breaks, but to stay fully aware in whatever you're doing, whether you're eating, walking, or having a conversation. Kim advises focusing on the moment rather than juggling multiple tasks or worrying about what's next. This practice helps clear the mental clutter that builds up from always being connected and busy.

One of the things Kim recommends is making time for stillness. This could be as simple as spending a few minutes each day sitting quietly, meditating, or reflecting. In a world that never seems to stop, these moments of stillness can help calm the mind and reduce stress. Kim believes that regularly practicing stillness can lead to better mental health by allowing your mind to rest and recover from the constant demands of life.

One of Kim's most helpful but simple pieces of advice is to focus on self-care. Many people, in their rush to stay productive, overlook activities that bring them joy and relaxation. Kim stresses that self-care is not just a luxury, but it's a necessity. By making time for things you enjoy, like hobbies, spending time outdoors, or ensuring you get enough sleep, you create a more balanced life. This balance helps repair the damage caused by constantly consuming fast, short-term content, which can leave you feeling impatient and stressed.

His idea and work are supported by HelpGuide.org, which includes research from Harvard Health, shows that being completely engaged, even during stressful times, can increase awareness. This awareness helps people manage the constant distractions and impatience that come with modern life. The study explains that mindfulness isn't about waiting for the perfect moment to relax but about choosing to be aware and present in everyday situations, even when it's challenging.

By simply applying these ideas to your personal life like slowing down, being mindful, and taking care of yourself, you can start to counteract the negative effects of living in a fast-paced world. This approach helps you regain control over your attention, reduce stress, and live a more fulfilling life. It's not about giving up productivity; it's about finding a healthy balance that lets you be intentional with your time and energy.

By focusing on today like what we can control, we pave the way toward achieving tomorrow's goals. The key is to start now, to take that first step towards mastering our attention, and to embrace the journey toward a more intentional and focused life.

The truth is, there's no such thing as the "perfect time." I've told myself plenty of times, "I'll start tomorrow" or "I'll do it later," but that mindset only pushes things further away. If tomorrow became today, I'd probably make the same excuse and keep delaying. The more I've thought about it, the more I've realized that the only perfect time to start is now, because the best definition of "perfect time" is simply the time you have in this exact moment. This second right now, that's the only time with which you can work. As soon as that second passes, the next one becomes your new opportunity.

An hour from now isn't the perfect time, and two hours from now won't be either unless you use this moment to prepare and plan for what's ahead. We can schedule and organize, sure, but action can only happen in the present. The only perfect time that exists is the time you have right now.

Working as a delivery driver has helped me understand the little things in life and how important they are in navigating the small stresses that often add up. Things like my prayer life, school studies, and so many other obligations can pile up and become overloads. I say "little things" because it depends on how you perceive these difficult tasks. Our brain is the most powerful organ in the world. With its timeless and immense power, we have the choice to either magnify our problems or minimize them, and it all depends on the strength of our mindset. The little packages I delivered, whether small or large, served as a reminder that even the smallest things like an hour in a day can make a big difference if I am intentional.

There was one stop during my delivery route that I still remember more than most. I had to drop off a large, three-piece trampoline set in a nice neighborhood on the east side of town. It was one of those bulky boxes that takes patience to maneuver out of the back of the truck without dropping it. I remember using my hand truck, lowering it gently to the ground, and then slowly working my way toward the customer's front door.

As I approached the steps, the front door swung open, and this tall man greeted me with a big smile. His name was Jason Wheeler, and right away, he seemed friendly, almost too friendly. He thanked me for the delivery and then said, "Hey, come in for a second. I want to give you a cold bottle of water." I was hesitant to step inside since delivery drivers aren't allowed to enter someone's home for liability reasons, but he said he'd give me a cold bottle of water if I came in. Since my truck didn't have A/C and the heat was brutal, the kind of Arizona heat you get in the middle of July, I figured why not cool off for a bit and take a short break. So, I nodded and followed him into the house.

The moment I stepped inside, Jason casually said, "Don't worry, they won't attack," and I wasn't even sure what he meant by *they* until three large dogs came charging toward me, barking like I had just bro-ken into the place. We were standing right under a ceiling vent, and the cold air pouring down made me want to stay a little longer. It was definitely below 70°. It felt amazing. He handed me the water bottle, and before I could even take a full sip, he said, "I want to show you something really quick." That quick moment turned into a full tour of his home, room by room, as if I were there for a scheduled visit instead of just dropping off a package.

As we walked through the house, his three large dogs kept barking at me on and off. One was a German Shepherd, another an Australian

Shepherd, and the third was a Belgian Malinois mix, or at least that's what he said. The German Shepherd kept barking loudly behind me at one point, each bark made me jolt, and it went on for at least two minutes straight like I was some kind of threat. I turned slightly to see what was happening. Out of nowhere, Jason, standing several feet in front of me, dramatically rushed over to the coffee table near the kitchen, picked up a water gun, and just after I turned back toward Jason, he quickly reached forward and gave that dog a good sharp squirt. For a split second, I flinched hard, and my heart jumped. I genuinely thought he was about to shoot me with a real gun. I didn't know what was going on, and I was freaking out. I acted like I wanted no part of it and stayed out of the way. He smiled at me and said, "They stop barking when I shoot them with water; it works every time."

Terrified and slightly shaking in fear, I continued following him through the house, showing me souvenirs from his travels, artwork on the walls, and even a few ambient lighting devices around the living room and kitchen. There were lights above the cabinets, on the shelf edges, and even around the baseboards. He had remotes sitting on the coffee table that could instantly change the lights' colors, and he seemed pretty proud of that setup. He even showed me the packaging from where he bought them: Timu, Amazon, and Walmart were all part of his collection.

Eventually, we made our way outside to the backyard. He had a nice pool, a covered patio area, and some landscaping that looked like it had just been trimmed. While we were standing there, he shared a quote that he said came from his daughter, who liked writing and drawing. The quote stuck with me. She had said, "If you can think of anything you can do in two minutes, just do it now. Don't waste the time, just get it done." I thought that was kind of brilliant.

He went on talking for a while about all kinds of random things, how the pest control was on their way to take care of something around the house, his favorite travel spots, how he was remodeling his shed, just jumping from one topic to another like we were old buddies catching up. My delivery truck was still running out front the whole time with the hazard lights on. I must've been there for twenty-five minutes, just listening, nodding, and sipping the cold water under that strong AC vent.

Finally, he asked, "Hey, do you mind using your hand truck to help me get the trampoline into the backyard?" I paused for a second, but it was already too late to say no. He had already opened the side gate and cleared a path. So, I said sure and wheeled the box all the way around to the back of the house, making sure it didn't tip or hit any of the plants.

When it was all said and done, I thanked him for the water, waved goodbye, and walked back toward my truck. As I was leaving the backyard and stepping through the gate, the pest control guy was already pulling up, trying to get through the front. I climbed back into the driver's seat and pulled away.

As I drove off to the next stop, something caught my attention. I thought about the conversations, the lights, the dogs, the quote from his daughter, and all the random stories. Then it clicked. That's why he did all of that: the water, the long chat, and the house tour all strategically warmed me up before asking for help rolling the trampoline from the front door around the house to the backyard. I had been distracted by friendliness and stories, and next thing I knew, I was hauling a massive box into someone's backyard. I laughed and said, "Man, I just got played." At that point, I was already halfway down the street, and there was no undoing it. I figured, oh well, I guess I'm just a nice guy.

That quote Jason shared with me, "If you can do anything in two minutes, just do it," stayed with me even after I clocked out from work. It's strange how we can spend more than two minutes just thinking about whether or not we should do something that would take less time to finish. Instead of acting right away, we go back and forth in our minds, weighing it out, delaying it, and letting it sit there longer than it needs to. If we simply took those same two minutes to get it done, it would be over, and we wouldn't have to think about it again. That one small action would free up space in our minds and give us room to move on to the next thing without that task quietly bothering us in the background. It's a simple but powerful way to break the habit of procrastination, and it starts with noticing just how often we waste time deciding instead of doing. The longer you think about something you know you need to do, the more weight it begins to carry in your mind. That task, that idea, that responsibility starts to feel heavier the more you let it sit, and when it becomes heavy, it feels harder even to try. When you act right away, you keep it light, and something that could have weighed you down ends up being as easy to handle as a feather.

I kept thinking about how true it was, especially small, simple actions that can improve your day. Whether making your bed, wiping down your desk, or preparing your space to focus better, those quick two-minute tasks build momentum and can lead to lasting habits that take you much farther than you expect. It's so interesting how even my day-to-day work experiences can teach me things that carry over into my personal life. Sometimes, it has nothing to do with time management or anything specific, just small lessons from random interactions like delivering to someone's house. Moments like that remind me how much I can learn by simply paying attention.

Becoming aware and intentional about every package that needed to be delivered taught me a powerful lesson, one that has reshaped my perception of each day. This transformative insight didn't just change the way I approach my daily routine; it also shifted my entire perspective, making me more intentional and mindful in how I live.

FOCUS YOUR ENERGY ON WHAT MATTERS TODAY

John C. Maxwell, an expert on leadership and the bestselling author of *Everyone Communicates, Few Connect,* shared his Rule of 5 during one of his speaking engagements. It immediately grabbed my attention. The concept is simple but powerful and can completely change how you approach your goals. Imagine there's a big tree in your yard that you want to chop down. Instead of wearing yourself out trying to bring it down in one exhausting day, you decide to take five swings with your ax each day. At first, it might seem small, but with each intentional swing, you're making progress. Eventually, the tree will fall, not because you did it all at once, but because you were consistent and deliberate.

This idea isn't just about chopping down trees; it's a practical way to approach everyday life. Think about five things you can do each day that move you closer to your goals. Maybe it starts with something simple, like waking up and making your bed, which sets the tone for your day with a small victory. Then you might spend time in morning devotions, connecting with the Lord and setting a positive, focused tone. After that, you take your kids to school, knowing that you're giving them the momentum they need for a good day. From there, you dive into your studies or your job, focusing on the tasks that matter most for your growth.

Each of these actions might seem small, but they matter. By focusing on these five specific tasks every day, you're not just going through the motions; you're building a habit of growth. One of those five daily actions could even be planning for your future: thinking about where you want to be, setting goals, or working on a business idea. That step ensures that you're not just living day-to-day but actively shaping your what's ahead.

The beauty of the Rule of 5 is that it grounds you in the present while keeping an eye on what's ahead. Each small, intentional step you take today becomes a brick in the foundation of your future. By staying consistent with these daily actions, you're not just getting things done; you're building something real. This approach keeps you focused on what really matters, allowing you to balance the demands of today with the dreams of tomorrow. Still, if you're not careful to guard your focus, the weight of worry can slowly drain your energy.

WORRYING CAN LEAD TO MENTAL ENERGY SPILLAGE

Over the years, I've come to understand that worrying about tomorrow's affairs leads to energy spillage, demotivation, and a loss of focus. The simple analogy of leaving your house doors and windows open during the winter with the heater running paints a powerful image of what happens when focus is lost. Much of the warm air escapes, cold air will rush in, and it takes far longer to warm the house again. In the same way, worrying about tomorrow drains your mental focus; focus that should be dedicated to solving today's problems. Just as an overworked heating system struggles to keep a house warm when doors are left open, your mind becomes less effective when focused on the future. Instead, use today's time to plan for tomorrow, keeping your mental energy anchored in the present moment.

Many people find themselves mentally drained simply because they're focusing on the wrong things. For instance, if you spend a lot of time gossiping, worrying about what someone else said to you, or picking apart other people's flaws, you're using your mental energy in a way that doesn't benefit you. These activities might seem harmless, but over time, they slowly drain your focus and leave you feeling tired, distracted, and unproductive.

It's easy to get caught up in these low-level distractions; things like gossip, jealousy, or even judging others. These are choices we make, and they reveal where we're choosing to place our mental focus. Instead of investing that energy into yourself and your future, you end up spending it on things that don't matter in the long run. That kind of focus doesn't just drain you; in fact, it holds you back from achieving your full potential. That kind of negative focus traps you in a cycle of low energy and stunts your growth.

Imagine what could happen if you chose to use your mental energy in a positive way. What if, instead of dwelling on what's wrong, you focused on what's right? What if you invested that mental focus into improving yourself, developing your skills, and working toward your goals? That kind of focus not only boosts your energy; it drives you forward in life.

Think about how often small things distract us and drain our focus. It might be something as simple as an argument with a friend, a misunderstanding at work, or a minor inconvenience at home. These things can easily consume our thoughts and lead us down a path of negativity. If we choose to approach them with a solution-oriented mindset, we can conserve our energy and use it in a way that benefits us.

It's important to recognize that our thoughts and focus shape our character. The way we handle everyday challenges, how we interact with others, and where we choose to direct our mental energy, all contribute to who we are. If we constantly allow distractions and negativity to take over, it will be difficult to build the life we want. On the other hand, if we focus on what matters: personal growth, positive relationships, and meaningful goals, we begin to move toward a brighter, more purposeful future.

When you're intentional about where you focus your mind, you'll start to notice changes not just in your energy levels but in your overall quality of life. For instance, if you wake up every morning focused on what you can accomplish today, rather than dwelling on yesterday's problems or tomorrow's worries, you set a positive tone. That kind of intentionality helps you stay present and make progress, rather than getting bogged down by things you can't control. I mean, solving problems can only be done when you solely focus on them without distractions.

The same idea also applies when you become mindful of your future. If you're constantly worried about potential problems, you'll miss opportunities to grow and succeed. If you focus on setting clear goals, developing smart strategies, and taking actionable steps toward your dreams, you'll find that your mental energy is used in a way that brings you closer to where you want to be. The way you use your mind and where you place your focus determines the greatness of your future.

Excessive worrying about the future can deplete your mental energy, hindering your ability to focus and solve today's tasks.

A study published in *Behaviour Research and Therapy,* a peer-reviewed journal by Elsevier, found that worry impairs problem-solving capabilities. Participants who were asked to worry about a current problem generated fewer effective solutions and were less likely to act on them, compared to those who approached the problem with a calm and objective mindset. This highlights how worrying can create a cognitive overload, making it challenging to concentrate on immediate tasks.

This cognitive overload does not just affect major life decisions. It also impacts how well you function in everyday situations. You might notice it when trying to remember a simple task at work, staying focused during a conversation, or making decisions when things feel overwhelming. The mental strain builds quietly, and over time, it becomes increasingly difficult to stay sharp.

Think about someone who is constantly worried about an upcoming bill or something that feels urgent. They become so mentally preoccupied with the stress that they forget to respond to important emails or miss a meeting without realizing it. Their mental energy is not being wasted because they are lazy. It is being drained because their focus is stuck in the wrong place. Worry takes their attention away from what they need to handle right now, and as a result, they struggle to move forward.

Anxiety activates the body's "fight or flight" response, diverting energy away from cognitive functions and toward perceived threats. This response makes it harder to concentrate and solve problems, similar to how a heating system struggles to maintain warmth when doors are left open in winter.

WHEN LIFE SHOWS UP AT WORK

It was the summer of 2015, and I had just started my shift at the Subway restaurant where I worked. As I walked in, the smell of freshly baked bread filled the air, it was a familiar scent that usually brought a sense of calm and routine. That day felt different, like something was off the second I walked in. The moment I stepped behind the counter, I felt a tension that was almost tangible. Alyssa, my coworker, was already there, and she seemed unusually tense.

Alyssa and I had worked together for a while, and she was typically cheerful, always quick with a smile or a joke. Today however, her demeanor was off. She didn't talk much and when she did, her words were sharp and clipped. She was busy making bread in the oven proofer, going through the motions of her tasks mechanically, without her usual enthusiasm. Something was clearly wrong, but she wasn't saying anything.

The atmosphere in the restaurant had noticeably shifted. Customers coming in for their usual sandwiches could sense it, too. They glanced at Alyssa, then at me, clearly trying to figure out what was going on. One customer even asked Alyssa if she was okay. She snapped back with a loud, "I'm fine!" The abruptness of her response startled everyone, making the already heavy air even thicker with unspoken tension.

As the lunch rush approached, the situation only got worse. We were slammed with orders, and the lack of communication between us made the shift feel endless. Alyssa started barking instructions at me, her tone was sharp and bordering on hostile. I couldn't help but take it personally. I'm a sensitive person, and her attitude made me feel like I had done something wrong. I started to worry, wondering if I had unknowingly upset her. The constant stream of customers and the pressure to keep things running smoothly only added to my anxiety.

I remember one specific point in the day, around noon, which was the busiest part of our shift because of the lunch rush. A line of customers stretched to the door, and Alyssa was preparing sandwiches with a speed that felt frantic. I stood at the register, scrambling to keep up with the orders. Every time she handed me a sandwich, it came with a huff, like she was barely holding back her frustration. The customers could sense her mood, and a few even gave me sympathetic looks, almost like they were silently saying, "Hang in there, kid."

The hours dragged on, and our lack of communication made everything feel ten times harder. We were supposed to work as a team, but that day felt like we were each in our own separate worlds. I kept worrying as my mind spun with thoughts about what I might have done to upset her. Was it something I said? Or something I did? The more I thought about it, the more anxious I became.

Finally, the shift ended. I felt a sense of relief as I walked out of the restaurant, but the day's tension lingered. The next day, I couldn't shrug it off, because I needed to understand why Alyssa had been so different, why she had been so hostile and uncommunicative. I needed an answer because I couldn't stop overthinking.

When I approached my manager, Christina, I hesitated, unsure of how to start the conversation. I knew I needed to get to the bottom of it. "Is Alyssa okay?" I asked. "She was really rude to me and the customers yesterday, and she didn't talk to anyone. It was like she was a different person."

Christina let out a long sigh and gave me a serious expression. "Alyssa's grandmother is dying," she said quietly. "She's been really worried about her. She was called into work yesterday but didn't want to be here. That's probably why she was acting that way."

It was then, when everything clicked into place, that a paradigm shift changed how I understood the situation. Alyssa's mood, her behavior, it all made sense. She wasn't just being cold or unfriendly; she was carrying something heavy on her heart. Her mind was divided between her worry for her grandmother and her responsibilities at work. Her mental energy was drained, leaving her unable to focus or communicate effectively.

She was completely blindsided; so caught up in her own stress that it became a blind spot, keeping her from noticing the reality unfolding around her. Alyssa's mind was preoccupied with her grandmother, and as a result, she couldn't engage with her work or her coworkers. If she had communicated what she was facing, perhaps we could have found a way to help her, and to ease her burden.

Experiencing stress is completely normal, and in many cases, a healthy and balanced level of stress can be helpful, as long as it is managed well and kept in proper perspective, since what matters is how we respond to each situation and where we choose to place our focus. A certain amount of stress keeps you alert, keeps you moving, and can even be a good thing, as long as it does not overflow and begin to consume you, especially when you choose not to let it build up beyond what's needed.

HOW CAN WE STOP WORRYING?

Before diving into the six steps on how to stop worrying, I first want to start by pointing out something that often gets overlooked. I don't want to go off topic here, but it's important to first recognize how much your mental state shapes your ability to make rational decisions and stay calm, especially in serious long-term relationships like marriage, where being mentally sober makes it much easier to keep worry in check.

Being sober-minded, as the Bible describes it, is not only about staying away from substances, but also about how you choose to think. Being sober-minded is more psychological than most people realize. It has everything to do with how you allow yourself to think, how you approach each thought, and how you either give it room to grow or shut it down before it spreads. The mind is complex, but the way we handle it can be very simple, and depending on how you approach it, that simplicity can either work against you or become one of your greatest blessings.

The idea of being sober minded involves mental focus, emotional stability, and the ability to respond with wisdom and discernment, which means that worry, fear, or racing thoughts can rob you of that clarity and pull your mind in several directions at once. The Greek word used in the Bible is sōphroneō, which means to think clearly and sensibly, with sound judgment and self-control. This is the kind of mindset Paul refers to in places like Titus 2:6, where he urges people to be sober-minded and focused. Thinking with clarity is not just a mental discipline, but a spiritual posture that reflects a heart aligned with God. Every decision you make should involve every part of you, fully present, fully aware, and led by both the truth of God's Word and the power of the Holy Spirit.

This kind of intentional thinking is a form of worship because when your thoughts and actions are rooted in God's truth, you are honoring God with the mind He gave you. The reason I say this is the best form of worship is because worship can be broken down into what I like to call *worth-ship*, where you think and live in a way that shows God is worth it all, and He honors that kind of mindset because it reflects that He holds first place in your life.

Being sober means thinking rationally and being whole, where every part of you is engaged and aware of the thoughts you are allowing, without confusion or inner division, so your mind remains clear and fully present.

One of the biggest threats between people, especially in relationships, is not just what happens but how it's interpreted. This is called a perceived defense, when someone close to you uses a certain tone or expression that feels personal, even if they never meant it that way. If it's not addressed quickly with effective communication, the mind starts to rehearse it over and over until it solidifies into what Scripture calls a *vain imagination*, something that feels real because of the emotion behind it but may not be true at all. If it continues like this, it can lead to a pointless argument the next morning that has no sense of direction. Eliminating these vain imaginations that were caused by perceived defenses is one of the greatest ways to stay sober-minded.

Recognizing that worry divides your focus is the first step in helping you understand why you might feel mentally overwhelmed, and realizing this truth will help you move forward with a stronger mindset and a clearer sense of direction.

The six steps I am about to share with you are incredibly powerful and can really transform your life, especially when you're intentional about applying them daily. John C. Maxwell emphasized that adding value to others ultimately brings value, comfort, and a sense of peace back to you. By prioritizing the needs and concerns of others, you are doing more for yourself than you might think.

1. **Practice Selflessness Through Mindful Listening:**
   When you're overwhelmed at work, stressed and worried about something else, think about the person you're interacting with. Practicing mindful listening is a selfless act that can work wonders when you feel out of control. Instead of letting worry divide your mind, focus on the other person. This difficult yet simple act creates healing in your body, mind, and spirit. After all, it's better to give than to receive.

2. **Pray**
   Give your worries to Jesus because He cares about your soul, spirit, and body. Jesus cares about you as a whole, not just your mind. Prayer is simply a conversation with God, like a child would speak with their father. Tell Him your needs, because He is the source and Prince of Peace. Then, wait patiently for His response. His ways are higher, and His timing is different than ours. *"Cast all your anxiety on Him because He cares for you." - 1 Peter 5:7*

3. **Consider Others' Situations**
   It's important to understand that everyone faces their own struggles. When you realize that others around you are also dealing with problems, it creates a sense of shared humanity and can be very grounding. This empathy helps you stay present and not get lost in your own worries. It creates this paradigm shift, reminding you that there is often so much happening behind the scenes in someone else's life that you may never see.

   So, imagine you're having a hectic morning, like dropping off your kids at school, running late, and feeling frazzled. When you finally get to work, instead of carrying that stress with you, take a moment to consider your colleagues. Perhaps a coworker is dealing with a sick child, or another just got some bad news. By showing concern and offering a listening ear, you not only support them but also shift your focus from your own stress. That paradigm shift allows you to step outside of your own worries and view things more clearly.

4. **Limit Distractions by Helping Others**

    Helping others can be a powerful way to limit distractions. When you help someone with their problems, you momentarily put aside your own worries. This act of selflessness can be incredibly rewarding and can provide a much-needed break from your own concerns.

    Let's say you didn't do well on a final exam, you're feeling defeated, and then you head to work. Instead of letting that disappointment affect your whole day, redirect your energy towards helping a coworker with a project, or assist a customer with their needs. This redirection not only makes you feel useful but also eases your own stress.

5. **Be Present and Make Positive Eye Contact**

    Being present means fully engaging with those around you. One of the simplest ways to connect and show you're listening is by making eye contact with the person you are talking to. This connection fosters mutual respect, understanding, and makes your interactions much better.

6. **Thankfulness and Counting Your Blessings**

    These are great antidotes to worry. They shift your focus from what you lack to what you already have. Giving thanks fosters a sense of contentment and helps you recognize the abundance in your life. When you are content, you become more aware of your blessings. This diminishes feelings of distress and anxiety. Gratitude cultivates a positive mindset, allowing you to appreciate the present moment and dispel the fears that often accompany worry. In this way, embracing thankfulness can lead to a more peaceful and fulfilling life.

Speaking of thankfulness, it's one of the most powerful weapons against worry. There's a story in the Bible about King Jehoshaphat, the ruler of Judah, who faced a situation that made him extremely worried. Suddenly, he heard that three powerful armies, like the Moabites, Ammonites, and people from Mount Seir had joined forces and were coming to attack his kingdom.

The news of these approaching armies terrified Jehoshaphat. He knew that his own army was too small to stand a chance against them. The thought of possible destruction to his people and land filled him with fear and worry.

In the midst of his fear, Jehoshaphat took a very important step; he turned to God. He called for a national fast, asking all the people of Judah to come together and seek God's help. They gathered at the temple, and Jehoshaphat led them in prayer. He openly admitted that they were powerless against such a great multitude and that they didn't know what to do.

Yet, he also expressed his trust in God, saying, "Our eyes are on You." Jehoshaphat's worry was clear, but so was his faith. He knew that only God could save them from this threat.

As they stood there, a prophet named Jahaziel spoke up, filled with the Spirit of the Lord. He delivered a message from God that was both surprising and comforting. He told them not to be afraid or discouraged because of the vast army, for the battle was not theirs, but God's. Jahaziel instructed them to go down to the battlefield the next day, but they wouldn't need to fight. Instead, they were told to stand still and see the salvation of the Lord. The people must have been shocked and curious. How could they win without fighting?

The next morning, Jehoshaphat and the people of Judah did as God instructed. Instead of leading with soldiers armed for battle, Jehoshaphat placed singers at the front of the field. These singers were not warriors; they were there to praise God. As they marched toward the battlefield, they sang a song of thanksgiving: "Give thanks to the Lord, for His lovingkindness is everlasting." This wasn't just a simple song; it was a declaration of their faith and trust in God. Despite the fear and uncertainty, they chose to focus on thankfulness.

As they sang, something incredible happened. God caused confusion among the enemy armies. The soldiers from Moab, Ammon, and Mount Seir began to turn on each other. They fought among themselves, completely forgetting about their common enemy, Judah. By the time the people of Judah reached the place where the battle was supposed to happen, they saw only the dead bodies of their enemies. Not a single enemy soldier was left standing. The mighty armies that had once terrified them were gone and defeated without Judah lifting a sword.

The story of Jehoshaphat and the people of Judah shows how effective thankfulness can be. Their decision to praise God in the midst of their fear didn't just bring them comfort; it brought them victory. Thankfulness turned their focus away from the terrifying armies and reminded them of God's everlasting love and kindness. It helped them to replace worry with trust, fear with faith. When they sang "Give thanks to the Lord, for His lovingkindness is everlasting," they weren't just expressing gratitude; they were declaring and acknowledging their belief that God was in control.

This act of thankfulness wasn't just a nice gesture; it was a weapon. It was a spiritual weapon that defeated their fear and allowed God to work in miraculous ways. When we choose to be thankful, even in difficult times, we invite God's presence into our situation. It helps us to see beyond our problems and remember that God is greater than any challenge we face. Just like Jehoshaphat and the people of Judah, we can use thankfulness as a weapon against worry. It can shift our perspective, bring us peace, and open the door for God to do amazing things in our lives.

FINAL THOUGHTS
Take back your mind.

Your thoughts shape your choices,
and your choices shape your life.

→ If you do not pay attention to what is running through your mind, it will start directing your day without you even realizing it.

→ When you slow down, step back, and choose what deserves your focus, you begin to take real control of your life.

HOW DEEP BREATHING CAN HELP YOU REGAIN MENTAL FOCUS

Never underestimate the power of getting back to basics.

MANY TIMES, we rush through our day without realizing it, jumping from one thing to the next, but slowing down might be the best place to start when it comes to finding calm and focus. I believe God placed something beneficial inside our bodies, a natural rhythm we often overlook, and it's called taking deep breaths. Deep breathing has the power to slow down your mind, and that is exactly how God designed it to work. There is a fine connection between the lungs and the brain, and when you inhale deeply, that connection helps quiet racing thoughts and gently vents out the stress that builds up inside. It is like a natural system God placed within us to help us reset, clear our heads, and stay present in the moment.

Deep breathing, personally for me, has been one of the simplest and most effective ways to stay present. Do most of us do it? Not always, in my opinion, especially during tough and heated moments of despair. Taking deep breaths in and out helps you gather yourself, regroup, and slow things down, even when life feels overwhelming.

Recent findings show how powerful deep breathing can be for reducing stress and improving focus. Dr. Richard P. Brown, an associate clinical professor of psychiatry at Columbia University, explains that deep breathing exercises stimulate the parasympathetic nervous system, promoting calm and relaxation. Slowing down your breathing also slows down your thoughts, bringing your attention back to the present moment. I've tried this myself, especially after a stressful situation like the car accident I was involved in back in March 2022.

I was on my way to work early in the morning, driving south toward my dispatch station in Phoenix, getting ready to take the I-10 eastbound from Reems Road and eventually exit on 75th Avenue. At the time, I was driving a 2012 Scion iQ, which for those who may not know, is one of the smallest four-seater cars ever made. It only has two doors, but surprisingly, there's room for two small seats in the back. I had even managed to fit two of my adult friends in there once. It's compact, but it does the job.

That morning, I pulled up to a four-way stop. Just as I was heading through the intersection, a red Jeep Wrangler coming from the west didn't wait for her turn. The driver, who I later found out was a nurse running late for work at Banner Estrella Medical Center, rushed through the stop sign and hit me head-on. I was already in the middle of the intersection. Her front bumper was built like a rock, solid and unyielding, from what I remember, and an impact at just 7 miles per hour completely totaled my car. My left shoulder slammed into the B-pillar, and everything happened so fast I barely had time to think. My adrenaline kicked in, and I was trying to make sense of what just happened, even though my entire front bumper was nearly torn off and dragging as I slowly backed the car onto the dirt shoulder. I could still hear the radio playing inside, even as that thick plastic bumper scraped along the road. Hearing thick plastic dragging after a crash, even in a small accident, is one of those sounds that makes you wish you could reverse everything and stop it from happening in the first place.

I wasn't seriously injured, but I remember how hard it was to breathe. My chest was tight, and my thoughts were all over the place. When I called my manager to let him know what happened, the very first thing he said wasn't "Are you okay?" He simply told me, "Breathe slowly." He wasn't being cold. He just knew I needed to calm down so I could think clearly and explain the situation, and it worked. Within a few minutes after catching my breath, my mind began to settle. I could focus, describe what happened, and take the next steps I needed to take. That moment taught me something firsthand: slowing your breathing helps you return to yourself.

This kind of calming effect is something researchers have been studying for years, including Dr. Patricia Gerbarg, co-author of *The Healing Power of the Breath*. She highlights how regular deep breathing can help manage anxiety, improve mental clarity, and enhance overall well-being. It's a simple tool, but it can make a big difference. Her work highlights how regular deep breathing is not just a relaxation technique, but something that improves focus, lowers anxiety, and helps bring the body and mind into a calmer rhythm.

When your breathing slows down, your thoughts begin to settle, and your ability to think clearly starts to return, which is why so many people feel more balanced and level-headed after just a few intentional breaths. Deep breathing clears out the mental fog that stress brings and creates space for better thinking, which can lead to more focused decision-making and stronger emotional control. I want to take a moment to show you exactly how this works on a biological level by explaining what happens in your body and brain when you take a deep breath and how that process helps calm the mind.

When you take a slow, deep breath, your lungs expand and your diaphragm moves downward, which activates pulmonary stretch receptors and baroreceptors found in your chest and blood vessels. These receptors send signals through the vagus nerve to the brainstem, mainly to a part called the medulla oblongata, which helps calm your body by turning on the parasympathetic nervous system. This response lowers your heart rate and slows the release of stress hormones like cortisol and adrenaline, while also increasing oxygen and balancing carbon dioxide levels in your blood. All of this helps calm the amygdala in your brain, which slows down your thoughts and brings your body into a state of peace that God built into you for moments of stress.

These sensors are tiny nerve endings designed to detect pressure, stretch, and movement within your body. You can think of the pulmonary stretch receptors like little switches along your airways that sense how much your lungs are expanding, and the baroreceptors are more like pressure gauges that sit in your arteries and keep track of your blood flow. The reason this system works so well is that your body is designed to look for signs of safety, and deep breathing constantly sends a signal that you are not in danger, which tells your brain to slow everything down.

It's amazing to think about how God designed this system to work on its own, even while we're asleep or going through our daily routines. You don't have to voluntarily control your breathing, your heart rate, or any of the internal functions happening in your body. It all runs involuntarily, like it was built to support you from the inside out. All you have to do is live, stay connected to Him, and trust that every part of your body was created to help carry you through life with peace, because God made it simple to live. Everything you need is already working for you.

FINDING CONFIDENCE IN SMALL THINGS

God created us to lean in and take ownership of even the smallest things in life. Have you ever noticed how someone's posture can tell you a lot about how they're feeling? When someone is hunched over, shoulders slouched forward, and their head down, it's almost like their body is saying, "I'm having a rough day." That kind of posture can reflect a lot, maybe they're unsure of themselves, maybe they're stressed or exhausted.

On the other hand, when someone stands tall, with their shoulders back and head held high, it's a completely different story. They look confident and steady, like they know where they're going, even if life feels chaotic.

It's fascinating how much posture influences not just how others see us, but how we feel about ourselves. I remember my former pastor at Zion City Church once said, "Smart people walk fast and have good posture." That stuck with me. It's true, when you see someone walking purposefully, head up and shoulders aligned, they give off this quiet confidence. It's not just for show. That kind of posture sends a signal to your brain: "I'm intentional, I'm focused, and I believe in myself.

Posture isn't just about confidence or appearances; it's about how it affects your body and mind. When you take a moment to straighten your spine and align yourself, something shifts. It's almost like everything starts to fall into place. You breathe a little easier, your body feels steadier, and your mind begins to calm down. What's amazing is how simple this adjustment is, yet it has such a powerful impact.

Your spine plays a huge role in this. It's not just there to hold you upright; it's the central highway for all the signals traveling from your brain to the rest of your body. When your spine is aligned, everything flows smoothly. Your nervous system functions the way it's supposed to, your muscles aren't under unnecessary strain, and you feel more balanced overall. When you're slouching or hunched forward, it's like putting a kink in a garden hose. That misalignment disrupts the flow, and before you know it, you're dealing with shoulder tension, shallow breathing, or just a general sense of unease.

This reminds me of what I've mentioned earlier about the importance of breathing. If you think about it, when your chest is compressed because of poor posture, it makes it harder for your lungs to fully expand. You end up breathing shallowly, which can increase feelings of anxiety or stress. It's like your body gets stuck in a loop of tension. When you straighten your spine and open up your chest, you give your lungs the space they need to take in deep, calming breaths. That kind of breathing does wonders, because it slows your heart rate, steadies your mind, and helps you feel more in control.

What's happening here is connected to something called the parasympathetic nervous system. This part of your nervous system helps your body relax and recover. By breathing deeply and aligning your posture, you're essentially flipping the switch from "fight or flight" mode to "rest and digest" mode. It's your body's way of saying, "Hey, everything's okay and you can take it easy now."

The best part is that this doesn't require any special tools or techniques. It's as simple as pausing for a moment, checking your posture, and taking a breath.

This is more than adjusting your body, because it also means paying attention to the small seconds and moments in your day. We tend to rush through life, feeling like we don't have time to stop, but the truth is, we have more time than we think. The little moments that we often overlook, such as the seconds between tasks, the pauses in conversation, or even the brief breaks during a busy day, are opportunities we can use to reset.

When you pause and check your posture, you're not straightening your spine; you're pausing to reconnect with time itself. You're becoming familiar with the seconds you thought you didn't have but are right there, waiting for you to notice them. So many of us skim over these moments because we're busy. We make the mistake by convincing ourselves there's no time. When we stop, even briefly, we realize how much those small moments can add up.

BREATHE WITH YOUR CREATOR IN MIND

It's interesting when you stop and think about how our lives are made, we're not just physical bodies walking around, living day by day; beneath the surface, we're more than that. There's so much more to us than what we see on the outside. We're not just human in the sense of flesh and blood; there's a greater part of us, something deeper and more purposeful: that's our inner man, our soul. That's the part of you that remembers, the part that's conscious and aware, the part that's fully present right now. As you're reading this, it's your soul that's actively taking in these words, processing them, and making sense of them. That's the real part of you, the part that matters most.

Your physical body, while important, is just the biological part of you. It's your outer layer, which is considered to be a vessel, but it's not everything. The best way to describe what a vessel is would be to compare it to something like an artery or a vein. It's a simple tube, extremely clean and clear, that moves liquid from one place to another. It's a part of you that holds and carries what's inside. Your spirit, the eternal part of who you are, is the core of your being, and it's far more significant than the physical shell we tend to focus so much on.

Here's what makes this so incredible: when you engage in small moments like deep breathing, you're not just doing something good for your body. You're creating space for something much greater to happen. You're inviting Christ into those little seconds, the ones we often overlook, and allowing Him to bring peace into your life. It's not always about the big, life-changing moments where you surrender something major to God—though they are very important. Sometimes, it's about recognizing how important even the smallest pauses can be.

When you think about it, these little pauses like these moments of deep breathing are like a reminder of Philippians 4:6-9, where it says, *"Be anxious for nothing, but in everything by prayer and supplication, with thanksgiving, let your requests be made known to God; and the peace of God, which surpasses all understanding, will guard your hearts and minds through Christ Jesus."*

That verse captures the heart of what happens when you stop, breathe, and allow God to meet you where you are. Even when your mind feels cluttered with anxious thoughts, pausing to breathe and inviting Him into that moment can shift everything.

I can tell you from my own experience that this has been life-changing for me. When I take those moments to breathe deeply, fix my posture, and ask God to meet me in that moment, I feel something shift inside me. It's like I'm being refueled, not just physically but spiritually, too. It reminds me that God cares about every detail, every second, every breath, and nothing is too small for Him to be a part of.

So, as you're reading this, I want to encourage you to give it a try. Take a deep breath, focus on your posture, and ask Christ to meet you in whatever situation you're in. These little seconds are the ones we often overlook, yet they are where peace begins, where your strength is renewed, and where God quietly shows up.

It's incredible, and it's something you can take with you wherever you go.

I think it's amazing how God designed our bodies to be so complex. It's like every part of us reflects how great and infinite He is. When you stop and think about it, it's kind of humbling, because this intricate design shows us just how intentional and powerful God really is. It's almost like He's saying, *"I created you and every detail matters."*

Honestly, it reminds me of intimacy with God. When you spend time with Him, you start to notice things you didn't before. You become more aware, not just of your surroundings, but of time itself. Every second feels important, like it has purpose. It's funny, though, because while you're focusing on Him, it's almost like time disappears. You're so caught up in the moment with God that you're not thinking about how much time is passing, because you're just *there* with Him.

This is exactly what God is talking about in Matthew 6:6, where Jesus says, *"When you pray, go into your room, close the door, and pray to your Father, who is unseen. Then your Father, who sees what is done in secret, will reward you."* God doesn't need big, elaborate displays of faith, because He simply wants intentional moments with you. Even in the smallest, quietest seconds, He's there, and He treasures those times.

Think about when you're driving in the car, feeling stressed, or going through a heated moment. If you take an intentional deep breath, fix your posture, and silently invite God into that second, He sees and honors it. The fact that you're trusting Him, even in those difficult moments, matters to Him.

What matters most is the heart you bring into it, because the sincerity behind your time with God carries more meaning than how long you spend. Even a quiet pause to breathe and trust Him means so much to God, so take a moment to give it a try and see what happens when you open your heart to Him. Take a breath, let go of the tension, and allow Him to meet you right there, in the middle of whatever you're going through. It might seem small, but to God, it's significant.

There's a scripture from the book of Psalms that really reflects what we've been talking about. Psalm 37:23 says, *"The LORD directs the steps of the godly. He delights in every detail of their lives."*

Isn't that amazing? God doesn't just guide us through the big moments; He delights in every single detail of our lives. Every step we take, no matter how small or insignificant it might seem to us, matters to Him.

It's incredible to think that God, in His infinite greatness, chooses to care about the little things we do, like taking a deep breath to regroup, or inviting Him into the stressful moments of our day, even while driving. These tiny acts of trust and connection aren't overlooked. God sees them, He delights in them, and He honors the fact that we're turning to Him in those moments.

I remember my friend Bill saying something during a Bible study we had at a coffee shop one Tuesday night, it's something we do every first and third Tuesday of every month. He said that focusing on God and trying to hear His voice is a lot like adjusting the frequency on a radio. It's like fine-tuning your spirit to better hear what He has to say to you.

This is exactly what deep breathing and fixing our mind on Christ can do. We allow our spirit to tune in and connect with God on a deeper level.

THE MOMENT I REALIZED TIME
WAS SLIPPING AWAY

When you narrow your focus, even small actions lead to big results. I used to think I had all the time in the world. Growing up, I spent a lot of time hanging out with close friends, which was great. A lot of those moments were spent sitting around and doing nothing. We'd play video games for hours, scroll through our phones, or just hang out without any real purpose. I enjoyed being with them—don't get me wrong—but something in the back of my mind always nagged at me: was I really using my time in the best way? It wasn't until I hit twenty that this question really hit me hard.

I remember that day so clearly. I was at my friend's house, like usual. We had a routine: video games, movies, snacks, repeat. It was what we did to pass the time. We weren't working, so there were no obligations. It was just a way to relax and enjoy ourselves.

However, that night, something changed.

As I sat there, with my gaming controller in hand, I looked around the room. My friends were glued to the screen, completely locked into the game. Nothing had changed; we were doing the same thing we'd been doing for years. For the first time, I wasn't lost in it. I saw it differently. It felt like we were stuck in this loop, repeating the same thing over and over. I thought, *how much time have I spent like this? How many hours have I given to this without even thinking about it?* That thought didn't leave me.

The next day, I started paying attention to my habits. I noticed how much time I spent scrolling through social media, watching pointless videos, reading comments that added nothing to my life. I saw how often I defaulted to playing video games instead of doing something productive. It wasn't that any of these things were bad, but I started to realize how much energy I was pouring into them, energy that could've been used for something more productive.

I realized that time isn't unlimited, and we don't get to hit pause or rewind, because every moment we spend on something is a moment we can't get back. That's not to say we shouldn't enjoy life or have fun, but it made me think twice about how I was using my days.

Scheduling your time wisely means making room for the things you enjoy, like playing video games, while also giving priority to the things that help you grow and make a positive difference in your life. It's very sad to see many people throw away their time into a black hole that won't give them anything back in return.

I think a lot of people don't realize how much their small, consistent choices shape their future. It's easy to think that what we do today doesn't matter, but it does. The small choices we make every day add up over time. If we keep pouring our mental energy into things that don't help us grow, we're robbing ourselves of opportunities, like the ability to focus on what matters.

It's like trying to ride a bike with low air in the tires. When a tire doesn't have enough air, it sinks in slightly, creating more resistance against the ground. That extra drag makes it harder to move, so your legs have to push with more force just to keep a normal pace. You might not notice it right away, but over time, it wears you down. The problem isn't that you're weak or not trying hard enough. The problem is that the tire isn't doing what it's supposed to do. You end up spending more energy than necessary on something that could have been fixed with a little attention. Once you stop and deal with the real issue, the ride becomes easier, smoother, and far less exhausting. Now your energy can go toward the road ahead, not the drag behind.

It's the same with everyday life. When you stop putting your energy into distractions or things that don't deserve your attention, you begin to see what needs your focus. There are so many situations pulling at your thoughts that don't even matter in the end. When your attention is scattered, your energy gets spread thin, and that creates a kind of low compression in your mental strength, making everything feel more difficult than it really is. When you clear away those distractions and focus on one thing at a time, your energy becomes more concentrated, your thinking becomes clearer, and your momentum begins to build in a meaningful way. That is how you move forward with purpose. That is how you begin to go farther than you thought you could. That is how you retake control of your life and begin making progress that lasts. That's something I've had to realize for myself, and it's changed the way I approach how I spend my time and what I choose to focus on.

Now, I don't want to look back and wonder what I could have done if I had just been more intentional. I don't want to regret the time I wasted when I had the energy and ability to do more. That's why I've committed to using my mind in ways that serve me. Whether it's reading, writing, learning new skills, or having conversations that challenge me, I want to invest in things that will benefit me down the road.

I still see people around me stuck in the same cycle I was in, like scrolling endlessly, playing games for hours, wasting mental energy on things that don't bring them closer to their goals. I get it, because I was there plenty of times. Still, there is something you have to understand. Time doesn't wait for anyone, and every day we let slip by is a day we can't get back.

So, my question to you is this: Where are you pouring your mental energy? Are you using it in ways that will benefit your future, or are you letting it slip away, little by little, without even realizing it? One day you'll look back and hopefully be able to say that you used your time wisely. I hope you can say that you didn't take your mental energy for granted, because that's a decision only you can make.

A SIMPLE DECISION THAT CREATES MOMENTUM

*"One small step in the right direction can turn into
the journey of a lifetime."*

—UNKNOWN

IT WAS in September of 2024 when I decided to begin writing and building my weekly newsletter on Substack, which in many ways reflects this book you're reading right now. Starting this newsletter was far from easy. When I first created my account on the platform, everything seemed empty, and even though I stayed consistent, I had no traction or engagement for five months straight. It honestly felt like I was talking to a wall, but I kept choosing to go forward because I was hoping that eventually something would break and some kind of progress would start to happen. Every month, I would post updates, sharing little nuggets of what this book was about. I'd include excerpts, ideas, insights, and it slowly started to draw a lot of attention. After seven months of hard work, I was gaining over fifty new subscribers every week, and my subscribers were quoting and sharing my work.

For those unfamiliar with Substack, it's a platform you can use on your phone or computer that's designed entirely for writing and publishing. The way it works is there's a newsfeed on your screen, similar to Facebook, X, or Medium, but instead of random posts and distractions, it's filled with long-form content: newsletters, articles, personal reflections, and even short notes. It's a place where writers can grow a community of readers who genuinely support them, interact with their work, and build something special over time.

What's really amazing about Substack is that it gives every writer a chance to create their own space. This platform is full of purpose, with people who are chasing their dreams and using their voices to do something different. It's the most productive social media platform I've ever used in my life. You get to interact with people who support your vision, have real conversations, and connect with readers on a deeper level. When you're working on something big, like a book, a blog post, or even your fitness journey, it becomes the perfect way to bring people along for the ride. It allows you to create excitement and momentum by keeping people informed and sharing progress well in advance, long before your work is finished or ready to share.

Over time, I've built a solid community made up of people who not only supported my work but were impacted by it in real ways. Some of them even reached out to me directly through Substack. They would message me privately and share how much the notes I posted meant to them, especially during difficult times. More than once, someone told me that every time I post something new, it lifts them up and gives them the encouragement they needed for that day. Messages like that remind me why I started, and I appreciate hearing that the words I'm putting out are making a difference in someone's life.

I gained subscribers, followers, and friends who genuinely support my work. What surprised me the most was that not everyone on Substack was an author. In fact, many were simply passionate about writing. They weren't trying to sell anything or trying to become famous, they just wanted to share their thoughts, inspire others, and grow as individuals. It was unlike any platform I had ever used before.

I started noticing how much effort people put into their posts. I'd see beautifully formatted newsletters with bolded text, italics, and well-placed images that made their writing feel alive. People were writing every single day, and they weren't just sharing surface-level content, they were putting real thought into their words. What amazed me even more was realizing that many of these writers were teenagers in high school, while others were in their twenties and early thirties. They made a solid choice to avoid the toxicity of social media and devote themselves to this platform.

My mind was completely blown when I realized just how supportive and kind the people on this platform were. Coming from social platforms where arguments and negative comments sometimes run wild, this felt like stepping into a whole different universe. On most social media platforms, people will say anything behind a keyboard.

Newsletter platforms like the one I've been using for a while now are completely different. They're filled with like-minded people who are focused on growing, finding their voice, being heard, and building something that matters. There's even a built-in group chat section in the app where you can create your own chat room to talk about specific topics or ideas, and it honestly feels like a family. People are kind, they support each other, and it's amazing to see how much they care.

Now granted, this didn't happen to me right away. I had to be intentional about finding the right people, and it took time to build those kinds of connections. Since I kept searching and stayed consistent, I eventually found a community that aligned with what I was looking for, and even though it didn't come easily, it was the result of patience, effort, and being open to the right people when they showed up.

One of my most popular newsletters was called, *What If?* In that post, I talked about how people often hold themselves back with negative "what if" questions. *What if I fail? What if this doesn't work? What if something goes wrong?* I challenged my readers to flip that perspective. *What if I succeed? What if this goes better than I imagined? What if I push myself and go further than I ever thought possible?* That simple shift in mindset can make all the difference.

That post resonated with a lot of people. It got shared multiple times, and I received messages from readers saying it helped them move past their doubts and take action. That's the power of surrounding yourself with the right community. When you're in an environment where people are constantly pushing themselves, learning, and growing, it becomes easier to do the same.

I realized that progress isn't just about motivation; it's about where you place yourself. If you're surrounded by people who are lazy, unmotivated, and constantly making excuses, it's easy to fall into that mindset. When you're surrounded by people who are actively working toward something, who are pushing themselves every day, it starts to feel natural to do the same. Being part of this community showed me how much environment matters. The people you surround yourself with will either push you forward or hold you back. When you're in the right space, things start to feel easier because you're no longer carrying everything alone. Looking back, I'm grateful I took the time to build this community. It wasn't just about gaining followers or growing a newsletter. It was about creating something that will last, something that can inspire others.

As I move forward with this book, I know that this community will continue to play a huge role in shaping its progress. At the end of the day, what matters most is not what you create, but the people you share it with and the way it connects to something bigger than yourself.

So, take a moment to sit down, go somewhere quiet, maybe your room, maybe a peaceful spot outside, and ponder. Think about the power you have. Right now, at this very moment, you have the ability to change your life. Not tomorrow, not next week, but right now. That power comes from the choices you make. Every single decision is an opportunity, and it's up to you whether you use it or let it slip away. Time will always decide against you if you don't act on what you know you need to do, because no one else will do that thing for you. The clock never stops, and it doesn't rewind. Time is like gravity, it's always pulling you downward, and unless you keep moving with purpose, even one decision can feel heavy, like a helicopter losing lift the moment its blades stop propelling.

So many people don't realize this. They let their days pass by, thinking they have all the time in the world. They let their dreams fade because they never take action. They let time control them instead of grabbing hold of it. You don't have to be one of those people. You have a choice to take control, to create traction in your life instead of just watching time slip away.

Think of it like tires on the road. When you have traction, you move. You grip the road, and every decision you make keeps you moving forward. Without traction, you're just sliding around, wasting time, and going nowhere. The difference lies in the choices you make, and whether you stick to them.

THE POWER OF CHOICE IS A GIFT FROM GOD

Now think about this: animals have choices too, like how a lion chooses to hunt, a bird chooses where to build its nest, and a dog chooses whether to sit or stay when it is commanded by their owner. The thing is that animals don't have the ability to intentionally change the course of their entire life the way you do, because they act on instinct and immediate needs. They don't sit down and reflect on their future. They don't make a decision to completely transform their lives through commitment and consistency.

A lion doesn't wake up one day and say, *I want to be a better hunter, so I'm going to train every day to be faster and stronger.* A dog doesn't decide, *I want to improve my life, so I'm going to develop better habits.*

You were created in God's image, which means you have the ability to step back, evaluate your life, and make intentional choices that can completely shift your direction. If you wanted to start a healthy diet, you could choose to do that. If there's something in your life that's been holding you back, you have the power to walk away from it. You can create discipline, develop new habits, and change the entire course of your future by simply deciding to move in a different direction and staying committed to it. You were given a mind that can plan, reflect, and make intentional choices. You have the mental capacity to think deeply about where your life is going and to make decisions that shape your future. That ability is a gift from God. It separates you from every other living creature on this planet. That's why it's such a shame when people don't use it properly.

God didn't create you to just go through the motions, repeating the same patterns without rational thought. He gave you the ability to dream, to create, to improve, and to make conscious choices that lead to a better future. If you don't use that gift, then you're wasting one of the most powerful abilities you have.

So, take time every day to pause, to reflect, and to remind yourself of this power you've been given. Even just five minutes of sitting in silence, quietly thinking about your life, your goals, and your choices, can shift your entire perspective.

Every smart person you admire, every great leader, every person who has achieved something big, got there because of the choices they made. They didn't get there by making some rare or dramatic decision that only a few people can make, but instead small, consistent choices made over time by people who had the same power you have right now. The question is will you use it? Will you make intentional decisions that move you forward? Or will you let time slip away, watching life pass you by, just like so many others do? The power to make a real shift in your life is already in your hands, and sometimes all it takes is simplifying your mindset, quieting the noise, and choosing to stop overthinking so you can just start moving in the direction you already know you need to go.

How you spend your time plays a huge role in how effective you are each day. The way you see others also affects your productivity. If you spend time judging people or talking negatively about them, you're wasting precious time. As human beings, we're wired to share ideas and support one another, so it's important to use your mental energy wisely every single day, because that's what determines your positive growth. Instead of spending hours on video games or scrolling through social media memes, try using that time to read a good book.

Getting involved in small groups or surrounding yourself with like-minded people who have big dreams can completely transform your productivity. How you invest your time makes all the difference. Even small moments spent on the right things can create momentum that shapes your future.

That's why how you spend your downtime is so important. A lot of people turn to entertainment when they have free time, and that's not a bad thing. The time you spend in those moments can either push you forward or hold you back. How you prioritize your downtime makes all the difference.

Sometimes we tell ourselves we don't have enough time, but the truth is, we often have small pockets of time that go unnoticed. It's those quiet seconds, like when we're about to gossip, scroll on our phones, or play video games, those could be used for something more productive.

If you need to rest or sleep, then do it, because taking care of yourself is important too, and that's a much better use of time than getting caught up in distractions. What if you chose to use those moments to focus on things that help you grow or support someone else? Maybe it's finishing your homework, checking in on a friend, or working on a goal you've been putting off. These small things may seem insignificant, but when you're consistent, they can become incredibly meaningful and shape your future.

A lot of the small, consistent steps I took in high school, like building good habits, staying productive, and focusing on my goals, are what led me to where I am today with writing books, growing my business, and staying productive. In my opinion, it's worth it. Utilizing even the smallest amount of time available to invest in yourself when you are heavily occupied with a busy schedule is best. The busier you are, the more productive you become. Your brain connects the dots and creates similar patterns to form compound effects to take on more challenges. That is how you stay productive and intentional today, even with a busy schedule.

The whole idea is to take hold of small opportunities available and accomplish them so you can create momentum for yourself. Once you build a significant and robust momentum, you will no longer procrastinate. Every single day is packed with potential, but most of us go through life missing so much of it. It's easy to fall into routines or habits that make our days blur together, but there's so much more just waiting to be uncovered.

Imagine if you could unlock parts of yourself and your time that you didn't even realize were there, those hidden layers of creativity, energy, and ability that seem just out of reach. Sometimes, the things we want most feel impossible to achieve, but they're not as far away as we think. It's like opening a window you didn't know existed and suddenly seeing a view that changes everything.

I remember watching the movie *Click* with Adam Sandler, and man, that movie was hilarious. Adam Sandler has always been one of my favorite actors, and I love watching his movies when I'm taking a break or just relaxing. What really stuck with me about *Click* was how much deeper it was than just a comedy. Sure, it had all the typical funny scenes you'd expect from Adam Sandler, but the message behind it really made me think about how we use our time and what we prioritize.

At the beginning of the movie, Sandler's character, Michael Newman, is this overworked architect who's constantly trying to climb the corporate ladder. He's so focused on getting ahead in his career that he barely gives any attention to his wife and kids. His family is right there, wanting his time and love, but he's too busy stressing over work and chasing dreams.

Honestly, that's something a lot of us can relate to in some way. We get caught up in trying to "get ahead" or handle responsibilities, and we tell ourselves, "I'll make time later." That "later" keeps getting pushed further away. Then comes the crazy part of the movie. Michael gets this universal remote that can control his life by skipping through time. At first, it's all fun and games, like pausing, fast-forwarding, and rewinding through life's little annoyances. Who wouldn't want to skip through traffic or mute an argument, right?

Soon, the remote starts skipping parts of his life automatically, especially the parts he's shown he doesn't care much about, like family dinners or spending time with his kids. He doesn't even realize how much time is slipping away because he's so focused on getting through things he thinks are "in the way." The worst part is when he fast-forwards through years of his life and suddenly wakes up to find everything's changed. His kids are grown up, his marriage is falling apart, and he's missed out on so many things he can't get back.

That part of the movie really means something. You can see that deep regret on his face. He's standing in this version of his life where he got everything he thought he wanted career-wise, but it cost him the relationships that mattered. His family became strangers to him, and he couldn't believe how much he missed because he was too busy.

What makes it even more heartbreaking is that there's this scene where Michael watches a memory of his dad, played by Henry Winkler. In that memory, his dad is trying to spend time with him, but Michael brushes him off, thinking he'll have more time later, even though *later* never came. Watching that scene, you can feel how much Michael wishes he could go back and appreciate those moments. That part really made me think about how often we do the same thing, we think we have all the time in the world to be with our family or friends, but life doesn't wait for us.

Eventually, Michael realizes how badly he's messed up. He starts begging for a second chance to live his life differently. When he finally gets that chance, he wakes up in the bed at Bed Bath & Beyond, and it's like none of the fast-forwarding ever happened. After what he had just experienced, he doesn't waste a second. He's fully present with his wife and kids, soaking in every moment and being intentional with his time. He's laughing with them, making memories, and you can see that he finally understands how valuable those small moments are.

That's the part of the movie that really connects with what I'm talking about here. We all have these hidden moments throughout our day, like little pixels of time that we often overlook because they seem small or unimportant.

Looking back, I realize that some of the small, consistent choices I made in high school helped shape where I am today. Whether it was choosing to write instead of wasting time, focusing on personal goals, or staying productive. Those habits built the foundation for me to write books and work on my business now. At the time, those decisions didn't seem huge, but staying consistent with them made a big impact.

It's just like the movie *Click;* Michael didn't realize how much those small moments with his family mattered until he lost them. We don't have to wait for a wake-up call to figure it out. We can start now by recognizing those "hidden" pockets of time and using them wisely. Whether it's improving yourself, helping someone else, or just being present with your loved ones, those small, intentional moments can shape your entire future. In my opinion, it's worth it.

Once you start shifting your mindset, you'll notice something incredible: it feels like you suddenly have more time in your day. By becoming aware of the seconds instead of just hours, you realize how much time there actually is to work with. Instead of letting those minutes slip by unnoticed, you begin to see opportunities where there were once excuses. This way of thinking encourages you to take action rather than procrastinate or compromise. You're more willing to make a productive move because you understand the value of every second, and that awareness inspires you to get started instead of delaying.

Think of it like discovering a key to a locked door in your life. You've always had the key, but now you finally realize what it opens. Behind that door isn't just a more productive day; it's a version of you that is confident, capable, and clear about what matters. The best part is, this isn't about perfection or having everything figured out. It's about taking small steps that unlock bigger opportunities and using those to build toward the life you've always wanted.

The truth is that time isn't the barrier we think it is. Often, the real barrier is how we see it. When you start to focus on the seconds within your day, you stop thinking in terms of "later" or "someday" and start realizing that every minute counts. What if you began to notice the moments in your day that could be redirected toward what matters to you? What if the goals and dreams that seemed distant could suddenly feel within reach, simply because you've learned how to use your time more intentionally?

Life isn't about waiting for the perfect moment to arrive. It's about realizing that the moments you have *right now* are the ones that will build the life you want.

Your day isn't just something to "get through." It's a chance to discover your strengths, overcome your challenges, and realize just how much you're capable of. You don't have to do everything at once, and you don't need to figure it all out today.

What you *can* do is start uncovering what's already there, like the opportunities, the abilities, and potential that have been waiting for you all along. By thinking differently about your time, you set yourself up to accomplish more, procrastinate less, and build momentum toward a life that changes more than just your own.

FINAL THOUGHTS
20/80 Vision

What you see in front of you is only about twenty percent of the full picture, which is what makes sense now. The other eighty percent is unseen and includes God's promises, His plans, and everything He's already prepared for you long ago. Most people live only by what they can see, but faith means trusting God with the part that hasn't been revealed yet.

Today is the only piece with which you can work, so make it count.

LOST TIME

Lost time is never found again.

- BENJAMIN FRANKLIN

TIME WORKS the same for everyone, but when something matters to you, it's used differently.

In early 2019, after a few years of working as a sandwich artist at a Subway restaurant in Tucson, Arizona. I was the pre-closer, scheduled from 4 p.m. to 8 p.m., and every minute mattered. As the pre-closer, I had to make sure the store was in good shape before it officially closed. I cleaned the popcorn machine, wiped down the counters, scrubbed the oven, refilled the entire deli station, swept the floors, and mopped, all while still handling customers as they came in. My coworker, the official closer, would work alongside me, but I carried the bulk of the early shutdown. At the time, I was dating my girlfriend, and two nights a week after my shift, I had planned to spend time with her. I was determined to get everything done on time; I never knew if I'd get hit with a sudden rush of customers, so that sense of urgency pushed my mind to move fast and stay focused. I wanted nothing more than to clock out at exactly 8 p.m. and make the most of the night ahead. I was genuinely interested in investing my time with her, and building something real, after all, it was my first relationship.

Then we had our very first Valentine's Day together, and it turned out to be one of the most special nights we ever shared. I had taken her to Harvest Restaurant, a nice place for dinner in Oro Valley on a rainy night. A few hours before our dinner, I made a trip over there to personally hand the chef a gift basket I had prepared. In the woven decorative basket was a large stuffed bear, surrounded by all her favorite snacks and chocolates, and on each item, I had placed a small sticker note with a personal message that simply expressed thoughts about her that came from the heart. I did not buy a pre-made gift basket from the store. I spent nearly four hours at home crafting everything by hand, cutting the stickers, writing the notes, and carefully picking out her favorite chocolates, snacks, and stuffed bear separately. The time and effort I put into it was the most thoughtful way to show how much she meant to me.

We arrived at the restaurant that night and it was pouring down rain. I came prepared with an umbrella, walked her to the front entrance, and made sure she never touched a single door handle, hoping I'd score a few extra points for that. During our meal, the chef unexpectedly brought the basket out, just as I had planned. As he walked through the dining room, weaving between tables with the big basket in his hands, the entire restaurant seemed to pause. People turned their heads, whispering things like "aww" and "how sweet," as all eyes followed him table by table until he reached ours. While I was talking to my girlfriend, the basket caught her attention as it approached our table, and she turned to look with a soft glow on her face, immediately drawn in.

She was speechless.

The moment the basket was placed at the center of our table, her hands covered her face in disbelief as she let out a breathless laugh, her eyes teary, wide and full of emotion, completely overwhelmed by the surprise. She kept saying "oh my gosh" repeatedly, almost like she didn't know how to express how happy she was. I remember seeing people at the other tables turning to look at us. Everyone around was just quietly enjoying their dinner, but what I had planned stood out. Right then and there, it felt like something different was happening, and it was something I'll never forget.

Then, two months after our first Valentine's Day together, I was working out at the Planet Fitness gym that day and following my usual routine. I had just started doing tricep dips on the machine where you hold onto the side handles and lower your body up and down while suspended. I was mid-set when I felt my phone buzz in my pocket, so I got down, pulled it out, and checked to see who it was. Sure enough, it was her. Normally, whenever she texted me, she'd say "babe" or "hey honey," but this time the message started differently. She said, "Hi Jon," and immediately I felt something was wrong.

There was a strange distance in the way she addressed me, and it didn't feel right. It sounded more like a message from a friend than someone in a relationship. Then I read the rest. It was a short text where she said, "Hi Jon, I feel like we need to go our separate ways." That was it. No call, no in-person conversation, just that one short message. I stood there, stunned, and the energy in me dropped. I didn't even finish my workout. I had only been about fifteen or twenty minutes into it, and I normally stayed at the gym for close to an hour.

I grabbed my things, walked out, and sat in my car for thirty minutes. I tried not to cry, and I didn't move. I just sat there, trying to put the pieces together, and attempting to figure out what I had done wrong. Everything felt surreal. I kept thinking, is this real? Did she just end it like that? I was genuinely confused as to why she suddenly wanted to end it all so quickly after only five months of dating. Although I thought about calling her to find out what was really going on, I didn't. Something in me just accepted that she had made her final decision, and as much as I wanted clarity, I chose not to ask why.

Just like that, she wasn't mine anymore.

Funny enough, this book was born out of that breakup. I started reflecting on the urgency I felt every single day, just trying to finish my shift at Subway so I could see her. That urgency shaped something in me. Before we dated, I didn't really think about time. I moved slowly and honestly didn't care much about my work performance. I was one of the worst workers at Subway. I was quiet, shy, and hesitant with customers. I never projected my voice. I didn't have a reason to care, so I didn't. But once I started dating her, everything changed. I had a reason, which created a fire inside me. I became fast, sharp, and focused, not because someone trained me, but because something mattered to me. That urgency came from wanting to spend time with her after work. I had no idea back then that this was shaping how I viewed time and productivity.

After we broke up, everything shifted again. At the time, I was working as a bellman at the Hilton El Conquistador Hotel in Oro Valley. I remember one morning clearly. It was early, the air was breezy, and I stood outside staring at the mountains. I started thinking about those long workdays and how much I used to accomplish in such a short time, and I realized something. I had the ability to do a lot with very little time, and I had never noticed it. It wasn't about the hours I had; it was about how I used the minutes. I became great at doing so much with just a few minutes, and it happened naturally, simply because I had a reason to care. Once the relationship ended, that drive faded. I no longer had something to look forward to after work, so I started slowing down again. That contrast made me realize how powerful a sense of purpose can be. It wasn't about being talented or gifted. It was about having a reason that truly mattered. That was the beginning of this book. That was the moment I realized that if something matters to you, you will find a way to get it done, and often, you'll do it faster than you ever thought you could.

WHEN EVERY MINUTE COUNTS

Now and then, I reflect on those days as a sandwich artist when I worked with such urgency, racing the clock to get everything done before 8 p.m. so I could spend time with my girlfriend. It amazes me, especially now, with everything I'm juggling, including writing books, managing newsletters, preparing podcast appearances, organizing book signings, and keeping up with social media content. Sometimes I scratch my head and wonder how I pulled it off back then. It almost felt like I had a superpower, like I was locked into a rhythm where every minute had weight. Over time, I've come to see that I'm not the only one who thinks that way; people around us today live with that same intensity and intentionality. When you surround yourself with those kinds of people, you realize that managing time well isn't just something you once did; it's something you can learn from, carry forward, and keep applying with purpose.

WHEN PURPOSE MEETS THE CLOCK

In a single day, regardless of who you are, we each have 24 hours, 1,440 minutes, 86,400 seconds. Every moment is an opportunity, yet so often, we let these moments slip by unnoticed and unused. Many mindful people refuse to let that happen, one of them being Elon Musk. What sets Elon apart is the ability to harness time and make the most of every second, helping him accomplish more. It's something anyone can do. It just comes down to understanding how it works.

Now watch this: if you knew you had 86,400 opportunities each day to make little progress, to move forward, to achieve something extraordinary, would you let them pass you by? Musk doesn't. He sees time as a finite resource, something more precious than any material wealth. That's why, even when he eats, he's not sitting idly, savoring each bite. Instead, he combines that time with something productive, often reading or working as he eats.

Musk's approach to time management isn't just about efficiency. It's about deeply understanding that every second counts. Over the years, many observed Musk's time strategies; how he structures his day using tools like the five-minute rule or time blocking. Think about that for a moment. The five-minute rule is simple, yet powerful: if you don't want to do something, tell yourself to do it anyway, but only for five minutes. Make sure you say it out loud. There's something different about speaking out loud that makes you believe it.

Say, "I'm going to do so and so for five minutes," and see where it takes you. In fact, if there's something you know you can finish in five minutes or less, like starting a load of laundry or clearing off a counter, tell yourself you'll do it, then just do it immediately. This trains your mind to take simple initiative and builds strong momentum overtime.

You'll be surprised at the results, whatever they may be, whether you're in school, a single parent doing chores, working on your endeavors, or pursuing hobbies. This small shift in mindset can lead to significant productivity gains. For Musk, those five minutes can turn into major breakthroughs. Using this throughout your day can really boost your productivity. When you break tasks into small time chunks, it makes things feel less overwhelming and helps you build momentum. I've tried this myself, and it's amazing how effective it can be. This method helps you stay focused on the present and be more intentional with your time, like how Elon Musk manages his day.

There was one time, back in 2015, when I worked at Discount Tire out in Tucson near Ina and Thornydale. I was part of the crew that replaced tires, rebuilt tire sensors, buffed out wheel hubs, rotated tires, reapplied wheel weights, and rebalanced everything to keep vehicles running smooth on the road. It was fast-paced, hands-on work, and honestly, it taught me a lot about pressure, precision, and staying sharp when everything around you is moving a hundred miles an hour.

I still remember there being about five managers on shift every single day, and it wasn't even rare to get yelled at. Honestly, it felt like a normal part of the day. Even if I were doing something right, they'd still tell me to pick up the pace, move quicker, or just flat-out bark orders across the bay. That was just the nature of the job: high energy, no room for hesitation, and very little grace for anyone falling behind.

In all fairness, Discount Tire was still a solid company with a great reputation. The founder, Bruce Halle, who has since passed away, was known to be a man of faith in Christ. He built a culture of integrity, customer service, and hard work, and that trickled down through the ranks. I remember offering water bottles to customers during the summer heat, doing free tire checks, and making sure people were taken care of. There was something about those small actions, like handing someone a cold bottle of water while they waited that stuck with me. It reminded me that even in a high-pressure job, small gestures could still make a big impact.

There was one moment that sticks out clearly in my memory, this time when I had to do a nail repair on a customer's tire. There was a nail lodged deep in the tread, and I had to remove the entire wheel, unscrew the lug nuts, and dunk the tire into this water tank we kept on site. That's how we'd find the leak, you'd watch closely for bubbles, and wherever the air was escaping, that's where you'd mark it with a piece of chalk. Then you'd grab the repair kit and patch it up properly.

I was still new at the time, and I wasn't fast. It took me around thirty minutes to finish the repair, which in that environment was way too long. One of the managers, who was ex-military, heard about it, and not long after, he pulled me aside and just tore into me. He was dropping f-bombs, yelling at me to hurry up, pushing me to move faster, and it felt a little ridiculous. I mean, I was doing my best, but in that place, there was no room for being slow.

Yet, what amazed me the most was how some people thrived in that environment, like this one girl named Samantha. She was sharp, quick, and rarely seemed tired. I remember approaching her once while she was finishing up a tire install, tightening the lug nuts with the impact gun, and I asked, "How are you always so quick with everything?" At first, she just kind of brushed it off and ignored me. The next day, during one of our early morning meetings before the store opened, we were chatting again, and she told me something that stuck with me.

She had been doing these five-minute workouts every morning around 5:30 a.m., five days a week. Ten exercises—thirty seconds each—nonstop. They involved compound movements like push-ups, burpees, jumping lunges, high knees, wide push-ups, all back-to-back with no breaks. She said it wasn't just about burning calories; it was about starting the day with intensity. It got her heart pumping, sharpened her focus, and made her feel more in control of her energy throughout the day.

That conversation meant something to me. I decided to try it myself. At the time, I weighed about 190 pounds, and I was around twenty-three years old. I started doing those workouts each morning and stuck to a healthy diet. A month later, I'd dropped nearly twenty pounds. More importantly, I felt sharper, more alert, and even my performance at work improved. The mental fog started clearing. I was making better decisions. I had more energy.

Honestly, it's wild how something so small—just five minutes—can make that kind of difference. It's tough while you're doing it. Your heart races, your breathing speeds up, and you've got to walk it off afterward. It changes your day and it shifts your momentum. It's not about doing everything; it's about doing something, giving it your best in that small window, and letting that effort carry you into everything else you face.

I found that working out early in the morning brought me the most benefit, far more than doing it later in the day. In the evening, your mind tends to be cluttered with the experiences you've already gone through, and there's usually a sense of fatigue that makes it harder to give your best. In the early morning, your mind is clear, calm, alert, and it almost feels like it gets a head start before the rest of the day even begins.

It wasn't about how long I worked out, but about how much effort I gave in that short window. If I could give my absolute best in those five minutes with no breaks, maintaining good posture, controlling my breathing, and pushing myself to stay sharp, then I felt like I could handle anything else the day threw at me.

It helped me build mental endurance and made me more alert. I began noticing small improvements in how I handled multitasking, such as writing my book, answering emails, organizing my newsletter, or just managing the overall pace of my day. I wasn't as easily frustrated when dealing with complaints or unexpected issues in my business. I started handling things with a clearer mind and a steadier approach. Over time, that small habit made a big difference. It sharpened my awareness, helped me stay focused, and slowly turned into one of the most effective routines I've picked up.

One interesting study from the University of California, Santa Barbara showed that short bursts of morning exercise helped boost brain function, memory, and attention. This is especially good to know if you're trying to cut down on caffeine intake. Starting the day with short bursts of exercise helps jumpstart your metabolism, giving your body a natural boost in energy and alertness. It also promotes faster calorie burning throughout the day, helping you stay more active, focused, and physically refreshed well into the afternoon.

I was reading online while doing some more research on this topic and came across this study from *JAMA Network Open,* and I thought it was interesting. They found that even short bursts of regular movement reduced brain protein buildup, like beta-amyloid, linked to memory loss and helped people think more clearly. It surprised me to learn that beta-amyloid buildup, often seen in the early stages of Alzheimer's disease, can start forming quietly over time without symptoms, which makes even light movement a powerful way to support long-term brain health. If someone you know is dealing with early memory issues or signs of Alzheimer's, this kind of simple daily movement might be a helpful way to support their brain health.

If you're reading this, I highly suggest that you try doing that five-minute workout yourself, it could be a game-changer for you. It helped me become more attentive in my daily responsibilities, whether it was at work, during worship sessions at church, or just in everyday life, I started noticing things I used to overlook. It sharpened my cognitive performance and overall awareness, and honestly, I think that's one of the most incredible benefits that came from something so simple. Even though I don't have Alzheimer's or memory loss, I'm always looking for ways to protect my brain and stay sharp.

Small efforts add up by simply using small increments. Even if you don't feel like starting a task, telling yourself to do it for just five minutes while saying it out loud can make a big difference. You might be surprised by how much you can get done. The key is to apply this rule to different tasks throughout your day, whether it's work, chores, or personal projects. As you keep practicing it, you'll likely notice that your productivity improves, and you'll accomplish more. I'm confident that if you stick with it, you'll see great results. The more often you do it, the more progress you'll make, and you'll find yourself moving closer to your goals.

By taking control of your time in these small ways, you can really make a big impact on what you achieve. This precision with time isn't accidental. Musk's method of dividing his day into these micro-units allows him to focus intensely on tasks while minimizing waste. He's constantly aware of how much time he has and how much of it is left, which means he's always thinking ahead, planning, and adjusting. It's a mindset that few adopt, but it's what allows Musk to run multiple companies, innovate in fields as diverse as space travel and electric cars, and still find time for his family.

Take, for example, his famous lunch meetings. While most people see lunch as a break from work, Musk views it as another opportunity. He'll eat during meetings, ensuring that not a minute is lost. For him, multitasking isn't just a strategy—it's a necessity. The idea of sitting down and relaxing during lunch might seem absurd to Musk because he knows that time is always ticking. Every second spent not working is, to him, a second wasted, which he sees as a moment that could've been used to propel one of his ventures forward.

I'm not saying to work every waking second of your life. I'm saying to choose a large portion of your day and give it your best, even in small increments.

Imagine watching Elon Musk go through a typical day. He wakes up around 7:00 AM after about six hours of sleep, which according to him, is just enough to stay sharp and productive. Within minutes, he's already checking his phone, scanning through emails, and prioritizing what's most urgent for the day.

On a personal note, I always start my day by reading the Bible and spending time with the Lord, but his work ethic still motivates me.

By 7:30, he's in the shower, a simple habit, but one he considers an essential part for clearing his mind and preparing to dive into work. By 8:00 AM, Musk is already in the thick of it, often skipping breakfast and jumping straight into meetings, emails, and decision-making. His mornings are intense, filled with rapid-fire discussions and problem-solving sessions that require his full focus. Every conversation has a purpose, every meeting is intentional, and there's no time wasted on small talk or unnecessary details. It's all about efficiency, like moving from one major decision to the next, ensuring that things keep progressing at the pace he expects.

For lunch, if he even has it, is never a sit-down affair. He's usually eating during a meeting or while reviewing plans, keeping his focus on the work rather than the meal in front of him. By the afternoon, he shifts into deeper work: whether it's engineering discussions at Tesla, reviewing rocket designs for SpaceX, or making critical adjustments to ongoing projects. This is the part of the day where he's not just leading but actively contributing, getting hands-on with the details that could make or break a project. As evening rolls in, there's no winding down and no slow transition into relaxation. Instead, Musk is still working, still engaged in high-level discussions, still making decisions that will impact the future of his companies. Even when he attends business dinners, it's not about unwinding, but it's another setting to exchange ideas, brainstorm new concepts, and push things forward.

Despite his packed schedule, he carves out time for his children, making sure he's present with them, even in the middle of everything else he's juggling. By midnight, he's finally starting to shift gears, maybe reading or having conversations that challenge his thinking, but even then, his mind never fully stops. He finally goes to bed around 1:00 AM, only to do it all over again the next day. During the most intense periods when everything is on the line, when deadlines are looming, when success or failure is hanging in the balance, he doesn't just work long hours; he immerses himself completely. When he was developing the Falcon 1 rocket, he didn't waste time commuting or checking out early. He literally slept on the factory floor, staying as close to the action as possible, making sure not a single second was lost.

Now, obviously, most people aren't running billion-dollar companies or trying to send rockets into space, but there's something about his approach that anyone can learn from. It's not about filling your day with tasks just to feel busy, but it's about making sure the things you spend your time on move you forward. Instead of trying to do everything at once, it's about narrowing your focus to what matters, such as cutting out the distractions and unnecessary obligations that take up time without adding real value. Whether you're building a business, working toward a big goal, or simply trying to be more productive, the key isn't to do more, but to be intentional with what you allow into your day and make sure your time is spent on things that matter.

I mean, if you look carefully at Musk's lifestyle, it becomes clear that his growth isn't just due to his intelligence or creativity. It's his awareness of time, shown in his ability to break down his day into moments and use each one with purpose that sets him apart. Most people see time as something that just passes by, but Musk sees it as something to be mastered, something to be controlled. He's intentional with every second he has, using it wisely because he understands that life can only be lived and controlled by the seconds that you have right now. Once a second passes, it becomes the past, and there's no getting it back.

Now, not everyone can operate at the level Musk does. His approach may be extreme, and it's not something that everyone can—or should—replicate entirely. What it does is show people that it's possible to push themselves beyond their own limitations. Even if you can't match his intensity, you can still learn and be inspired from his mindset. By becoming more aware of how you spend your time, by seizing those moments instead of letting them slip away, you can accomplish far more than you might believe possible.

This idea ties directly into making tomorrow a reality by being present with the time you have now. Musk understands that the only thing you can truly control is the second that you're in. By focusing on how you spend your time today, you lay the groundwork for the breakthrough of tomorrow. It's a mindset shift that can lead to profound changes in how you approach both your life and work.

After all, time waits for no one. If you learn to master it, as Musk has, you can achieve extraordinary things.

ELON MUSK'S APPROACH
Making Every Minute Count

On June 19th, 2018, Elon Musk reportedly said that he and his brother, Kimbal, slept in his office and showered at the YMCA while starting their first company, Zip2, as mentioned in the *CNBC Make It* article by Tom Huddleston Jr.

Even years later, after selling Zip2 and PayPal, Elon had many milestones behind him and growing success from his earlier ventures. He continued to avoid luxury and stayed focused on the mission. He even went so far as to sleep under his desk at his Tesla Fremont factory in California, so that his employees could see him sleeping on the floor during shift changes. His motive was to show his team that he wasn't relaxing at a luxury resort overseas or sipping a glass of champagne somewhere. He wanted to communicate, without saying a word, that he took his job seriously and was willing to suffer more than anyone else on the team.

Elon worked the front lines for nearly three years in Nevada and Fremont while trying to build the Tesla Model 3. Although Tesla is internationally recognized for producing the fastest-accelerating car in the world, it has faced a relentless challenger from the very beginning—time itself. Time shows no favoritism. Elon Musk takes his day so seriously that he consolidates his time by skipping breakfast and integrating his meals into daily meetings. Rather than eating at home, he uses this approach to save time and ensure every minute is productive.

His sleep, daily hygiene routines, meals, and interviews are all woven into his busy work schedule to maximize every moment. Musk has mentioned that he doesn't want to waste time driving home to shower and sleep. Instead, he uses that extra time to stay at his Tesla factory in Silicon Valley, working on the Tesla Model 3. This model posed the greatest challenge for him, and he spent countless nights under difficult conditions to ensure the best quality for the vehicle.

Why does Elon Musk take time so seriously? The answer is evident in his production line, which is expanding and improving at an impressive rate. In 2022, Tesla delivered 1,313,851 vehicles to customers worldwide, marking a 40% increase in deliveries compared to the previous year, according to an article by *Investing.com*. By selling 491,000 cars in America in 2022, Tesla secured the title of the US luxury sales leader. Elon thinks differently than others, but his approach is quite simple. Many of us struggle to understand how Musk achieves so much, even though the answer is right in front of us. The reason Elon utilizes his time so effectively is not a mystery; it's incredibly simple. Everyone has access to time.

This simple secret, practiced by many great minds to build their empires, is available to anyone not just entrepreneurs or business leaders. It's accessible to anyone who wants to accelerate their day and see massive results, whether you're a single parent, student, employee, or anyone else. You are about to embark on an effortless yet powerful journey that will change and shape your mindset. The answer is this: Have a powerful vision for your future and use today's opportunities with a clear sense of direction to make it happen.

Elon Musk foresaw the future: producing electric cars and helping humanity become a multi-planetary species. Things didn't happen overnight for him, though it might have seemed that way as he worked tirelessly in the factory. He remained steadfast and determined to turn his vision into reality by taking his time seriously.

There's a proverb that speaks to this: *"Where there is no vision, the people perish: but he that keeps the law remains happy"* (Proverbs 29:18). Without a vision, there's no reason to push forward and pursue your God-given dreams. You must know what you want before going after it, just like pursuing the person you hope to marry. That person must possess the personality, traits, and physical attraction you desire. That's the person you strive to win over every day in marriage. It's the same with any goal, big or small, that you want to accomplish, whether it's long-term or short-term.

Elon Musk faced harsh criticism during his career, but it didn't stop him because he had a strong vision. His vision was so clear and compelling that he used people's negative criticism as fuel to pursue his long-term goals. He had such a strong sense of direction that he confidently gave a facility tour to YouTube tech reviewers like Marques Brownlee, along with Hollywood figures such as Leonardo DiCaprio, who visited in person.

SETTING RIGHT EXPECTATIONS

In 2008, Elon Musk faced a critical decision: He had to choose between letting go of either Tesla or SpaceX due to severe financial difficulties. Instead of abandoning one company, Musk decided to split the small amount of remaining funds between the two, risking the possibility that both might fail. Despite the odds, his bold move ultimately paid off, allowing both companies to survive and thrive.

To provide context, in 2008, the financial crisis was at its peak, and both Tesla and SpaceX were on the verge of bankruptcy. Musk had invested millions of his own money into these ventures, and failure seemed imminent. His decision to divide the remaining funds was a last-ditch effort to save both companies, demonstrating his relentless determination and belief in their potential. This pivotal moment set the stage for Tesla's eventual success in revolutionizing the automotive industry and SpaceX's achievements in advancing space exploration.

Eventually, after working things out with Tesla investors, Elon signed a $1.6 billion contract with NASA to keep moving forward. In an article I came across by *The Verge,* Elon kept both companies alive during one of the most challenging times in American history.

Interestingly enough, during the 2008 financial crisis, Tesla made it through without any government help by relying on Elon Musk's own money. Ford also avoided the main federal bailout by securing private loans ahead of time, which helped it stand out from General Motors and Chrysler, who both needed direct government aid to survive.

What does this tell us?

It shows how hungry Elon Musk was to achieve his goals, even during the most challenging times, especially when other companies like Ford were also fighting to survive. Why? Because Elon had a vision and a clear direction for reaching his dreams and protecting them from failure. Some people can achieve their dreams, but few can protect and maintain them. Amid the chaos, Elon was focused on the small things. He knew exactly what needed to happen to save both of his companies. He planned accordingly and adapted during a challenging situation by signing a new contract with NASA. This was only possible because

Musk had a simple vision, a clear direction, and a relentless drive to achieve his dream, no matter how difficult the journey.

The main thing to remember is that time is the great equalizer. People from all walks of life, with different worldviews and from all parts of the world, use time differently. Everyone on Earth, regardless of their success or location, shares the same twenty-four hours each day. We can't control the amount of time we're given, but we can manage it effectively. With the time he had, Elon Musk cherished it as though it were gold. Before he ever started his businesses, he took the time to sit down and carefully consider the challenges ahead long before taking action. This wasn't something he rushed into. It was after he graduated from college, at a time when he was still a shy kid, so shy that even the thought of going to job interviews made him nervous. Instead of forcing himself into uncomfortable interviews, he thought, *why not just start my own company?* Even then, he didn't just jump in blindly. He used that time wisely, thinking through the risks, the struggles, and the obstacles he might face.

Musk once said that starting a business is like *"eating glass and staring into the abyss."*

That statement alone tells you everything you need to know about his mindset. He wasn't expecting it to be easy, he was already preparing for the uncertainties ahead. Why did he describe it that way? When you start something new, especially something as unpredictable as a business, you're stepping into the unknown. There's no clear roadmap, no guaranteed outcome. The "glass" represents the pain and struggle you have to endure, and the "abyss" is the uncertainty of not knowing how things will play out.

That's exactly why Musk took the time to count the cost early on. He knew that stepping into business meant stepping into uncertainty, and the only way to handle that was to expect the struggle before it arrived. He understood that if he didn't prepare himself mentally, the weight of those challenges could break him. He anticipated the difficulties; he was able to push through them instead. That's why his time was so valuable, because he invested it in preparing for the future. He wasn't just hoping for instant growth; he was bracing himself for the struggle it would take to get there.

THE RIGHT EXPECTATIONS CAN PREVENT DISAPPOINTMENT

Many people get discouraged when things don't go as planned. They hit a roadblock and start second-guessing themselves, wondering if they even made the right choice in the first place. If you already expect challenges before you begin, they won't knock you down as easily. There's an old saying: *"Anything that can go wrong, will go wrong."* That's called Murphy's Law, and while it might carry a negative connotation, it's actually a great tool for planning. It doesn't mean you should assume everything is going to fail. It just means you should be prepared for obstacles, so they don't take you by surprise. This is exactly how Musk operates. He never assumed Tesla would be an instant success, instead, he knew there would be setbacks. So, when things started going south, he didn't freeze up; he adapted. He had already factored the struggle into his plan.

Disappointment is just an unmet expectation, a moment when something you were hoping for to happen doesn't. When you think about it, it's almost like you're setting a mental calendar in your brain. You're making an appointment with an event or outcome, telling yourself, *this is going to happen at this time.* That expectation becomes locked in your mind, just like setting a date for something important.

Here's the problem: life doesn't always follow your schedule.

So, when the moment arrives and what you expected doesn't happen, that mental appointment gets canceled. Just like that, you feel disappointed, because the expectation wasn't met. That's exactly why disappointment hits so hard. It's not just that something didn't work out, it's that your mind was already set on it happening.

What if you reversed the process? Instead of only expecting good things to happen, what if you also set a mental appointment for challenges? What if you expected obstacles to show up? Then, when that challenge happens, you won't be caught off guard. You won't feel disappointed because you already knew it was coming. It's not an interruption; it's part of the schedule.

That's the key: disappointment happens when you don't expect difficulties, but when you do show up, they don't shake you as much because you're prepared. Instead of feeling defeated, you're able to face it head-on and keep going. It's the same thing with having kids. Everyone loves the idea of having children, it sounds beautiful, fulfilling, and meaningful. What most people don't fully realize is that having kids is one of the biggest sacrifices you will ever make.

Even before a child enters the world, your life is already changing. You have to plan, prepare, and shift your mindset. Some people don't count the cost beforehand. They think about the cute baby pictures, the little laughs, the bonding moments, and all the good experiences. They don't always stop to really consider what they're signing up for. Once that baby is here, everything changes.

Your hours of sleep begin to fade, your free time no longer belongs to you, and your patience is tested every single day. The baby cries through the night, leaving you exhausted for work the next morning. Then, just when you get used to the baby stage, they grow up into a toddler who throws tantrums in the grocery store over a candy bar. Before you know it, they're a teenager talking back, breaking rules, pushing boundaries, and you're standing there wondering, *what happened to my sweet little baby?*

If you don't count the cost before you have kids, you'll be blindsided when those challenges happen. If you sit down beforehand and really ask yourself, *Am I ready for this? Am I willing to give up my time, my sleep, and my own desires to raise another human being?* Then, when the hard days come, you won't feel like the world is collapsing on you. Would you rather deal with it now or later?

I was listening to a story on *Family Life Radio* about intentional living while I was driving to the grocery store. A father was talking about his daughter and how she never listened to him, no matter what he said. She constantly disobeyed, talked back, and pushed him to his limit. He reached a point where he was so frustrated, he just wanted to kick her out of the house. This was always part of the journey. He just hadn't fully realized it when he became a parent.

This is the thing people need to understand: challenges aren't an accident; they're part of the process. If you don't mentally prepare for them before they come, then when they do, they'll feel unbearable. It's kind of like saying, *I want to be a doctor,* but never thinking about the years of medical school, the long nights of studying, the stress, the debt, and everything that comes with it. If you don't fully understand what you're committing to, then when the struggles come, you'll be asking yourself, *why is this happening?*

If you count the cost beforehand, then when the difficulties arrive, you won't feel like everything is falling apart, you'll know that this is just part of the journey you signed up for. This is why so many people give up on things. They didn't plan for the obstacles ahead. Some people start a business thinking it's going to be fun and exciting, then they realize it's stressful, risky, and exhausting, so they quit.

See, if they had counted the cost and expected the first couple of years to be tough, they wouldn't be so discouraged. They would have been mentally prepared for slow months, setbacks, and financial struggles. They only planned for the best-case scenario, they feel like they've failed even if they're making progress.

This is why Musk's mindset was so powerful. He never expected everything to go perfectly. He knew there would be failures. He was mentally prepared for them; those failures didn't shake him. If you expect only smooth sailing, you're setting yourself up for a hard fall. If you go into something expecting both highs and lows, you'll be able to handle setbacks without feeling like you've been knocked off course.

Let's think about it in another way.

Your mind has to build momentum by preparing for the worst. When you get a flu shot, you're basically putting a little bit of the virus into your system. Why? So that if you ever catch the actual flu, your body already knows how to handle it. That's exactly what happens when you mentally prepare for obstacles before they happen. When you take the time to think, *okay, what could go wrong? What's my plan if this happens?* You're giving yourself a "mental flu shot." So, when those problems come—and they will—you don't panic, because you've already built-up immunity to setbacks.

This is why Musk was able to make tough decisions without hesitation. He wasn't just reacting in the moment; he had already built up the mental resilience to push through challenges before they even showed up. It's not about expecting everything to fall apart; it's about being steady when it does. When you train your mind to anticipate challenges, you also sharpen your ability to adapt. You start noticing patterns quicker, responding with clarity instead of emotion. That kind of mental preparedness doesn't just help you survive the tough moments; it helps you move through them with purpose. Over time, that steady, grounded mindset becomes one of your greatest strengths.

This is the real question: How far are you willing to go when things don't go as planned?

Let's be honest here, if you're only willing to keep going when things are easy, you're not going to make it very far. Positive transformation isn't about whether you'll face obstacles. It's about what you do when they show up.

Musk didn't make it because things just magically worked out for him. He made it because he was prepared to push through when things *weren't* working out. He had already wrapped his mind around the fact that this was going to be hard. That's the kind of mindset you need if you want to make something happen in your life. You can't just hope everything works out, you must expect challenges, prepare for them, and keep moving forward anyway.

STARTS WITH SMALL STEPS

Focusing on the small moments within each hour is powerful, but true growth comes from combining those moments with consistent, steady steps over time.

I remember watching a documentary on YouTube some time ago about the start of Amazon. It showed how Jeff Bezos started with almost nothing, just an idea, a garage, and a few people helping him pack boxes. In fact, when Bezos launched Amazon, his journey was anything but grand. He had to borrow money from his parents, who invested $245,573 from their life savings into his idea. That may seem like a lot of money for many people, because it is, and his parents drained their savings for Jeff. At the time, it seemed like a major risk, especially since Jeff was starting small, taking little steps to build something that didn't even exist yet. He had a plan, and he was putting in the work to make it happen. His parents believed in him and were willing to give what they could, even though that money was a huge portion of what they had. It was everything they were able to offer, which was a difficult leap of faith in their son's vision, not knowing if it would amount to anything. Still, they knew Jeff would make something out of it, and to them, that was all that mattered.

At first, Amazon wasn't even called Amazon. Bezos went through a couple of different names before finally settling on "Amazon," inspired by the Amazon River in South America. He first considered the name Cadabra, hoping that people would understand the magic behind how his website functioned, that it could hold an infinite number of books, unlike traditional brick-and-mortar stores, which were still the norm at the time. Unfortunately, people kept mishearing it, often misunderstanding it as a reference to a dead body. The confusion surrounding the name led him to adopt a new one, Relentless, a name he felt captured the company's unstoppable drive; however, that name didn't resonate well either. Eventually, he settled on Amazon, which carried a vision of something much greater.

Another reason for this name was because the Amazon River is one of the largest and most powerful in the world, stretching across multiple countries, full of life and constant movement. Bezos wanted his company to represent something just as vast, something that would keep growing and expanding over time.

When Bezos first started, there wasn't anything glamorous about the operation. He and his small team worked tirelessly, putting books into boxes and shipping them out by hand. There were no massive warehouses, no automation, just a handful of people assembling packages on the hard concrete floor. They didn't even have tables to work on. They were doing everything on their knees, stacking boxes, taping them up, and getting them ready to ship. After hours of this, one of his early team members finally suggested a simple but game-changing idea: "Why don't we buy some packing tables?"

Then came that laugh, Bezos's distinct, loud, almost exaggerated chuckle that you can hear in countless interviews and clips online. It's the kind of laugh that makes you do a double take, half amused, half surprised at how unique it sounds.

After hearing his team member's suggestion, he let out that famous laugh and said something along the lines of, "Packing tables, of course. How did we not think of that?" It was such a simple solution, yet they had been working on the floor for so long without even considering it. So, they invested in tables, and just like that, a small improvement was made.

That part of his story resonated with me because it showed how Bezos valued practical solutions and small progress. It wasn't about making huge, sweeping changes all at once, it was about fixing one problem at a time, making things just a little bit better every step of the way.

Amazon's journey wasn't just about these small adjustments; it was also full of setbacks. As the company grew, new challenges kept coming. There were legal and regulatory issues to navigate, logistical problems with deliveries, and even accidents involving Amazon's delivery drivers. I remember hearing about incidents where drivers crashed, packages were lost, and unexpected problems kept surfacing. But instead of letting these obstacles slow him down, Bezos tackled them one at a time.

I saw a video review from one of Amazon's early customers that shocked me. This was back when Amazon had just started expanding beyond books, aiming to become the go-to online store for everything. They were still figuring things out, learning how to handle all kinds of products and deliveries. One customer had ordered a hair blow dryer, expecting just a normal, everyday product. When they turned it on, instead of just blowing hot air, it literally shot out flames. Now, I have to admit, as crazy as that was, part of me couldn't help but laugh. I mean, seeing a blow dryer burst into flames is not exactly what you expect when you buy something online. At the same time, it was kind of scary. Imagine expecting a simple tool to dry your hair, and instead, it operates like a mini flamethrower.

The customer even recorded a video review, showing exactly what happened. Honestly, it was one of those moments where you realize, even a company as big as Amazon wasn't immune to setbacks. That's the thing about setbacks; they're just part of the process. Mistakes happen, things go wrong, and unexpected challenges come up. That's normal.

What matters is how you handle them. For Amazon, this was just another step in learning how to improve its business. Maybe it meant collaborating with better suppliers, double-checking product quality, or finding ways to ensure things like that didn't happen again. Every setback, no matter how big or small, was an opportunity to adjust and improve.

That's exactly how progress works. It's never a straight path. There are always going to be bumps along the way. Each challenge is just another chance to refine the process, fix what's broken, and move forward. That's something I've come to realize in my own life. Whether it's business, personal goals, or anything else, setbacks aren't a sign to give up, but instead they're just part of the journey.

Amazon had plenty of moments like this: times when things went wrong, when customers were unhappy, when mistakes were made. Instead of letting those situations define the company, Bezos and his team used them as learning experiences. They took one step at a time, solving problems as they came. They didn't try to fix everything all at once but stayed focused on the next step in front of them.

I think that's the biggest takeaway. Whether it's a hairdryer that blasts like a flamethrower or a delivery mistake, setbacks don't mean failure. They're just another step forward, another opportunity to grow, improve, and keep going. That's something that really stood out to me. He didn't panic, and he didn't try to fix everything all at once, he just focused on solving each problem as it came.

Out of everything he said in that documentary, one line stood above the rest. He was being interviewed in his office, which had small toys scattered across his desk, just random things that he was shipping out. He appeared to be a very simple guy, and then he said, *"Big things start small."*

It was unforgettable.

It's a biblical principle. There's a verse in Zechariah 4:10 that says, *"Do not despise small beginnings, for the Lord rejoices to see the work begin."* That verse has always stood out to me because it's a reminder that everything great starts small.

It's easy to overlook the early stages because they don't seem significant, but that's where the foundation is built. Without those early struggles or those tiny steps forward, the big things we admire today wouldn't exist. What I really admire about Bezos is how he valued those small beginnings. He didn't rush the process or try to skip ahead. He focused on what was in front of him and kept building from there. That's something anyone can do. You don't need to have everything figured out from the start; it's about taking one step at a time and staying consistent.

Many people give up too soon because they don't see results right away, but the ones who keep going, even when it feels insignificant, eventually see growth. Amazon didn't become a multi-billion-dollar company overnight. It took years of small steps, problem-solving, and constant adjustments. Even now, it's still growing. That's the thing, growth doesn't happen in one big leap. It happens little by little, through the small, daily decisions.

Watching that documentary really changed the way I see progress. It reminded me that no matter how small something seems at first, it matters. The key is to keep going, keep improving, and trust that the small things will eventually lead to something bigger.

Do you see how powerful this can be when you put both ideas together?

Elon Musk focuses on making every minute count, squeezing as much productivity as possible into short periods of time. Jeff Bezos, on the other hand, takes small, steady steps, building something great over time. What happens when you combine these two approaches? What happens when you learn to maximize the moments within each hour and take small, consistent steps toward a long-term vision?

That's where the real magic happens.

Think about it like this: Imagine trying to read a long book. If you sit there and think about how many pages there are, how much time it will take, how overwhelming it feels, you might not even start.

What if, instead, you focused on reading just a few pages each day? Maybe even just five minutes here, ten minutes there, fully engaged, making the most of the time you have.

Over time, those small reading sessions add up, and before you know it, you've finished the book. That's exactly how progress works in anything: business, fitness, learning a new skill, or even building relationships. You don't do it all at once. You do it little by little, moment by moment, step by step.

This is what makes people like Musk and Bezos so effective. Musk doesn't waste time; he looks at each minute as an opportunity to get something done. Bezos never rushes the process; he understands that small beginnings lead to big results. When you put those two perspectives together, you get an approach that allows you to be both highly productive in the short term and increasingly effective in the long run.

It's about mastering the balance between what you can accomplish right now and what you can build over time. The truth is, this works in any field, in any walk of life. Whether you're an entrepreneur starting a business, a student trying to graduate, or an artist perfecting your craft, this mindset can completely change the way you approach challenges. Instead of feeling overwhelmed by the big picture, you break it down into small moments. Instead of procrastinating, you act, even if it's just a little. You move forward, one step at a time, while making the most of every hour.

It's just like eating a pizza. You don't eat the entire thing in one giant bite, that's impossible. Instead, you eat it one slice at a time. Even then, most of the time, you don't eat it alone, you share it. The same goes for progress. You don't achieve everything at once, and you don't do it alone. You share your time, your journey, and your experiences with the people around you: mentors, friends, family, or even a community that supports your growth.

This is the mindset that separates those who get things done from those who just dream about it. You do not always have to work hard; it's about thinking differently. If you can start treating each minute as an opportunity while also committing to small, consistent steps, you'll be shocked at how much you can accomplish over time. So, whatever it is you're working toward, don't get caught up in how long it will take. Just start. Make the most of the minutes you have, take small steps every day, and trust that big things always start small.

However, the thing is, you always have to remember, there will be setbacks. There will be obstacles in your way, no matter how mindful or prepared you are. That's just part of the process. You must train your mind to expect challenges, to understand that things won't always go according to plan. Life happens. Just like it did for Jeff Bezos, unexpected problems will show up, like setbacks that shake your vision, slow your progress, or even make you question whether it's all worth it. That's why you must balance expecting the best with also being ready for the worst.

CHALLENGES DON'T BLOCK THE PATH, THEY ARE THE PATH

Many people encounter setbacks further down the road and think, *I don't think I'm cut out for this.* It'll help to understand that challenges will always surround you. They're necessary to build determination, strengthen endurance, and shape the character needed to keep going. The best food is often cooked under intense heat; you never expect to eat raw steak, do you? I didn't think so, and in the same way, it's often the pressure of heated situations that helps you grow into who you're meant to be.

If you expect the road to be clear, every roadblock will feel like a reason to stop. If you expect challenges from the start, then when they come, you won't be thrown off course. You'll understand that they're not something separate from the journey; they *are* the journey.

Let's be real, most people who want to write a book never finish. Not because they're not capable, but because life gets in the way. When they come to me for advice, they usually expect me to tell them something about writing techniques or motivation. What I tell them is this: *Expect obstacles. Count the cost before you start.*

People aren't only inspired by the achievement; they're moved by the struggle it took to get there.

The funny thing is, when people hear my story, they don't get inspired by the fact that I finished my book. They get inspired by the *obstacles* I faced along the way. They hear about my car accident, the long nights of writing even when I was tired, and *that's* what makes them feel like they can do it, too. It reminds them that fast growth isn't about everything going right; it's about pushing through when things go wrong.

People aren't moved by perfection. They're moved by perseverance. If I had finished my book with no setbacks, no struggle, no obstacles, it wouldn't mean as much. I went through something difficult and kept going anyway, it carries more weight. It speaks volumes. It was all about how I utilized my time wisely.

TIME IS LIKE PLANTING SEEDS

Every moment you have is an opportunity. Every hour, every day, every decision adds up to something. The problem is that most people don't think about time that way. They assume they have plenty of it. They assume tomorrow is guaranteed. They assume that life will keep going, just as it always has. The truth is, we have no idea when our time will be up. That's why making the most of your time *right now* is so important. Life will seem more meaningful if you build something that lasts. It's about using the time you've been given to plant seeds that will grow into something bigger than you.

Think of time like a garden. Every day, you have the choice to plant seeds. Some people spend their days planting good seeds: learning new things, working toward their goals, building relationships, making a difference. Others spend their days doing nothing, letting their time slip away. Here's the thing, whatever seeds you plant today will determine what you grow tomorrow. If you spend your time wisely, pouring your energy into things that matter, you'll eventually see the rewards. You'll have a strong foundation: a life filled with meaning and purpose. If you waste your time on distractions, negativity, or things that don't help you grow, then when the future comes, you won't have anything to show for it.

YOUR LIFE IS AN INVESTMENT

Think about how people invest money. They put it into things that will grow over time: stocks, real estate, and businesses. They do it because they know that even small investments, when made consistently, can turn into something huge. Time works the same way. Every second you spend doing something meaningful is an investment in your future. Every skill you develop, every relationship you build, every bit of knowledge you gain will all add up. Over time, those small choices become something powerful.

The same goes for money, if you waste your time, you get nothing in return. If you throw away hours scrolling through social media, watching pointless videos, or engaging in negativity, you're making a terrible investment. You're putting your time into things that won't help you grow, won't create anything, and won't leave a lasting impact.

So, ask yourself: Where are you investing your time? Are you putting it into things that will bring value to your life, or are you wasting it on things that don't matter?

MAKE TIME WORK FOR YOU

Time is going to pass no matter what. You can't stop it. You can't slow it down. You *can* decide how you use it. If you start now, right now, today, you can create something incredible. You can build a future of which you'll be proud. You can make an impact that lasts long after you're gone. If you keep telling yourself that you'll do it later, you'll most likely wake up one day and realize that ten years have gone by.

Don't let that happen; instead, use every moment wisely by planting the right seeds and investing your time into things that matter. One day, God forbid, when your time is up, the only thing left will be what you have built. If you do it right, that will be enough.

It really makes me stop and think that time does not wait for anyone. We go about life assuming we have time. We make plans, we push things off until tomorrow, we think that if something tragic happens, it'll happen to someone else, not us. That's not how life works. Nobody is guaranteed anything.

Look at Air Florida Flight 90. Back in January 1982, a Boeing 737-200 took off from Washington National Airport in terrible weather. The plane couldn't get enough lift because of ice buildup, and it crashed into the 14th Street Bridge before plunging into the freezing Potomac River. Seventy-eight lives were lost, including passengers, crew, and even people on the bridge. Only five survived.

These kinds of tragedies are still happening. At the time I was writing this chapter, just last week in Scottsdale, Arizona, a private jet owned by Vince Neil, the lead singer of Mötley Crüe, crashed into a parked Gulfstream 200 at the airport after losing control during landing. One of the pilots on Neil's Learjet 35A died instantly. Vince's girlfriend and her friend were on board but survived, though she suffered injuries.

They were just about to land like any normal flight. Then, in the blink of an eye, everything changed.

All these plane crashes and tragedies have really made me reflect on how fragile life is and how easily things can change without warning. People live like time is on their side, as though they'll always have another chance, another day. We don't know when our time is up. Seeing all of this happen just makes me want to live differently. I don't want to waste my time. I don't want to spend my mental energy on things that don't matter. I want to live intentionally, be more productive, and prioritize what really counts.

For me, that means spending more time with God and making sure my life is centered around Him. It means being productive with my days, using my time wisely, and not just letting life pass me by. You'll never know when your time will come. When that moment happens, all you have is the life you lived and the choices you made. So why not make them count?

SUCCESS COMES FROM ALWAYS PLANNING AHEAD

It's not just about the game; it's about being ready before it even begins.

Cristiano Ronaldo, one of the greatest footballers in the world, is known not just for his extraordinary talent on the field. He's recognized even more for his strict discipline and relentless preparation off the field, where everything he does behind the scenes directly reflects how he performs on the field. Ronaldo's approach to time management is methodical, and it's one of the key reasons behind his long-standing progress. Imagine a man who could easily have someone else do everything for him, yet he chooses to be deeply involved in every aspect of his preparation. This isn't just about playing football; it's about creating a lifestyle that supports his excellence.

Take his time at Real Madrid, for example. Ronaldo was famous for how he handled his meals. Yes, he had a team of chefs at his disposal, but this wasn't just a luxury; it was a smart choice. He didn't just leave it all up to them; he worked closely with his chefs to make sure every meal was tailored exactly to his dietary needs. The goal was clear: to perform at his best every single time.

Now, could he have cooked these meals himself? Of course. Many athletes and gym enthusiasts do it every day. Ronaldo knew that the time spent cooking could be better used elsewhere: on the field, in the gym, or recovering from intense training. It's a perfect example of doing two things at once; he wasn't just saving time by planning ahead; he was also making sure his body got exactly what it needed to perform at its best. By having his meals prepared in advance, he ensured both time efficiency and top-level nutrition. It wasn't just about the meals.

Ronaldo is also known for how dedicated he is to recovery. He doesn't just work hard; he works smart. Using advanced recovery techniques like cryotherapy and massage therapy is a regular part of his routine. For Ronaldo, rest and recovery are just as important as training, and by focusing on these, he ensures he's always in top shape.

What makes Ronaldo stand out is how intentional he is with everything. Every single thing he does is carefully thought out. His meals, his recovery, and his training were all part of a bigger plan, mapped out weeks or even months in advance. This kind of planning isn't just about filling his schedule; it's about achieving a return on his investment when he steps onto the field.

Think about it: every amazing goal you see him score, every record he breaks, is the result of work done long before the game. If Ronaldo didn't plan his week ahead of a match, he'd lose time and the sharp edge that turns him into that player. Without that kind of planning, his meals wouldn't be ready, his recovery would be incomplete, and his game strategies wouldn't be as sharp. There would be no order, no structure, and certainly no room for the excellence Ronaldo expects from himself.

ROUTINE IS A GREAT USE OF TIME

I've watched several of Cristiano Ronaldo's performances, both during live games and in behind-the-scenes training clips, and I'm always surprised by how sharp and focused he appears in every moment. There is a quiet intensity in the way he moves, not just with his feet, but in the way his whole body follows his mental preparation. It is clear that his performance on the field is the result of everything he has prepared for long before stepping onto the pitch. What stands out to me is not only his athletic skill but the mental strength that fuels his discipline. It is not about reacting on the spot. It is about entering the field with a vision already playing in his mind.

That kind of mindset stirred something in me. It gave me this deeper awareness of how far mental preparation can carry someone through pressure. While I am not playing soccer in front of millions of fans, I had come to realize that handling many packages also required structure, focus, and discipline. Before I even started the truck every morning, I took some time to mentally walk through the entire route. I thought through which businesses usually received large bulk deliveries, which neighborhoods had tight clusters of houses, and where I typically saw duplicate stops stack up. My focus in that moment was not just about making sure the boxes were loaded properly. It was about making sure my mind was aligned with the rhythm of that day. When my head was clear before that shift began, I already felt ahead.

Each morning began with reviewing my route sheet and giving full attention to the details. I studied the list to identify early pickups, heavy volume areas, and businesses that tended to open later or close early. I also checked the freeway conditions, especially the Interstate 10, since that was the main stretch between our Phoenix terminal and the neighborhoods I delivered to in Surprise, Arizona. If there was a crash, road closure, or heavy traffic, I had to figure out an alternative way to get to my route before leaving the building. Those early adjustments were part of how I stayed ahead. That mental preparation started about two hours before my first delivery.

Even with all that preparation, the truth is that no two days are the same. The unpredictability used to catch me off guard more often than I'd like to admit. I remember one morning when I arrived a few minutes late, expecting it to be a smooth day. What I walked into was a day packed with overflow boxes, a long list of pickups, and multiple added-on deliveries. I had no warning until I stepped into the building. That was the day I began to understand how valuable it is to train my mind for unpredictability. It is not enough to plan for what you expect. You have to build the kind of mental strength that can adapt when nothing goes the way you thought it would.

There have been mornings when I felt soreness in my back before even stepping onto my truck. Other times, I've had to navigate through heavy traffic, deal with road closures, or cross paths with customers who were simply in a bad mood. The pressure builds when other drivers cut you off or park in spots that block driveways. It is easy to become frustrated in those moments. In the past, I might have responded emotionally or rushed to make up time. Over time, I learned to make a different choice. As I mentioned earlier, I began waking up earlier to give myself more room to think, to stretch, and to plan. That small adjustment gave me more margin for unexpected problems. It gave me the space to stay calm.

As I began to create this routine for myself, the routine eventually began to shape who I was becoming. I was no longer just trying to survive the day. I was building a rhythm that I could take into every area of life. When something in my house stopped working, like the air conditioner failing or a leak in the roof showing up after a monsoon, I didn't panic like I used to. I own my house, and I understand that things can go wrong at any moment. Whether it is an unexpected bill, a last-minute repair, or a delay in services, those surprises used to throw me off. Over time, the mindset I developed while working with packages helped me navigate those problems with a clearer head.

That same mindset started to impact my relationships. Whether it was tension in the family, a misunderstanding with someone close, or simply the responsibilities of daily life piling up, I noticed I was no longer quick to overreact. I didn't let my emotions run ahead of me the way I once did. I had learned to pause and think. I had learned how to handle problems one step at a time without losing focus. That shift was not something I expected when I first started the job. It developed gradually, but it made a lasting difference.

My experience handling packages shaped more than just my ability to drive, sort, and deliver. It taught me how to keep my mind steady under pressure. It showed me how to prepare for the weight of the day before the day even begins. Most people look at a delivery driver and assume the job is simple: pick up the boxes, drop them off, and drive to the next house. What they don't see is the mental load that comes with it. We are checking traffic reports, scanning pickup windows, calculating neighborhood patterns, adjusting for weather, and making sure every stop counts. That kind of thinking happens quietly, but it defines how well the day goes.

When I reflect on everything I've learned, I realize that the most difficult part of this job was not the physical labor or long hours. It was the uncertainty. Not knowing what the day would bring. Not knowing whether the route would be light or packed with stops. Not knowing whether something would break down, whether the scanner would glitch, or whether a business would close unexpectedly. That uncertainty used to make me feel like I was behind before I even began. With time, though, I learned to expect that feeling and to push through it. The more I leaned into it, the more confident I became.

I trained myself to be mentally ready for anything. That mental strength became one of the most valuable tools I could carry with me, not just in my delivery truck, but in life. It gave me the ability to respond instead of reacting. It gave me clarity in moments where others might feel overwhelmed. It made me stronger where I used to feel weakest. That transformation didn't just help me get through the workday. It helped me grow as a person. True preparation does not remove difficulty from your path. It does not eliminate the unpredictable. What it does is give you a foundation to stand on when the pressure hits. It gives you a rhythm to move even when the pace changes without warning. That rhythm became internal, as though it were drilled into me like a built-in system I could rely on. It helped me carry a calm and steady pace through moments when others were rushing or losing their grip.

The more prepared I became, the more I noticed how rushed the world around me started to feel. Everywhere I looked, people seemed to be moving faster. They were looking for quicker answers, shorter commutes, faster service, and instant solutions. Convenience began to dominate everything. In many ways, it seemed like the easier things got, the more impatient people became. It started to show up in traffic. People were honking, speeding, and reacting more aggressively, especially when they knew the freeway was supposed to save time. The pressure to move fast became a normal part of life, but I started to wonder what it was costing us. That realization is what prepared me for the next thing I began to learn. When life becomes too convenient, the way we experience time starts to change. It does not just make things faster. It makes us expect everything to happen without delay, even when life is not built that way.

CONVENIENCE SPEEDS US UP, BUT DOES IT HELP US PLAN?

As convenience speeds up our lives and continues to reshape how we live, we often find ourselves rushing more, thinking speed will make up for lost time. True progress comes from a mix of convenience and intentional planning. For centuries, people have tried to save time, especially with the growing population and the need to move faster. We have highways with multiple lanes, faster cars, even instant communication, and it's all designed to save time. The problem is the more convenient our lives become, the more rushed we seem to be. The convenience of fast cars and quick communication has led us to procrastinate because we think we can make up for lost time with speed. This mindset isn't helping.

In the past, when people relied on horses or simply walked to get around, they understood that travel would take time. There was no rushing because there was no way to speed up the journey. Even sending messages took days, and people accepted that. Today, we're constantly in a hurry, trying to do more in less time, and often ending up with less time than before. The real issue isn't the convenience itself; it's how we think about it. We've become so used to instant gratification that we've lost the ability to value patience and thoughtful action. We believe that by speeding up, we're saving time, but we're just filling our days with more things to do and leaving us with even less time for what really matters.

So, what's the answer? It's about finding a balance between using the benefits of convenience and being mindful of how we manage our time.

CONVENIENCE CAN BE A TRAP

Convenience feels great in the moment, but it often steals time in the long run. Only intentional planning can save you time.

Convenience makes things even more challenging because it causes us to lose patience. When everything is instantly available at your fingertips, you're not used to waiting, so your tolerance for patience decreases. Another important factor to consider is one that will increase your understanding of how to save time. Believe it or not, convenience isn't always in favor of time. You may think it saves you time in the moment, it does. However, over time, convenience trains your mind to expect everything to be done quickly and easily.

We can't eliminate convenience, as it's part of our daily lives, and it's everywhere you look. Many entrepreneurs constantly seek ways to work less and make more money because they want more time with their families and don't want to live just to work. You see it everywhere. Millions of people worldwide are learning to make money online by creating social media marketing agencies, and selling products on platforms like Snapchat, and more.

Grant Cardone, a successful speaker and salesman, once shared during a meeting with the Ashley Furniture sales team that he was selling $5,000 worth of products daily through Snapchat alone. People all over the world are trying to make more money in less time, because what they want is more time for themselves and their families.

It's funny how in movies, the lead character is always in a mad rush, zipping through traffic, thinking they're saving time. Take *The Santa Clause*, for instance, Tim Allen's character, Scott Calvin, is speeding down an empty freeway in the middle of the night, trying to get home faster. He's pushing the limits, convinced he's making every second count, even though the road is completely deserted. It's such a classic scene, and honestly, one of my favorite parts of the movie during Christmas.

Then there's *National Lampoon's Christmas Vacation* with Clark Griswold behind the wheel of their old Ford Taurus Wagon, singing with his family. Suddenly, a couple of drunkards rear-end them. Clark's reaction is priceless as he gives them a cheeky finger wave and later plays a wild game of limbo with a semi-truck. It's chaos, but it's a classic.

These movie scenes are over-the-top, no doubt, but they do highlight something real: the urgency we often feel, whether we're driving or managing our time. Convenience often tricks us into thinking we're saving time. Take grocery shopping, for example. It's tempting to procrastinate because it feels easier in the moment. When you head out without a plan, the whole experience can turn into a time-consuming mess.

Back when I was at Bible school, sharing a house with five classmates, we figured out how to make grocery shopping efficient. Every week, we'd plan ahead. A few days before our Friday shopping trip, we'd use our small pockets of free time—between classes and jobs— to chat in our house group about what everyone needed. By the time Friday came, the person assigned to shop just followed the list, grabbing everything quickly and efficiently. We'd fill a cart with over $400 worth of groceries in less than an hour, getting good deals because we planned ahead.

I remember one of my roommates telling me about a clever trick some students used a few years before we moved in. They took their grocery money, which came from their tuition and was loaded onto a debit card they were only allowed to use for food, and lived off ramen noodles for months, using that food money to buy a PlayStation

4. They got caught and ended up in trouble, and since then, we have been given a restricted bank card that only works for food. Convenience can be a double-edged sword. While procrastinating might feel easy at the moment, it often ends up making things more complicated and time-consuming. Pre-planning might not always be convenient, but it's incredibly effective. By thinking ahead, you avoid the last-minute scramble and make better use of your time.

So, whether it's grocery shopping or tackling bigger goals, don't let convenience trick you into wasting time. The small inconvenience of taking a few moments to plan is nothing compared to the hassle of trying to fix things at the last minute. Just like firefighters don't wait for a fire before getting ready, we shouldn't wait for a crisis to start planning. Instead, take the time to prepare now, so when challenges come, you can handle them smoothly and efficiently.

In our own lives, we can take a similar approach. Whether you're setting ambitious long-term goals or just trying to get through your daily tasks, being organized and thinking ahead makes a huge difference. By anticipating challenges, you can develop strategies to tackle them proactively, saving you time and helping you avoid distress in the long run. Noticing the little things is the foundation of excellent pre-planning. It's about understanding what needs to be done and why it's important. Just like firefighters focused on their mission to save lives, we need to stay focused on our goals and aspirations. Time is precious, and it's up to us to make the most of it. Entrepreneurs know this well and they invest time and money into their businesses to create their return on investment and passive income, allowing them to buy back their time for what truly matters. We all have the same twenty-four hours in a day, but how we use that time can make all the difference.

Pre-planning is about preparing for the future, whether it's challenges, opportunities, or both. By adopting a proactive mindset and staying grounded in the moment with our actions, we can navigate toward our goals with confidence and purpose. Time is the most valuable resource we have, and how we manage it can determine the course of our lives. Everyone is given the same amount of time each day, but some people accomplish more because they make time work for them.

Use today's opportunities to shape your tomorrow. Just because tomorrow is on the calendar doesn't mean your dreams will automatically come true. You need to claim your tomorrow by first handling your moment, and the only way to do that is by being intentional with the frame of time you have right now. This circle of the present moment is all you have to make intentional choices and create positive results. Make today count. Use the time you have wisely, and make it work for you. The possibilities are endless.

FINAL THOUGHTS

There are two simple ways to manage tough moments in life:

First, focus on small minutes and moments as Elon Musk did, do as much as you can in a short amount of time. It's like placing a time grid over your day, using every little space wisely.

Second, focus on small steps. As Jeff Bezos says, big things start small, and with one step at a time, it all adds up.

→ **Use every minute wisely**

→ **Start small and grow steady**

Planning ahead is like investing in your future. Every small step you take now saves time later and secures your progress. Start now, stay consistent, and you'll thank yourself tomorrow for what you did today.

TURNING UNCERTAINTY INTO RESULTS

You don't have to be great to start, but you must start to be great.

—ZIG ZIGLAR

THE START of my official Barnes & Noble book signing tour, which began on November 18, 2023, in Tucson, Arizona, was the best day of my life, a day I'll never forget. I was making history in my own life, and it was so much fun. Standing inside the Barnes & Noble bookstore, surrounded by the buzz of readers and stacks of my newly released book, *Brave For Freedom*, gave me sense of accomplishment. This wasn't just another day; it was the fulfillment of a dream I had worked toward for years. Each signature and picture taken felt like a milestone: a tangible reality that this was only the beginning of something even greater.

The best part was when the store manager mentioned my name through the ceiling speakers, welcoming customers and announcing that I was in the building. I couldn't believe they were talking about me. People started getting in line to meet me, asking questions about my book, and I got to sign each copy for them personally. Throughout that day, there were a couple people who asked me to include their names in my next book, which happens to be this one. Their names appear in different parts of this book as part of the experiences and stories that came from meeting them, and if they're reading it right now, I hope they're smiling. I felt like I was living my dream; in this case, I was.

As I continued signing my books for my readers, I noticed familiar faces among the crowd, longtime friends who had come to support me, former roommates from Bible college, and even a few co-workers from my earlier days. Their presence at the Barnes & Noble store was a comforting reminder of the many chapters of my life that had led to this moment. We had shared so many experiences, both challenging and joyful, and now they were here to witness the culmination of one of my most significant achievements.

Standing there, I couldn't help but reflect on the many years that had passed before this moment. It was almost surreal how quickly the time had flown. I remembered the first book I independently published back in 2019. It was an incredibly challenging experience, not because I lacked the desire to write, but because I was battling something much more personal: self-doubt.

As I mentioned in the introduction of this book, I had struggled to feel confident in my academic abilities. This doubt often crept into my writing, making me question whether I could ever finish that first book. Deep down, I knew that writing was what I was meant to do. I had a vision, and I was determined to see it through.

Securing your achievement isn't just about reaching the finish line; it's about overcoming the obstacles along the way. As I worked on that first book, I reminded myself every day that the key to winning was consistency. It wasn't about writing the perfect chapter in one sitting; it was about writing one page at a time, day after day, no matter how difficult it seemed. Slowly, but surely, the pages turned into chapters, and the chapters turned into a completed book. When I finally held that first book in my hands, it felt like I had conquered not just a project, but a part of myself that had once doubted this was possible.

The journey didn't end there. Shortly after finishing my first book, I found myself diving into the second. This time, the process was smoother, though not without its challenges. I had learned so much from my first experience, and now I approached the task with a newfound sense of confidence. The doubt that had once plagued me was still there, but it was quieter and less intrusive. I was beginning to trust in my abilities more and more. Before I knew it, I had completed my second book, just over a year after the first. Now, whenever a new book idea comes to mind, I take initiative and begin brainstorming. From there, the writing process begins immediately, without hesitation or distractions.

Looking back, I realized that even though no one had ever said, "I'm proud of you," I was proud of myself. I had secured my breakthrough through sheer determination and focus. I had chosen to believe in my dream, to work toward it every day, and to overcome the doubts that tried to hold me back.

As I was saying about my experience at the bookstore, I was signing copies of my newly published book, I could see how far I had come. It was in that moment of reflection, surrounded by friends and supporters, that I fully understood the importance of acknowledging the past while not letting it define the future. Every hurt, every doubt, and every challenge I had faced was a part of my journey, but they were not the end of my story. They were simply chapters that had led me to this point. I realized that it was okay to feel the weight of those experiences, to heal from them, and to move forward with a renewed sense of purpose.

As I continued to think about my writing journey, I was amazed at how quickly it had all come together. Many people don't start writing until they retire, and some spend years working on a single book. Yet here I was, at twenty-eight years old, signing my newly published book in a bustling bookstore. It was a testament to the power of persistence and the grace of Almighty God. I hadn't done anything extraordinary; all it took was writing one page a day and remained consistent in my efforts. That simple, steady action had led me to this incredible moment.

A massive milestone isn't something that happens overnight. It's the result of securing your dream in your mind and working toward it every single day, no matter how small the steps may seem. It's about staying consistent and determined, even when the road ahead is uncertain. As I stood there, signing many books, I felt a deep sense of gratitude for the journey that had brought me here. The theme of securing completion is one that resonates deeply with me. It's about more than just achieving a goal; it's about the journey that leads you there. It's about facing your fears, overcoming self-doubt, and believing in your ability to turn a dream into reality. It's about taking that first step, no matter how small, and then taking another, and another, until you've reached your destination.

Many people struggle to trust themselves, particularly when trying to start something that seems daunting and they're not sure they can finish. Whether it's writing a book, a project, or something they've been wanting to start for the longest time but have been hesitant about it. They carry their past mistakes into today and assume the same will happen tomorrow. Sometimes the fear of failing again is enough to stop someone from even trying.

Here's something that might help you think about it differently. Walking, in its simplest form, is just controlled falling. You lift one foot, shift your balance, and catch yourself with the next step. That's all it is, one step at a time, moving forward, even when it feels uncertain.

Suppose you were a delivery driver stepping down from your truck and walking toward the recipient's house. With each step, you're falling slightly and catching yourself without even realizing it, because there's no heightened awareness telling you that you're falling. You're simply moving forward, without overthinking, and before you know it, all those small, controlled falls bring you to the doorstep. You made the delivery. As long as you keep going and stay consistent, you're not failing at all.

There's no need to overthink the fall, because it's those very falls that got you there, as long as you kept going.

CONNECTING WITH ACHIEVERS:
How One Encounter Changed My Path

Meeting like-minded people can transform your journey. Sometimes, all it takes is one conversation to give you that push you needed.

During my trip to Oro Valley, Arizona, following a well-received Barnes & Noble book signing, I had an unexpected encounter with a man whose life shows true determination and perseverance. Yet, it became one of the most inspiring experiences of my life. This man had a presence that commanded attention: not because of any loud declarations of his achievements, but because of the quiet confidence he carried. His demeanor was calm, yet there was an unmistakable intensity in his eyes, a focus that hinted at a lifetime of disciplined pursuit of excellence.

When I first introduced myself to him, I couldn't help but feel drawn to him. There was something about the way he carried himself: a sense of purpose that was both intriguing and motivating. It was clear that this was someone who had faced challenges head-on and had come out stronger on the other side.

I then learned that this man was Nordine Zouareg. His achievements in the world of professional bodybuilding are nothing short of extraordinary. During the 1980s, he claimed titles that many only dream of: Mr. Universe twice, Mr. World, Mr. Europe, and Mr. France. Yet, what surprised me wasn't just the accolades he had accumulated, but the humility with which he spoke about them. Here was a man who had conquered the world stage, yet he approached our conversation with a grace and simplicity that only someone confident in their journey can possess.

Beyond bodybuilding, he is also an internationally renowned fitness and wellness expert and a bestselling author of *InnerFitness*. He is the founder of the NZ90 fitness program, crafted to facilitate fat loss, boost well-being, and restore balance in life. His expertise in both physical and mental wellness is recognized worldwide, making him a beacon of inspiration in the fitness community.

He is also highly experienced in media and marketing, most recently demonstrated through the launch of his new podcast, *No-Limits Life,* on iHeartRadio. I was honored to be a guest on that show on June 3, 2025, which was an incredible experience. While I was there, I had the opportunity to walk into the iHeartRadio studio itself and step onto the recording set, which was an incredible experience. The atmosphere was energetic as we prepared for the episode, testing equipment, getting situated, and sharing a few laughs.

It was exciting to connect with Nordine in that environment and see a different side of him outside of the typical fitness or speaking setting. Getting to know him in that behind-the-scenes space made the experience even more memorable. It gave me the chance to meet highly influential people behind the scenes, including the producer, Emilio, and team members whose insight and professionalism left a lasting impression on me.

As we began talking, I realized that we were kindred spirits, both deeply committed to securing our dreams and goals. Nordine shared his life story with me, one that is a testament to the power of perseverance, focus, and an unshakeable belief in one's potential. His journey wasn't just about achieving physical feats; it was about mastering the mental discipline required to succeed at the highest levels.

When I told him about my dream of finishing the book I had written, a dream I had recently realized, his genuine interest in my story was palpable. He listened intently, and I could see that he recognized the same determination in me that had fueled his own growth. It was a moment of mutual respect, a shared recognition of the power of dreams, and the dedication it takes to bring them to fruition.

We stayed in touch. I had coffee with Nordine from time to time, and we spent some time catching up. During our conversation, he mentioned that he would be speaking at the Mind and Body Expo at the Tucson Convention Center. He told me he would love for me to attend, and I said I would definitely be there. I was excited to support him and curious to see what the event would be like.

On the day of the event, I showed up at the convention center, and the atmosphere was amazing. There were so many people there, and the energy in the room was incredible. I had the chance to meet a lot of interesting people, and the whole environment felt inspiring. After a while, I saw him walk up on stage. He looked calm and confident as he took his seat. iHeartRadio was there to interview him, and they asked him about his experience as a bodybuilder and some of the achievements he's had over the years. As he started answering their questions, I could tell he put a lot of thought into his words.

One thing that really stood out to me was something Nordine said in response to a question about his achievements. He said, "It's not so much the achievements that matter, but the journey and the growth that got me there that mattered most." Those words carried weight. As I listened, I started thinking about how much achievement happens behind the scenes. He didn't directly go into detail, but the way he spoke made me reflect on the work that happens underground: the quiet effort, the lessons learned, and the growth that no one else sees. That's what makes the achievements significant.

He wasn't overly impressed with his achievements; he was more thankful for the journey that got him there. Every struggle, every challenge, every painful moment he went through mattered because it built his character. That's something permanent. Achievements can fade, but who you become through the process stays with you.

This also got me thinking about expectations. We often put so much weight on what we want to happen, and when things don't go the way we planned, it's easy to feel disappointed. Nordine had a different approach. He planned his days and weeks, sure, but he didn't set unrealistic expectations for how things would turn out. Instead, he expected difficulties. He didn't just hope for the best; he prepared his mind for the struggles ahead. That way, when obstacles came, they didn't feel like a reason to quit. He had already accepted that tough times were part of the process.

It's almost like he used a psychological trick on himself. By expecting challenges instead of avoiding them, he made them easier to face. He wasn't caught off guard when things got hard; he had already wrapped his mind around the idea that setbacks, pain, and rejection were inevitable. That mindset made him more willing to push through. It's the difference between walking into a storm unprepared versus knowing it's coming and putting on a raincoat. When you see challenges as a natural part of the journey, they don't shake you as much.

His years as a bodybuilder, especially in the 80s when he was competing worldwide, were full of difficulties. The intensive training, dieting, traveling, and facing rejection was all part of his journey. He expected those hurdles; he didn't let them break him. He embraced them. In doing so, he built not just a strong body but a strong mind.

That perspective really made me rethink how I approach my own challenges. It's easy to hope everything will go smoothly, but if you only expect good times, you'll be thrown off when things get hard. On the other hand, if you expect difficulties, you'll be mentally prepared to face them. It's a simple, but powerful shift in mindset. Nordine's words reminded me that massive growth isn't just about reaching a goal; it's about the process of becoming the person who can handle whatever comes. That's what really lasts.

Nordine's response made me realize that it's not just about reaching the top or getting recognition. It's about what you do along the way to grow, mature, and gain experience. It's the unseen process that really matters because it's what shapes you into the person who can achieve those goals. What made it even more impactful was how he spoke. He wasn't in a rush; he spoke slowly, choosing his words carefully. You could tell he cared about everything he said, and that made his message even more powerful. What he said was powerful, but the way he said it brought the message to life and gave it even greater impact.

I left the event feeling inspired. Listening to him speak was an incredible experience, and it gave me a lot to think about. It reminded me to focus on the process, not just the results, and to appreciate the growth that happens in the background. His words motivated me to keep working on my own journey and to value the small steps that lead to bigger achievements.

The Mind and Body Expo was a great experience overall. From the people I met to the inspiring atmosphere, it was a day I won't forget.

By intently observing his focus and the priorities he sets before him, I realized that people who live their daily lives intentionally secure their milestones. That was what I noticed about him. Nordine had a secret that I discovered while talking to him. He went on to tell me about his bodybuilding days and how he outworked all his opponents every single time. The secret is to have the finish line in mind. The whole idea is to envision your long-term end goal throughout your journey.

As Nordine explained his personal experience to me, I realized that he uses this concept to always keep the end goal in mind. For instance, when writing the manuscript for my book, I think about how the front cover design will look. The reason is that it sparks curiosity in my mind and motivates me to keep writing and eventually finish the manuscript so I can finally get to the design portion of the project.

As I talked about earlier, securing your achievement is biblically recorded in Scripture, as mentioned in Proverbs 29:18: *"Where there is no vision, the people perish."* This verse refers to the context in which those who do not have the revelation of God's law live their way instead of God's way. That said, the idea of vision can still speak to personal endeavors and purpose as well. How true is it when applied to long-term goals? Imagine what the finished product would look like in the end.

While I was writing my last book, *Brave For Freedom*, my greatest curiosity was to eventually finish the book so I could begin the design part of the process. Finding a way to spark that curiosity and excitement made all the difference because I was full of imagination. Even before I started writing, I envisioned myself holding the finished book and recording promotional videos. That's exactly what happened. I stayed persistent and used that vision I had to secure my end goal, and eventually, the book was finished. I fulfilled that vision by holding the completed book and going on book tours with Barnes & Noble across Arizona. This mindset does wonders.

In the same way, during Nordine's bodybuilding days, he trained for hours each day, month after month, leading up to his championship performance. He had to envision how he would look months from then to spark the curiosity and hope that would drive and empower him to reach that result and win.

During that season, he was in Singapore at the time, getting ready for a photoshoot for a magazine. He was training and intentionally thinking about why he was there and how he would prepare and win. That time in Singapore was five months before his world championship in Switzerland. Nordine had the end in mind. He envisioned his win ahead of time so that his curiosity and excitement could secure his growth. Not only did he keep the end prize in mind, but he cherished every moment he had. Every set and repetition in the gym mattered to him. Every morning when the alarm clock sounded, he woke up with a reason.

The power of having the end goal in mind goes beyond just bodybuilding or writing. It's a principle that can be applied to every area of life. Whether you're working on a personal project, advancing in your career, or even nurturing relationships, the ability to visualize the desired outcome can be the driving force that keeps you going. It's about more than just setting goals; it's about living with purpose and intention every day.

Nordine didn't just focus on the physical aspects of his training; he was also deeply intentional about his mental preparation. He understood that the mind is just as important as the body in securing advancement. By visualizing his victory and believing in his ability to achieve it, he created a mental blueprint that guided his actions every day. This mental discipline is what set him apart from his competitors and allowed him to achieve the extraordinary.

The idea of keeping the end goal in mind is something that resonates deeply with me. It's not about rushing through life or constantly striving for the next achievement. Instead, it's about being present in the moment, fully engaged with the task at hand, while always keeping your eyes on the prize. It's about finding that balance between ambition and mindfulness, between planning for the future and appreciating the journey.

As Nordine shared more about his life and his approach to massive achievement, I realized that his methods weren't just about winning bodybuilding titles or writing bestselling books. They were about creating a life aligned with his values and vision. It's about staying mindful of each step, in every decision, every action, and every moment. This is the key to not just achieving what you've been fighting for, but also to living a fulfilling and meaningful life.

Reflecting on my own experiences, I see how this principle has played out across different areas of my life. The times I've seen the most accomplished were when I had a clear vision, no matter what obstacles came my way. It hasn't always been easy. The challenges almost derailed me, but the reward has always been worth the effort.

KNOW YOUR WHY, BE INTENTIONAL, BOOST PRODUCTIVITY

Nordine had his *why* firmly established in his mind to become the world champion in bodybuilding so he could teach others how to train their minds for peace, freedom, and massive achievement. Focusing on your *why* and staying rooted in it is the only way to thrust yourself beyond the finish line. He knew he would win that championship in Switzerland. He had mentally reserved his victory, setting an unbreakable appointment with constant growth in his mind. That championship was already his, because he first won it in his mind before ever stepping onto the stage.

Learning the importance of having a clear *why* helped me consider my mental priorities throughout daily life. To achieve long-term goals successfully, it's crucial to maintain mental organization. This means managing your daily routine effectively, so you don't become overwhelmed by the pressure of your ambitions. By concentrating on the task at hand and embracing the present moment, you can enhance productivity and reduce stress levels.

For instance, my objective is to eventually finalize and publish this manuscript. Breaking down the process into manageable chunks, such as writing a page per day, makes this goal more achievable. When engaging in various activities throughout the day, such as household chores or socializing with friends, it's essential to remain fully immersed in those tasks without letting your thoughts drift toward your long-term goals. Even if your objective is raising your kids or going to school, these goals and objectives still require focus and intentionality. You can prevent distress and maintain a clear mindset by staying present during these activities. This mindful approach ensures that when you work on your homework, go to the gym, or spend time with your kids, you can dedicate your full attention and energy to the task at hand.

Adopting this intentional and focused mindset allows you to navigate each day with purpose and peace. By breaking down your long-term goals into manageable steps and staying present during daily activities, you can effectively balance progress toward your aspirations while maintaining a sense of calm and control. This proactive approach not only enhances productivity but also fosters a healthier mindset, enabling you to tackle challenges with confidence and determination. This is all part of securing your breakthrough. By doing these things, you are taking control of the outcome through careful planning and using proactive measures to ensure you successfully reach the end goal you had in mind.

As I mentioned, this method works for anyone who adopts Nordine's approach to reaching the finish line. While watching his Instagram Reels, he often talks about peace. Maintaining the peace that God has gifted you is key to creating a smooth journey toward reaching your goals.

So, whether you're balancing multiple responsibilities or simply trying to make the most of your time, you know that focusing intentionally and maintaining a clean, organized space helps clear your mind and enhances productivity.

Training your mind to focus by valuing each small effort and creating a tidy environment can make a significant difference. This approach will ease your brain from distress. Walking into a clean room with a made bed, a refreshing fragrance, and an organized desk space with clothes put away, allows your brain to relax and become capable of taking on new challenges.

Start by doing chores and organizing your drawers and closet before tackling your daily goals. This simple habit motivates your brain and prepares you to take on challenges. When your space is in order, your brain will run smoother and more efficiently. After tidying up, you'll often find your mind becomes hungry for more productivity, making it easier to focus and get things done. This is a tremendous, natural motivation booster, and it only takes about five minutes. Whether you're a busy parent or a student, cleaning and organizing your space before diving into tasks can give you the peace and drive to stay on track.

Here's how it works: When you tidy up, your brain notices patterns and processes information, which stimulates neuron growth, much like a workout for your brain. As you organize or simply make your bed, clean the kitchen, wash your dishes, or handle small tasks around your home, your brain learns to categorize and prioritize, improving cognitive function. Even small tasks like sweeping the kitchen or tidying your desk engage your mind. Each action strengthens neural connections, making you more efficient and focused.

As I began researching this online, I came across a study from Columbia University's College of Physicians. They suggest that learning or doing something new can generate new neural activity patterns, leading to higher performance in achieving your goals. Engaging in tasks you've never done before, or haven't done in a while, can also improve brain activity and boost motivation.

For example, when I'm practicing behind the drum kit for a church worship set, it's too much for my brain to handle. Each song requires memorizing different beats, using proper strokes on the snare drum, toms, and getting every fill just right. After repeating the same song over and over to perfect it, then moving on to five more songs by the end of the week, my brain feels fried. My wrists and feet are sore, and I'm sweating from the mental and physical effort. So, I usually take a break by doing something easier that I've rarely done before, like reading a short poem or spending ten minutes reading a fiction novel, then I'll spend another ten minutes simply relaxing before getting back to the drums.

Much like after a hard run, you don't stop immediately; you go on a short walk to cool down so it's easier on the heart. In fact, if you consistently stop too suddenly after a long run, it can be bad for your heart, which is why it's important to slow down gradually. It's the same with your brain. It needs time to ease out of intense focus before it's ready to jump back in again.

UNLOCK YOUR BRAIN'S FULL POTENTIAL DAILY

When you learn something new or try different activities, even small ones, your brain performance gradually improves and can defer cognitive aging. This change happens through a process called neural plasticity. Neural plasticity means that your brain can adapt and improve by forming new connections between its cells, known as neurons. These connections help you think more clearly, solve problems, and achieve your goals more efficiently.

When you engage in learning or challenging activities, your brain doesn't just passively absorb information. Instead, it actively works to build and strengthen connections between neurons. Imagine your brain as a network of roads, with neurons as the cities and the connections as the highways. Every time you learn something new, it's like constructing a new highway between cities or widening an existing one to allow more traffic. These stronger connections make your brain faster and more efficient at processing information, making decisions, and handling various tasks.

This process is ongoing. Every time you push yourself to learn something new or take on a challenging activity, your brain continues to change and improve. The more you engage in these kinds of activities, the better your brain handles them.

So, if you usually brush your teeth with your right hand, try switching to your left hand for a few days and rotating the brush in a different direction. You can also try tying your shoes in a different way or using a new knot. Make small changes around the house, like making your bed differently or experimenting with new cooking techniques. By simply doing everyday tasks in a different way, even for a short time, you give your brain a chance to adapt, grow, and improve in positive ways.

Over time, this can significantly improve your cognitive abilities, such as better memory, quicker thinking, and enhanced problem-solving skills. These improvements aren't just limited to the tasks you're learning, the benefits can carry over to other areas of your life as well, making you more capable and adaptable in different situations. One key aspect of neural plasticity is that it's not limited to any specific age. Whether you're a child, an adult, or in some cases during your senior years, your brain can continue to adapt and improve as long as you keep challenging it.

Granted, depending on the person's health, mental state, or situation, some might see faster progress, while others might take more time, but the benefits are still there either way. This is why lifelong learning is so important, it keeps your brain active and helps maintain its health and functionality over time.

Every time you learn something new or try a challenging activity, you're not just gaining knowledge; you're physically changing your brain. These changes help you handle future tasks more effectively and can even improve your mental and physical health. Columbia's research emphasizes that this process is key not only for personal growth but also for developing better treatments for a wide range of conditions.

The power of neural plasticity means that you're never stuck with the brain with which you were born. You can improve and adapt throughout your life, as long as you keep challenging yourself. Whether it's learning a new skill, picking up a hobby, or simply trying something outside your comfort zone, every new experience can help make your brain stronger and more capable.

Understanding how the brain works has opened new possibilities for enhancing performance in various fields.

Even athletes show us how this can work. Take Michael Jordan, for instance. I'm not saying you need to become some world-class icon or leave behind a huge legacy. That's not the point. What matters is the small decisions he made during those quiet hours when no one was around and no one was watching. He trained very hard every day, pushing himself to his limits to make the high school varsity team. Even after all that, the coach still cut him from the team.

That could've ended him right then and there. He could've decided to walk away completely. After all, he had pushed himself day after day, only to get cut from the team. Maybe it just wasn't meant to work out. Walking away and pursuing another career would've been the easier option. If he had made that choice, there would be no Jordan sneakers, no brand, no name references in mainstream songs, and no legacy.

You might be thinking he could've created a legacy somewhere else. The thing is, if he had walked away at that point in his life, when it hurt the most, he probably would've walked away the next time things got tough, too.

The name, Michael Jordan, would have been just another name that faded into the background, one that might've never meant anything to anyone.

That rejection is what opened the door for something new. Instead of sitting in that disappointment, he made a split-second proactive decision to move forward before that discouraging thought had a chance to mature. It gave space for neural plasticity to kick in.

At 15 years old, during after hours, he packed his bag every night and headed out to the basketball court with a new mindset every time. With no one cheering him on, just the sound of crickets in the background as he worked with every second and every minute he had, practicing by himself under the night sky.

Michael didn't train the same way he was taught by his coach or follow what the other players were doing during practice. Instead, he started thinking differently by creating new footwork and trying sharper angles. He trained in a new way that broke away from everything the team had been doing. It was behind the scenes that he slowly became the player the world would later recognize.

So, as you can see, committing yourself to targeted practice and learning, people can fine-tune their neural connections, becoming more efficient and effective at what they do.

The brain is not a static organ, but a dynamic one that can change and improve with experience. Whether you're focused on personal growth, mental health, or physical rehabilitation, the principles of neural plasticity provide a powerful framework for understanding how you can take control of your brain's development and unlock your full potential.

The research I had just mentioned offers hope and inspiration for anyone looking to enhance their abilities, overcome challenges, and lead a more fulfilling life. After doing these things, you'll likely notice that your brain picks up faster. This concept applies to everything, no matter what you're doing. It's useful for students, busy parents, business professionals, or anyone who uses time to get things done. A clean space and surroundings will help your brain relax and avoid becoming overwhelmed.

Walking into a messy home or work environment robs your mind of positive energy. If your workspace is chaotic, your brain will become chaotic, too. How clean and organized you are in your daily life reflects how clear and organized your mind is. You don't need to have obsessive-compulsive disorder to benefit from this approach, but those who do may have a head start in maintaining a clear mind. Practicing this method allows you to work with a peaceful and focused mindset, leading to more efficient work and saving time by improving your performance in whatever task you're working on.

No matter your age or situation, prioritizing a clear mind and space can enhance your ability to achieve your goals. Organizing your environment before starting work sets a positive tone for productivity. Whether you're juggling family responsibilities or academic pursuits, creating a simple workspace can help you stay motivated and focused. Remember, it takes time to make time. Taking the time to clean your surroundings to boost your mind's motivation and clarity will save you plenty of time in the long run if you consistently practice this idea daily.

HOW A CLEAN ENVIRONMENT AND GOOD SPACE BOOSTS YOUR BRAINPOWER

It was one of those long, draining days at work where the hours seemed to blur together, and the entire shift felt like it would never end. I remember starting my day early in the morning, and by the time I clocked out, the sun had already set, and I was physically drained. The deliveries never seemed to end, and it felt like I was hauling endless boxes in and out of the truck. The Arizona heat didn't help either; it was one of those days where the temperatures soared into the triple digits, and every step felt heavier than the last. By the time I finished, it was 8:30 p.m.—much later than usual—and I was exhausted. I drove home, looking forward to nothing more than a hot shower, a quick bite to eat, and crawling into bed.

My car was spotless, as usual. I like to keep it that way because, to me, a clean environment equals a clear mind. The ride home, though tiring, gave me a bit of time to decompress after the chaos of the day. I arrived at my house, hoping for some peace and quiet, but what greeted me was the exact opposite. As soon as I stepped inside, it felt like

I had walked straight into a whirlwind of mess. The house was a disaster zone. The chairs around the dining table were all out of place, and some were not even pushed in. The sight of it stopped me in my tracks. I just stood there for a moment, staring at the mess, trying to process what I was seeing.

It was as if my brain short-circuited. I've always been the kind of person who needs order to think clearly. My surroundings have a huge impact on my ability to function. When things are clean and in their place, my mind feels sharp, focused, and ready for whatever task I need to take on. When things are chaotic, like they were that night, it's hard for me to concentrate. Walking into that mess after such a long day at work made me feel overwhelmed, and my brain didn't know how to handle it.

I wandered into the kitchen, hoping maybe it wasn't as bad as it first seemed, but it only got worse the more I looked around. The counters were cluttered with random junk, old receipts, and empty food containers. The dishes hadn't been touched in what felt like days. There were pots and pans stacked in the sink, and the floor hadn't been swept. No one else was home at the time. My roommates had gone out for the evening, leaving behind what looked like the aftermath of a tornado.

I found myself just pacing back and forth, trying to figure out how to even begin cleaning or if I should just leave it for tomorrow. My brain couldn't settle. It was too much for me, especially after such a long day. My energy was completely drained from work, and seeing the mess only added to my frustration. I could feel the tension in my body as I tried to figure out how to calm my mind and refocus.

I always keep my surroundings clean for a reason, because it gives me peace and allows my brain to focus, which helps me think clearly.

After standing there, feeling mentally cluttered for a few minutes, I decided there was nothing I could do about it that night. I was too tired to even think about tackling the mess. So, I headed upstairs to my bedroom, hoping that at least there I could find some peace. As soon as I stepped into my room, it was like a weight lifted off my shoulders. My bedroom was exactly how I left it: clean, spacious, and organized. My king-size bed was neatly made, and the soft scent of fresh fragrance filled the room. I felt a wave of relief wash over me.

I got ready for bed, grateful to be in my own clean space where I could finally relax. The contrast between the mess downstairs and the calm, organized atmosphere of my bedroom couldn't have been starker. It was exactly what I needed. I climbed into bed, and as soon as my head hit the pillow, my mind began to clear.

In that quiet, tidy space, I could think again. I remember lying there, thinking about how much my environment affects my ability to focus. My clean, uncluttered room allowed my brain to breathe. It gave me the mental space to start thinking clearly again. That also helped spark some ideas for this book. I started brainstorming new concepts for my writing. My clean desk in the corner of the room was another reason I could focus. It was set up just the way I liked it: neat, simple, and ready for me to dive into whenever inspiration struck.

This whole experience made me realize why people often ask how I manage to do so much with my time, including how I juggled a full-time job, writing books, drawing cars, and keeping up with my hobbies. It's all about maintaining my environment. Keeping my surroundings clean and organized allows me to function efficiently. When everything is in its place, my mind is free to work without distractions.

I've always believed that a clean space equals a clear mind. Whether it's my car, my desk, or my home, I keep it tidy because it makes all the difference in how I feel and how productive I can be. That night, more than ever, I realized just how true that is. Even after a long, exhausting day, walking into a clean, organized bedroom allowed me to wind down, reset my thoughts, and prepare for the next day.

As I drifted off to sleep that night, I couldn't help but feel grateful for that small sanctuary I had created for myself. In a world that can sometimes feel chaotic and overwhelming, having a space where my mind can rest and refocus is a blessing. It's something that I believe everyone can benefit from. No matter how busy life gets, maintaining a clean and organized environment is key to staying on top of everything and keeping a clear head.

The next morning, I woke up feeling refreshed and ready to tackle the day, knowing that no matter what chaos awaited me outside, I had my own space to come back to, where my mind could thrive.

Your mind operates like a puzzle game, fitting pieces perfectly. Imagine those toys kids play with, matching shapes to holes. Just as a messy room can dampen your mood, clutter affects your brain. If you walk into chaos, like an unmade bed or dirty laundry, your motivation dwindles, sometimes even leading to feeling physically sick. Your brain mirrors its surroundings; a disorganized space leads to disorganized thoughts.

Where you study matters. Doing homework in bed signals sleep to your brain. Instead, opt for a bright, airy space like an office desk by a window. Sunlight and fresh air can boost productivity. Your brain thrives in environments that match the task at hand.

Think of your brain like a sponge. It soaks up whatever's around it, whether that's distraction or focus. When you're in a cluttered or unorganized space, your brain is soaking up the chaos, making it harder to focus on the task in front of you. If you place that same sponge in a clean, dedicated area designed for work or study, it absorbs productivity, focus, and calm. So, creating a space specifically for studying isn't just about separating work from play; it's about giving your brain the right fuel to absorb what it needs.

Another way to think about it is to picture your environment like a stage. Before a performance, the stage is set, the lights are adjusted, and the actors know their cues. Everything is in place for the show to run smoothly. Your workspace operates in the same way. When you set the stage for studying or working by having a clean, organized environment, you're allowing your mind to perform at its best. It's like telling yourself, "Alright, time to focus," without even saying a word.

Your brain loves routines and associations. Just like how you wouldn't expect to fall asleep in a noisy coffee shop, it's hard to concentrate if your environment sends the wrong signals. By consistently using a specific space for work, you create a mental shortcut, and your brain begins to automatically switch into "study mode" as soon as you enter that space. Over time, this helps you build stronger habits, making it easier to get into the zone without extra effort. Similarly, effective time management and maintaining a clean environment can apply to various endeavors or everyday activities.

ADDITIONAL WAYS A CLEAN SPACE ENHANCES YOUR WELL-BEING

I came across something helpful from a site called *Mile High Psychiatry*. They shared how decluttering your space can boost positive energy and help you release emotional baggage. That stood out to me because those are two things that many people struggle with more than they realize.

By the way, for those who are healing from past relationships or going through depression, I think this is something you can practice. Letting go of emotional baggage can start with your surroundings, and sometimes just cleaning your space can help release some of that emotional tension. I'd like to share a few thoughts on how mental peace can lift you up and help you show up for yourself and others.

Releasing Emotional Baggage Through Cleaning

The way that cleaning your surroundings helps release emotional baggage is when your brain releases dopamine after you feel a sense of peace from having a clean space. I understand that dopamine is sometimes frowned upon because it's often tied to unhealthy desires or too much screen time, but the truth is, dopamine is helpful when it's balanced. It can improve your life in a real way when it's tied to progress, peace, and self-control.

Also, dopamine released through short cleaning can help lower depression levels because it gives you small nuggets of purpose through simple, productive action, even if the change doesn't happen instantly.

Mental Health Benefits: Energy and Peace

- When everything's clean, your mind isn't distracted by mess or disorganization, so you're left with more mental energy for yourself, others, and what really matters. Clutter can cause distress because it makes your brain feel like there's still work to be done. Walking into a clean room gives your mind permission to relax and focus.
- Decluttering can feel therapeutic on its own. As you clean your space, it can feel like you're mentally clearing out dis-

tress and distractions. It's an opportunity to reset both your environment and your mind.

Better Sleep: Clean Space, Rested Mind

- Your environment affects your sleep, too. People who sleep in clean, clutter-free bedrooms tend to enjoy better rest. When your space is tidy, your mind can relax, leading to a more peaceful night's sleep. If you've been struggling with sleep, tidying up your room might help as part of your bedtime routine.

Productivity and Creativity: Space to Think Freely

- Creativity and productivity thrive in clean, open spaces. If your desk or workspace is full of distractions, your mind has to work harder to stay focused. On the other hand, a clean and organized space allows for better focus and clearer ideas. It gives you the mental room you need to dive into your work or creative projects.

FORM A SOLID MINDSET:
Cleaning for Long-Term Success

While cleaning may seem like just another chore, it's an investment in your milestone and well-being. Keeping your surroundings clean is a habit that helps with other areas of life: your work, relationships, and personal growth. It teaches you discipline and consistency, which are key to achieving your goals.

Make tidying up a daily habit. Whether it's a quick 10-minute cleanup in the morning or a bigger organizing session once a week, small actions add up. The more consistent you are with maintaining a clean space, the easier it gets. You'll start to notice how much your mindset shifts toward productivity and peace.

In the end, the connection between a clean environment and a clear mind is undeniable. Whether it's helping you stay motivated with fitness, improving your focus on personal development, or encouraging you to pursue your passions, a clean and organized space sets the foundation for realization. Your surroundings reflect your mindset, and by taking control of your environment, you'll see positive changes in how you approach your day, your goals, and your relationships.

The effort you put into maintaining a clean space is never wasted, it's a key step toward creating a balanced, focused, and fulfilling life.

TRAINING YOUR BRAIN TO MAKE TIME

Let's say you've always wanted to write a book, but you've convinced yourself that you just don't have the time. Or maybe there's another big goal you've been dreaming about, but it always seems too far out of reach because life is just too busy. What if I told you that the real issue isn't time itself, but how you're using it?

One great way to train your brain to make time for something is to start small with something seemingly unrelated, like reorganizing your room. Now, I know what you're thinking: *How does redecorating my room have anything to do with writing a book or achieving a goal?* Hear me out. The point is to teach your brain how to set time aside for a specific task and to follow through on it.

Let's say you decide to reorganize your room this weekend. You pick a time, make a plan to move the bed, rearrange the furniture, and maybe even add a few new decorations. This task, though unrelated to your bigger goals, is valuable because it teaches your brain how to commit to a task, plan for it, and see it through to completion. It also reinforces the idea that you can carve out time for something, even when it seems like your schedule is packed. You've trained your brain to prepare for something, take action, and then enjoy the results.

Now, when you move on to bigger tasks, like writing that book or chasing another dream, your brain knows how to handle the process. You've already shown yourself that you can make time, even in a busy life.

THE BIGGER PICTURE

When we say we don't have time for something, it's usually not about the time itself. It's about how we manage our priorities and how we train our minds to handle tasks. When you teach your brain how to make time, you're not just organizing your day, you're building the foundation for long-term conquest.

Once you get into the habit of making time for smaller things, you'll find it easier to tackle the bigger goals. Your brain will naturally start to recognize that you can make time, and it will become less of a struggle to stay committed to your ambitions.

So, give it a try. Start prioritizing your life first. Manage your own home by creating a cleaning schedule and maybe clean your car once a week. People often mention things like the 21-day mark or even a full year, but you'd be surprised how it doesn't always come down to the number. Sometimes, all it takes is showing up one day at a time. After one year of doing this, when your brain starts locking into a new rhythm, I guarantee you'll find yourself thinking bigger, feeling more driven, and ready to handle much bigger things. Even years down the road, while you're hitting milestones, you'll still find yourself cleaning and organizing your personal space. By the time you're ready to tackle your big goals, your mind will already be prepared to handle them.

MAKING TIME FOR WHAT MATTERS

At the end of the day, your brain is your most powerful tool. It adapts to whatever environment you put it in. When you create a routine of setting time aside for the things that matter, like reorganizing your room, working on a project, or just spending time focusing on self-improvement, you're training your mind to make the most of each moment. You'll be surprised at how much more time you seem to have once you stop feeling overwhelmed and start managing your priorities.

So, don't wait. Start cleaning up the space in your home, set aside time to learn something new, or finally sit down to work on that dream project. Your brain will thank you, and you'll start seeing the results sooner than you think.

FINAL THOUGHTS
Clear Space, Clear Mind

→ A clean environment helps reduce distress and boosts mental energy.

→ Keeping your car or workout space tidy prepares your mind for action.

→ Cleaning releases emotional baggage.

→ Clean spaces support spiritual growth, creativity, and productivity.

→ Decluttering can be therapeutic and improves sleep quality.

The real concern isn't a lack of time. It's how we choose to prioritize the time we have.

TAKE CHARGE OF YOUR TIME

Time is what we want most, but what we use worst.

— WILLIAM PENN

AFTER I graduated from Valley Vista High School in 2013, I moved to one of the most diverse cities in the world—Tucson, AZ. As you've already seen through some of the experiences I've shared, this city, known for its unique charm and tranquility, even attracted the attention of Bill Gates, who famously flew over just for a cup of coffee.

Tucson has a certain pull, a mix of serenity and beauty that draws in well-known figures. Adam Sandler, for instance, visits regularly to see his older sister Valerie, who lives in Tucson, and often dines at Firebirds Wood Fired Grill, located near the upscale La Encantada outdoor shopping mall, my favorite restaurant. I've been to that same location at least eight times, and it's always been a great experience.

My personal favorite is the Lobster Spinach Queso appetizer, a creamy blend of lobster, baby spinach, tomatoes, and pepper jack cheese, served with crunchy chips. It's one of those dishes that makes you want to come back for more. I'd recommend it to anyone. Tucson's calm atmosphere, combined with its natural beauty, also attracts many other well-known faces. Jimmy Kimmel has spent significant time here, and Hailey Baldwin was born in the city. Even the Beatles have a connection to Tucson, as Paul McCartney has owned a home here for years, a quiet ranch-style place that's small, secluded, and far from flashy. It's a place that has seen the comings and goings of many public figures, yet it maintains its humble, laid-back charm.

It's also a city with an impressive history of innovations and development, especially in defense technology. Raytheon, which has a major defense and missile business in Tucson, also develops advanced sensor systems at its facility in McKinney, Texas. One of those systems is the F-35's next-generation Electro-Optical Distributed Aperture System, which provides pilots with full 360-degree infrared vision.

So, as you can see, Tucson plays an important role in the defense industry, and the presence of Raytheon underscores how much this city contributes on a global scale.

What makes Tucson special, at least for me, is its connection to astronomy. The city's dim streetlights, approved by the town to help University of Arizona students study the stars at night, create a peaceful ambiance that's perfect for stargazing. I remember lying on the bed of my red 1990 Toyota Tacoma, looking up at the night sky. The stars were so clear, and the longer I focused on one spot, the more I began to see. It was like there were stars behind stars, layers of light stretching deeper and deeper. Some were dimmer and harder to notice at first, but eventually they appeared. The night sky looked incredibly vast, something I had never experienced anywhere else, it's remarkable. It was nothing like what I'd experienced back in Phoenix. The desert, with its quiet, open spaces, provided the perfect backdrop for moments of reflection and peace.

I lived in La Puerta Del Norte, just south of Marana, in a small trailer neighborhood during college. The simplicity of that place felt right to me. Almost every night, you could find me out in the dirt front yard, watching the stars or taking a prayer walk in the early morning, soaking in the quiet beauty of the sunrise. There was something about Tucson that gave me the space I needed to think, to reflect, and simply be.

Mount Lemmon, with its stunning beauty, was another favorite. I would drive up there to watch the sunset and see the mountain bathed in shades of purple and pink as the night was approaching. It was one of those magical sights that never gets old.

As beautiful as Tucson was, I found myself struggling. I had a hard time staying focused, juggling what I needed to do with all the distractions around me. Whether it was work, personal goals, or even just organizing my day-to-day tasks, I couldn't seem to get a handle on things.

After living in Tucson for nearly three years, I discovered Zion City church in October 2015. As I familiarized and settled myself with this large-scale church, I quickly made new friends and everyone there was genuinely friendly.

Little by little, things began to change when I became a part of Zion City. The people there were so intentional, from the way they greeted me to the way they spoke. They made me feel genuinely seen and special. It wasn't just surface-level conversation; it felt like every interaction had meaning. Seeing and experiencing their intentionality firsthand made me pause and reflect. It stirred something in me, making me wonder how I could have purpose in my own life. Their example made me think deeply about the areas where I had been letting things slip, and it sparked a desire to approach my own life with the same level of purpose.

A month later, I plugged myself into the worship team. I served as a drummer for nearly three years. I wanted to perfect my drumming skills on stage because walking into the sanctuary a month prior, I couldn't help but notice the drummer who was playing on stage. He was perfect, and he completely buried the tempo as he played. That inspired me to always perfect my drumming skills in such studio-quality performance, and I always had fun doing it.

About a year later, in 2016, I received a call from one of the church Bible college leaders, his name was Alex. Zion City had its own Bible college called Edge College, where students studied Berean School of the Bible materials through Global University, an online program based in Springfield, Missouri. Alex called because he noticed I frequently attended the church and served on the worship team. He thought I might be a good fit for that class, given how dedicated I was to what I was passionate about.

If you're wondering how Alex even got my number, it was because I had become friends with a couple of his other friends on the worship team, and I had also filled out a connect slip that was handed to me during my first visit to the church over a year earlier. I decided to take the opportunity to enroll in Edge College because I wanted to stretch my social skills and educate myself theologically. My long-term goal was to one day become a senior pastor and be a voice for my generation.

As August came around, I stepped into the world of Bible College to begin my journey, and honestly, I was very nervous. It was different from what you might think. I've always been an introvert, but it goes even further than that. I'm timid and quiet by nature. I had difficulty conversing with my peers and involving myself in group activities. It was challenging. There were many students in the class, and most of them were so outgoing and social that it felt overwhelming for someone like me. We'd often be placed into group discussions or shared activities. It was nerve-racking. Many people in my class thought I was strange because I was so quiet. Some would even joke by saying, "What if this kid is a killer? He's not saying a word."

Anyway, I had to learn how to socialize the hard way. The most important thing was that I got the stretch I needed, even if it felt like high school all over again with those awkward, tedious beginnings.

PASTOR WAYLON'S WORK ETHIC:
A Lesson In Time Management

Zion City stretched me entirely, socially and emotionally, as I learned more about myself. One thing I realized was that I needed to learn how to naturally engage in regular conversations and keep them going without allowing them to drop or die out. Eventually, I got better at it. I no longer worry about what people think of me, and I've grown much more theologically inclined. It is what it is, and I graduated from this program as a newer, better version of myself.

As I continued through the program, my class had in-person lectures by the Senior Pastor of the church, Pastor Waylon Sears. Many of us in the class, me included, were familiar with him because we were heavily involved as Bible students. As a result, he and the rest of the church staff treated us with great respect. During his class teachings, Pastor Waylon would often share things that he usually wouldn't say during Sunday morning services, mostly because we were a specially selected group. As students within the church, we collaborated closely with pastors and staff members, which gave us a unique level of access and trust.

What stood out to me most from all the time spent listening to him speak was when he shared a fascinating anecdote, one that offered a powerful life lesson, whether for the workplace, ministry or personal life. That story ended up changing my life. It helped me shift my mindset and gave me a practical way to start prioritizing my time more effectively, so I could get more done in a day or a week, and still have time left over for myself.

Pastor Waylon began sharing about his experience as a senior pastor and how he manages a very tight schedule. His busy schedule did not pertain to his pastoral role alone, although there are preparations involved. He also provided weekly consultations for congregant individuals in his office. These sessions ranged from marital counseling to personal growth. On top of all of that, he also maintained his pastoral staff and managed many other satellite campuses weekly.

So yes, Pastor Waylon had a lot on his plate. What stood out to me was the way he made it all work. He found a wise and strategic method to increase productivity and create more free time during his busy week. It wasn't by hiring someone to do everything for him. He didn't rely on an assistant to save him time. Instead, he had a remarkable strategy that allowed him to *make* time, even in the middle of a packed week.

You might be wondering how this can work. How can someone who is already stretched so thin suddenly create more free time? The answer is easier than you think, and it starts with how he structured his schedule. Pastor Waylon is one of the busiest people I've ever met, but he knows how to manage his time down to the minute. Even when his day looks chaotic on paper, he's calm and collected because he's present and aware of how every hour is being spent.

One day, while he was in his office during a hectic weekday, someone unexpectedly knocked on his door asking for help. The man didn't have an appointment, but he was desperate, his marriage was falling apart, and he needed immediate counseling. This was one of those last-minute walk-ins that could easily throw someone off. Waylon didn't flinch. He welcomed the man in and gave his full attention, never once seeming rushed or distracted.

How was he able to do that?

He had already structured his time in a way that gave him margin. He wasn't behind on his work; he was caught up. So even on a busy day, he had the flexibility to respond to someone in need. He knew how to create time because he had already *made* time.

As a student serving in the church, I carefully watched Pastor Waylon's work ethic and paid close attention to his anecdotes during our private class settings. What amazed me was how he could compile more spontaneous, last-minute tasks simply because he stayed focused on whatever was in front of him.

His method was simply expecting the unexpected. He handled one email, one phone call, or one document at a time, fully aware that a spontaneous walk-in could happen at any given moment. He had already accounted for those interruptions in his mind. He rarely seemed frustrated and often gave his full attention during those last-minute meetings. There was something about the way he worked that showed me the power of simply dealing with what was in front of me and making the most of it. I started to notice the same quality in others as well.

GRANT CARDONE:
Mastering the Art of Being Present

In early 2020, just before the global pandemic struck, entrepreneur Grant Cardone was featured on the TV show *Undercover Billionaire* on the Discovery Channel.

If you're unfamiliar with Grant Cardone, he's a well-known real estate investor, speaker, and business coach. He's also the bestselling author of *The 10X Rule* and *Sell or Be Sold,* and he hosts the massive *10X* conferences attended by thousands of entrepreneurs each year.

The show's premise was to test whether Grant—a multi-billionaire—could rebuild the American dream from scratch under challenging circumstances. He was flown to a secluded location in the United States with only a truck, a contactless phone, and a one-hundred-dollar bill. Stripped of his money, contacts, connections, and company resources, Grant was given ninety days to build a million-dollar business.

He was dropped off in Pueblo, Colorado, which was a small, unfamiliar town. Without knowing anyone and without any resources, Grant faced the immediate challenge of survival. Instead of rushing to build a business, he took a humble and human approach. His first priority was finding a warm place to sleep and something to eat. This focus on basic needs showcased a strategic mindset by addressing immediate concerns to build a foundation for future fulfillment.

Grant's initial days were spent searching for shelter and food, leading him to an RV sales shop where he made a positive connection. With a roof over his head and some food, he could now think about the next step: finding a job to earn money for his game plan. His approach was methodical, focusing on one task at a time. Whether searching for a job, looking for a meal, or washing dishes, he devoted himself wholly to each small step. This single-tasking mindset, I believe, is a hallmark of highly successful people. They dedicate their full attention to only one thing at a time, no matter how small, ensuring it is done to the best of their ability before moving on to the next.

A remarkable moment during the show occurred when Grant caught COVID-19. Quarantined in his rented house, he could have used the time to plan and strategize. Instead, he focused on the simple task of cooking eggs and bacon while he was recovering. He engaged in a self-dialogue, appreciating how well the bacon turned out and how delicious the eggs looked. His complete immersion in the present moment, enjoying his meal, was astonishing. As I watched, I was worried about the ticking clock and his dwindling time, but Grant was content and focused solely on his breakfast. This illustrated a profound lesson: even when multitasking, one can maintain a single-tasking mindset by focusing entirely on each aspect of what they're doing

Grant's story in *Undercover Billionaire* clearly shows that progress often comes from focusing on one thing at a time. While our modern lives often push us toward multitasking, our brains are naturally wired for single-tasking. This not only enhances productivity but ensures that each task is completed with greater attention and care. By not starting another task until the current one is finished, we can achieve more, with greater quality. Even when Grant ran deals from his rented home while cooking, he clearly focused on each task as it came. He wasn't worried about tomorrow; he was fully present in the moment. This approach helped him build a successful business within the ninety-day timeframe and highlighted the importance of mindfulness and dedicated focus in achieving great things.

Grant Cardone's journey on *Undercover Billionaire* is a testament to the power of single-tasking and the profound impact of being present in each moment, no matter the challenges or distractions life throws our way.

BEING PRESENT IN EVERY MOMENT

Grant's attention to the small details, even under pressure, reveals something deeper about how we handle what's right in front of us. That same mindset can shape everyday moments in powerful ways. Focusing on what's in front of you now is crucial if you want your future to become a reality. This idea revolves around mindfulness and the ability to fully direct your attention to the task at hand, whether it's cooking a meal, washing dishes, or cleaning your space. Concentrating on one activity at a time enhances productivity and ensures each task is completed with the highest quality and efficiency.

Imagine you're in the kitchen, preparing a meal. Instead of thinking about your business plans or the next task on your to-do list, you focus solely on the ingredients in front of you. You appreciate the aroma of the spices, the sound of the bacon sizzling, and the visual appeal of the eggs as they cook. This simple act of being present not only makes the cooking experience more enjoyable but also allows you to create a satisfying meal, because your full attention is directed at cooking, leading to better results.

This principle applies to all areas of life. When cleaning or washing dishes, focusing solely on one step can transform it from a mundane chore into a meditative practice. You might notice the smoothness of the plates, the warmth of the water, or the sparkling clean surface as you finish. By staying present, you utilize your mind's energy on what's important at that moment, reducing the mental clutter and stress that comes with thinking about everything else you have to do.

Being fully engaged in the present moment helps build a foundation for the future. When you give your all to the task at hand, you lay the groundwork for future wins. Each completed task, done with full attention and intention, moves you closer to your goals. This is where the idea of "Handling Your Moment" becomes vital. The actions and efforts you invest in today directly influence the reality you will experience tomorrow. To make tomorrow a reality, it's essential to be intentional with today. That means dedicating your focus and energy to your current work. You will never be prepared if you are not ready to start today. Readiness is not a future state; it's a present action. If you were truly prepared, you would already be taking steps towards your goals.

Procrastination often stems from the fear of imperfection or failure, but the truth is, starting now, no matter how small the step, is the only way to bring your future dreams to life. Focusing on what's in front of you now is vital because it harnesses your mind's energy, enhances the quality of your work, and builds the necessary momentum for achieving future goals. Homing in on the now, through your actions today, is the key to making tomorrow a reality. Remember, today is tomorrow. If you are unsure when or how to start, the best time is always now. Embrace the present moment, commit fully to your current assignment, and watch as your future unfolds with peace and purpose.

THE SIGNIFICANT INFLUENCE OF ASSOCIATIONS

Influence is far more potent than mere instruction or lectures. The people you associate with can profoundly shape your behavior, values, and habits, often more significantly than formal education or structured lessons. Influence need not have a negative connotation; it can be a potent force for positive change and growth. To shape your future effectively, it's crucial to surround yourself with individuals who exemplify the qualities and skills you aspire to develop.

Consider the case of Pastor Waylon's work ethic and ability to manage tasks, which inspired a significant change in my approach to daily responsibilities. Observing his focus and dedication taught me that letting go of tomorrow and working on today with each task-at-hand allowed me to handle more responsibilities efficiently. This realization came from watching him; not being told how to manage my time. His influence was subtle but profound, demonstrating that actions often speak louder than words.

In 2019, I embarked on my journey as an author while juggling two jobs and serving as a drummer on the church worship team. Despite the overwhelming workload, I managed to write one pages a day. I stayed focused on the moment I was in, focusing on each step without distraction. That's what I saw Pastor Waylon do. While working at Subway, I didn't think about my book; I focused solely on my job. This level of intentionality, inspired by Pastor Waylon's example, enabled me to manage my time more effectively and achieve my goals.

Influence is a form of learning through observation and imitation. When you spend time with people who exhibit the qualities you want to develop, you naturally begin to adopt their behaviors and mindset. For instance, spending time with entrepreneurs is beneficial if you aspire to become an entrepreneur. Their approach to problem-solving, risk-taking, and innovation approach can rub off on you, providing practical insights and motivation that are often more impactful than theoretical lessons.

In the same way, if punctuality and time management are areas you wish to improve, being around people who excel in these aspects can significantly influence your habits. Their disciplined approach to managing their schedules can provide a living template for you to emulate. This influence often goes beyond what a professor might teach in a classroom setting, as it involves real-world applications and consistent practice.

The same principle applies to academic or technical skills. If you want to excel in math, spending time with individuals with a strong grasp of mathematical concepts can be incredibly beneficial. Their passion for the subject, problem-solving techniques, and analytical thinking can inspire and guide you more effectively than traditional lectures. This immersive form of learning taps into the power of influence, making complex subjects more approachable and understandable.

Concentrating on small, steady progress today to make tomorrow a reality involves more than just planning, it requires aligning yourself with the right influences. By spending time with people who embody the qualities you wish to develop, you create an environment conducive to growth and improvement. This intentionality is not just about the immediate benefits; it lays the foundation for long-term victory.

In my experience, the influence of Pastor Waylon went beyond mere task management. It instilled a more profound sense of purpose and dedication in my daily activities. His commitment to his work, regardless of how busy he was, showed me the importance of being fully present and engaged in every step. This mindset helped me not only manage my time better but also to derive greater satisfaction from my efforts. The power of influence extends to all areas of life. Whether it's personal development, professional growth, or academic achievement, the people you surround yourself with play a crucial role in shaping your journey. Their habits, attitudes, and approaches to challenges can significantly impact your behavior and mindset. This influence is often more sustainable and meaningful than temporary motivation or external instructions.

To make tomorrow a reality, it's essential to be intentional about your associations today. Seek out individuals who can positively influence you and help you develop the skills and qualities you hope to possess. This proactive approach to personal development is about more than just achieving immediate goals; it's about cultivating a continuous growth and improvement lifestyle. When you are intentional with your time and the people you associate with, you create a supportive environment that fosters learning and development. This intentionality helps you focus on your priorities and manage your time more effectively. It also provides a sense of accountability, as being surrounded by motivated and disciplined individuals encourages you to stay on track and strive for excellence.

Reflecting on my journey, I realize that the influence of those around me has been a driving force behind my achievements. Observing Pastor Waylon's dedication and focus taught me valuable lessons I could apply in my own life. This kind of learning has proven to be more impactful and enduring through influence rather than direct instruction.

Influence is a powerful tool for both personal and professional growth. By intentionally surrounding yourself with individuals who exemplify the qualities you wish to develop, you can harness this power to shape your future. Whether learning to manage your time, developing new skills, or pursuing ambitious goals, the right influences can guide and inspire you more effectively than traditional instruction. Be intentional today to make tomorrow a reality. Choose your influences wisely to create a path toward continuous improvement and milestones.

FINAL THOUGHTS

→ You can still enjoy free time, even in a busy life, if you plan your week well.

→ A clean space and a clear weekly calendar make all the difference.

→ Focus on one thing at a time and get it done.

→ When last-minute things pop up, you'll have the flexibility to shift things around.

→ Good organization helps you to stay productive and flexible at the same time.

→ Influence shapes behavior more deeply than lectures or instructions.

The Power of Community and Influence

→ Surrounding yourself with focused, disciplined people helps you grow.

→ Learning by observing others is powerful. Actions teach better than words.

→ Who you spend time with can sharpen your mindset and discipline.

→ Influence helps you naturally absorb real-world skills through everyday interactions.

The people around you often teach you more than any textbook ever could.

THE POWER OF SHOWING UP EACH DAY

A year from now, you may wish you had started today.

- KAREN LAMB

I HAD BEEN getting sharp, stinging sensations in my chest for nearly a year. Sometimes it felt like a needle was pricking right at my heart; other times, it was more like a quick, stabbing pain.

It wasn't constant, but it always seemed to hit when I least expected it. Some nights, I'd be drifting off to sleep, only to be jolted awake by the sudden pain. Other times, it would creep in while I was at work, moving heavy packages. I'd be bending down carefully to set a box on someone's porch, and there it was, the quick, unnerving stab that made me pause. I'd stop, catch my breath, and try to shake it off. After all, I'd always been healthy, and I kept in good shape, drank plenty of water, ate well, and exercised regularly. So why was this happening?

The scariest moment came one night when I was sketching a car for a client who lives in Beverly Hills, and I was working on a $1,500 project that needed to be perfect. I was deep into the details, my left hand moving swiftly across the paper, when suddenly, it went numb. The tingling sensation crept up my arm, making my fingers feel like they were buzzing. Panic set in. I'd heard stories of heart attacks starting just like this, and my mind spiraled. What if this was it?

I did the one thing I probably shouldn't have: I turned to Google. You know how that goes. Within minutes, I was convinced I might be having a heart attack. The anxiety was overwhelming, especially since I had terrible health insurance at the time. I wasn't just scared of the potential health crisis; I feared the cost.

With my bad health insurance card in hand, visiting the hospital for something as serious as a heart issue could be financially devastating. I imagined the bills piling up, including the tens of thousands of dollars I might have to pay for treatment, surgery, or who knew what else. The pain wouldn't let up, and I knew I couldn't ignore it forever. So, I decided to make a visit the very next morning.

Walking into HonorHealth Hospital that morning, I felt a mix of nerves and relief. I was finally there, seeking answers, but I had no idea what those answers might be. The waiting room was quiet; the air filled with the low hum of hospital chatter. After what felt like an eternity, they called me in. They took my blood, ran some x-rays, and attached several stickers to my chest, the little sensors that connect to wires and monitor your heart's activity. It all felt surreal. I was only there for a basic checkup, but the process seemed more serious with every new test they ran.

The result of the hospital visit left me speechless, the doctors came back and told me that there was absolutely nothing wrong with me. My heart was fine, my blood work was perfect, and everything was clear. They told me it was just acid buildup near my chest, likely from the way I'd been eating. That was all it was. I felt a mix of relief and frustration. After all that fear, all those sleepless nights, it turned out that I was completely healthy.

A couple of months went by before I found myself at home, opening my mail, and I noticed a bill from my hospital visit: $7,000. My insurance didn't cover much at all. I kept calling them and fighting it for weeks. I thought they would've paid most of it, but there was nothing I was able to do in the end.

I remember sitting there, staring at the number, feeling my heart sink. I had no idea how I was going to handle that kind of expense. What I was left with was an unexpected mental battle: how to tackle the $7,000 bill now looming over me. I couldn't help but wonder if the visit was worth it. I'd faced a huge financial struggle without any real health issue to show for it.

On the bright side, I saw this as an opportunity to build my credit score. I paid the bill using my credit card. My credit score was just over 700, and I wondered if I could use this setback to push it even higher, maybe to 730 or even 740.

So, I made a plan. I decided to tackle it one paycheck at a time. I broke down the daunting $7,000 into smaller, manageable chunks. The full amount was hard to believe, like a wave of pressure I hadn't felt in a long time, so I told myself every single morning to stop fearing it and start focusing on how to handle it. It was simple in theory, but far from easy. I had to be intentional with every dollar I spent. I started tracking everything: groceries, gas, even my occasional splurge on art supplies. I was careful not to overspend and directed any extra funds toward the hospital bill.

At first, I decided to pay down the $7,000 by committing to $1,000 every month, hoping that steady contributions would eventually bring relief. As I started the process, I quickly uncovered a bad habit I hadn't fully recognized before. I realized how often I was spending money on small, unnecessary things, especially food. It wasn't just about hunger; it was more of a mindset that told me I deserved a little treat after a long day. Sometimes it was a hot dog and a drink at the gas station. Or on a special day, it was the Albanese gummy bears from Sprouts.

If you haven't tried those Albanese gummy bears, you're missing out. They're easily one of the best gummy bears out there. Super soft, moist, and the sweet aroma pops out of the bag the second you open it. It's a new experience every time. Just putting that out there.

These small purchases seemed harmless at first, yet they added up quickly. The real issue was that I was unintentionally creating negative momentum. It felt like every time I tried to push forward by making a payment, I was also pulling myself back by giving in to these small impulses.

Progress was slow at first because I was caught in a tug-of-war between paying off debt and maintaining daily habits that drained my wallet without me noticing. The truth was, I often found myself near gas stations or stores, so temptation was never far. I had to build a new method, one that required more mental strength than any financial trick. Honestly, I didn't rely on any complex budgeting tools or fancy financial plans. I simply chose to stop spending on things I didn't need. That choice started with one simple action: I left my debit and credit cards at home.

For a while, I carried nothing with me. No cash. No cards. Just empty pockets and a new kind of discipline. This was before I had Apple Pay set up, so there really was no backup option. If I didn't have the money on me, then I simply couldn't spend it. That restriction became a safety net. It helped me gain control over my impulses. When I needed to fuel up my car, I'd take my card with me for that day only. If I absolutely had to go grocery shopping, I'd allow myself to bring my card, but otherwise, it stayed at home. This one change shifted everything. There was no pressure to buy something when I didn't have access to my money. It sounds simple, but it became one of the most effective strategies I used to stop the small leaks that were quietly keeping me in debt.

The early months were tough. There were days when it felt like I was making no progress at all. I'd make a payment, then look at the remaining balance and feel like I'd barely made a dent. I kept telling myself to remain focused on the immediate step. Slowly, things began to change. I started to see the numbers drop, bit by bit. Each paycheck brought a little more relief, a little more confidence. The balance was shrinking, and I felt a sense of control returning.

It wasn't just about the money anymore; it was about the mindset. I realized that this approach could apply to other areas of life too, not just financial challenges. The idea of being present and intentional, focusing on small steps rather than getting overwhelmed by the big picture, started to make a real difference.

I remember checking the balance one morning and being shocked at how far I'd come. The total had dropped faster than I'd expected. It was like all those small efforts had finally added up. The months had dragged in the beginning, but now they seemed to be flying by. I still had to be careful with my spending, but the burden felt lighter.

Then, one day, it was over. The debt was paid, and I'd done it. It took me about eight months to fully pay off my entire credit card. One step at a time, just as I'd planned.

After the debt was finally paid off, that good habit that had been drilled into my mind stayed with me, and it carried over into the way I handled money moving forward. Even though I had no debt and didn't rely on any fancy financial tools or techniques, I kept living frugally, and over time, I was able to accumulate more money than I ever expected.

SMALL STEPS LEAD TO BIG WINS

When it feels like you have too much on your plate, taking things slow and steady really does make a difference. After learning how powerful small steps could be with my finances, I started to notice that same mindset helping me in other areas of life too, even something as simple as a detailed car drawing. I was honestly surprised by how much I was able to finish on this car drawing project, even though I took many breaks along the way. The deadline was tight, a week to be exact, and I knew there was no room for rushing. I had to keep my focus, stay consistent, and just trust the process. It was one of those detailed pieces, about sixteen inches long, so it required a lot of attention.

I had all my tools set up: different shades of markers, fine pencils for those precise lines, erasers, and everything else I needed. Having everything organized made me feel ready to tackle it. It's kind of funny how something as simple as a tidy workspace can calm your mind, especially when you're under pressure. I broke the drawing into small sections, focusing on just a few square inches at a time. I wasn't trying to finish it all at once; I wanted to make sure every part got the attention it deserved.

Even though I was in a race against time, I knew I needed to plan ahead by setting aside time for breaks. You know how it is. Working non-stop just doesn't work. I'd finish one small area, then take a quick break. Sometimes, I'd just stand up and stretch or grab a snack. Other times, I'd step outside for some fresh air, just to clear my head. I've found that giving yourself a breather, even during crunch time, helps maintain quality. It's as important as the work itself.

SLOW DOWN TO SPEED UP

Sometimes, taking a moment to pause can be the best way to move forward. It's kind of like driving. You can't just zoom past every stop sign or red light on your way to work, no matter how late you are for work. You've got to slow down at the turns, stop when needed, and then keep moving. That's exactly how I handled this drawing. I had to be mindful of when to pause, even if it felt like the clock was ticking louder by the minute. I kept working steadily, giving each small part of the drawing the focus it demanded.

There were moments when I felt tempted to push through without taking a break, especially when a section looked almost done. I reminded myself that the goal was quality, not just finishing fast. So, I made sure to step back and see how each piece fit into the bigger picture.

With many of my drawings, I must admit, I felt a real sense of accomplishment. They turned out exactly how I'd hoped: detailed, realistic, and just what my clients wanted. The real reward was finding a balance between effort and rest, which made the whole experience much more enjoyable. It was a solid lesson that you don't have to rush to create something worthwhile.

CONSISTENCY IS KEY, EVEN WHEN TIME IS TIGHT

Progress comes from showing up consistently, day by day, rather than focusing on how fast you go.

I've learned this lesson many times: it's not always about speed; it's about consistency. By taking it one step at a time and fitting in those necessary pauses, I avoided the mental burnout that often comes with trying to do it all at once. It's easy to feel overwhelmed when you're fixated on the end result, but when you focus on small, manageable tasks, everything becomes less daunting.

This approach works in just about any area of life, whether you're working on a creative project, meeting a deadline at work, or chasing a personal goal. The idea is to keep your eye on the next step, not just the finish line. Just like driving a car, you have to respect the stops along the way. It's those pauses that allow you to navigate safely, without crashing into burnout. In my experience, the balance between effort and rest is what gets the best results. Sure, it can feel slow at times, but it's a pace that works and keeps you moving forward steadily.

SMALL WINS BUILD MOMENTUM

When you celebrate the little victories, you're motivated to keep going, no matter how tough it gets. The process of completing a drawing reinforced what I've always believed: little actions, done consistently, add up over time.

Even with the pressure of a deadline and high expectations from a client, I managed to deliver something that exceeded what was expected. It was a reminder that sometimes, taking it slow and steady is all you really need. In the end, it came down to learning how to handle pressure, stay consistent, and maintain quality, even when time is tight. It's a lesson I believe applies to any kind of work, whether it's art, writing, or a big project at your job. The trick is to know your limits. It's amazing how much you can accomplish when you keep the smaller things in mind while also respecting the need for breaks.

SMALL STEPS, BIG IMPACT

When you break down the journey, each step becomes more achievable, making the end goal less intimidating. Sometimes, tackling a big task feels like trying to climb a massive mountain. When you break it down into smaller steps, it suddenly seems doable. You give yourself a chance to breathe, to regroup, and to keep going. It's like taking regular stops on a long road trip, because you don't just drive straight through. This approach not only keeps you productive but also keeps burnout at bay. Your brain gets a chance to reset, which helps your overall performance.

This is a method I've used for years, and it's one that anyone can adopt. By taking small, consistent actions every day, you start to build routines that support bigger goals. Think of it as planting seeds. Each small step leads to a larger harvest over time. With this approach, discipline and time management naturally become part of your routine.

This approach turns small efforts into meaningful progress by allowing you to build and multiply into something significant.

BEING PRESENT MAKES EVERY MOMENT COUNT

When you're aware of how you're spending your time, each minute becomes more valuable, and distractions lose their pull. I've noticed that breaking tasks into smaller parts changes the way I view time. You start to value each second and become more mindful of how you're spending it. True productivity means using each moment with intention, whether you're working or spending time with loved ones. This kind of awareness brings a sense of fulfillment to even the smallest tasks.

Then there's the joy of celebrating the little wins along the way. Each completed step, no matter how small, feels like a win. It's like giving yourself a mental pat on the back, keeping you motivated to push forward. Each victory builds momentum, making the bigger challenges feel less daunting. By consistently working in smaller chunks, I've found that I can adjust more easily. If something isn't working, I can pivot without feeling like I've wasted a lot of time. It's like steering a ship, you make small course corrections to keep moving toward your destination. This kind of flexibility not only keeps you on track but also allows for continuous improvement.

FOCUS ON WHAT MATTERS

Making the most of your time begins with learning how to prioritize what deserves your focus, rather than simply trying to add more hours to your day. A personal method I've relied on is keeping my space organized and breaking the process into smaller parts. It's about creating a structured plan that keeps you focused and reduces distress. When everything is in its place, it's much easier to make steady progress without feeling overwhelmed. Think about how worried you'd feel if your surgeon was unorganized during a procedure! I'm sure you'd be very worried. It's the same principle here: organization leads to better time management and more consistent progress toward your goals.

Developing a strong work ethic is another result of this approach. Consistent, small efforts build a habit of dedication that influences all areas of life. Over time, this commitment leads to significant achievements and personal growth. Working in smaller increments also teaches patience and persistence, which are two essentials when you're chasing big goals. Time is one of those things you can't create more of, it's a gift, and how you use it matters.

I remember hearing Billy Graham say in a sermon, "Time works against you." That got my attention, because it's true. The clock never stops. Whether you're actively pursuing your goals or just letting the day slip by, time keeps moving. So, why not use it wisely?

Using time effectively starts with setting clear goals. Know what you want to achieve today, this week, or this month. Without a clear aim, it's easy to let precious moments slip away. A good plan gives you direction while still leaving room to adjust when life takes an unexpected turn. Life is a long journey of intentional choices.

Managing a busy schedule matters but so does making space for the things that bring true value, fulfillment, and purpose in your life. I've caught myself just going through the motions without really pausing to reflect on what's taking up my days. Maybe work tops the list, which makes sense, but what about the other things? Maybe it's caring for your pet or finding moments for yourself to simply unwind. Those personal times of stillness are golden, aren't they?

Now, re-sorting priorities isn't exactly a walk in the park. We all know that change can be uncomfortable. It's like rearranging the furniture in your living room, it's awkward at first, but eventually, it feels fresh and better suited to your needs. As people, we're surprisingly adaptable. I've experienced this myself; even when it feels tough at first, the mind starts adjusting sooner than you'd expect. It just takes a little patience and a clear picture of the rewards waiting at the end.

I often remind myself that it's worth the temporary discomfort if it means reaching a more fulfilling outcome. Here's the thing, once you're clear about what matters, it gets easier to say *no* to things that don't align with your priorities. It's about creating space, not just in your schedule but also in your head. I've found that when I'm intentional about what's important, I feel less overwhelmed. I stop trying to do everything all at once and instead focus on what brings real value to my life.

It's a shift from being busy to being productive. Let's be honest, it's not about squeezing everything into a single step. It's about making sure the important things are fully taken care of.

So, what's the hardest part? It's figuring out what to let go of. It might be as simple as cutting down on time spent scrolling through social media. Maybe set a 30-minute time limit on your phone. Making time means being aware of your choices so your energy goes toward what matters most.

It's the small, consistent decisions that lead to big changes over time. As you work through these changes, don't be hard on yourself. It's never going to be perfect. Some days will feel like progress, while others might feel like setbacks, and that's okay. I've learned to embrace it as part of the journey.

The key is to keep returning to what matters, even if it's just for a few moments each day. By keeping your end goal in sight, you'll not only find more time for the things you want most, but you'll also experience a deeper sense of fulfillment knowing that your time is being spent in the best way possible. This might involve waking up earlier or cutting down on non-essential activities. It's about being proactive and looking for pockets of time that can be repurposed for more meaningful activities.

When you have thirty minutes of downtime, and you know there's something you've been meaning to catch up on, make the quick choice to start. It's easy to put it off but doing it first will later make your downtime seem more satisfying. Once it's done, you can relax knowing there isn't much left to be concerned about. These small moments can add up to significant progress over time. Saving time involves finding ways to be more efficient in everything you do. This could mean automating repetitive tasks, using technology to streamline processes, or simply being more organized. The more efficient you are, the more time you can save for other essential activities.

It's also important to recognize where you're wasting time and take steps to minimize those moments. This might mean setting boundaries to avoid interruptions. Being mindful of how you spend your time helps you stay focused and productive.

The power of now lies in its potential to shape our future. Focusing on the present moment and making intentional choices can create opportunities that pave the way for long-term transformation. Surrounding ourselves with positive influences and staying mindful of how we use our time are key elements of this process. Every action we take today builds the foundation for tomorrow's achievements.

By prioritizing our time and making conscious decisions, we can overcome the challenges of the past and create a brighter future. Time is a precious gift, and how we spend it determines the quality of our lives.

TODAY'S CHOICES SHAPE TOMORROW'S REALITY

Every decision you make right now, no matter how small, builds the future you're heading toward. It's all about what you do with the present moment that opens new possibilities.

In early spring of 2015, I was in Tucson, Arizona. The days were getting warmer, and I was looking forward to watching a movie and eating some chips with homemade guacamole. During a fast trip to the grocery store, I grabbed a few avocados and everything else I needed. Once I got home, I started making guacamole. I sliced an avocado open, scooped out the green flesh, and like always, I tossed the seed in the trash. Before I moved on to the next one, I stopped and picked up the seed again, then washed it off in the sink.

It was huge, taking up most of the space inside the fruit. I held it in my hand, feeling its smooth, solid surface. I had eaten avocados plenty of times, but I had never really thought about the seed itself. Something about it made me pause. It made me wonder: how do avocados grow? I had never seen an avocado tree in real life. I had no idea where they were grown or how long they took to grow. Out of curiosity, I went to YouTube and started searching. That's when I stumbled upon a video explaining how you could grow an avocado tree at home, using nothing but the seed.

I had always thought avocados came from faraway farms, something only professional growers could cultivate. According to the video, all I needed was a small foam cup, some water, three toothpicks, and a little patience. The process was simple: you insert the toothpicks into the seed at an angle, only about a quarter of an inch deep, and rest it on the cup's rim so that the bottom half was submerged in water. Then, you place the cup containing the avocado seed in a dark place at room temperature, around 70°F, preferably inside a cupboard. You'll also need to change out the water daily, since the seed slowly absorbs it over time. After about a month, roots would begin growing from the bottom, and eventually, a stem would sprout from the top.

It seemed easy enough, so I figured—why not? I grabbed a foam cup, filled it about halfway with water, and carefully stuck in the toothpicks. The seed balanced just like in the video. Now, I had to wait and change out water regularly.

At first, I was excited. Every day, I checked on it, expecting to see some kind of change. I'd swap out the water, making sure it was fresh, and look for any signs of growth. Days had passed, then weeks, and nothing happened. The seed looked the same as when it started. I began wondering if I had done something wrong. I had followed all the instructions. The temperature in my house was warm enough, approximately 77°F, which was supposed to be ideal for growth. Still, there was no progress.

By the second month, I was getting frustrated. I had been consistent, checking on it every day, yet there were no signs of life. I almost considered giving up and tossing the avocado in the trash, thinking maybe this method didn't work. Maybe I had a bad seed. Even so, a part of me told me not to give up.

Then, after nearly three months, I noticed a small crack at the bottom of the seed. It wasn't much, just a tiny split, but it was proof that something was happening. A few weeks later, the crack widened, and a tiny root started emerging from the bottom. That's when I realized that growth had been happening all along, just beneath the surface where I couldn't see it. For weeks, all the progress had been hidden. The seed wasn't lifeless; it was just taking time to build its foundation. Before anything could sprout upward, it had to first grow downward, sending out roots.

That was the moment when it all started to make sense. I started thinking about how life works the same way. When we make small, intentional choices every day, whether it's working toward a goal, building a habit, or making a change, we don't always see immediate results. It's easy to feel like nothing is happening, as though all the effort is wasted. That doesn't mean growth isn't taking place. Most of the time, change starts beneath the surface, where no one can see it.

Eventually, the top of the seed split open, and a small stem pushed through. What started as nothing more than a hard seed in my hand had transformed into the early stages of a tree. It took patience. It took consistency. Most of all, it took faith in the process, even when I couldn't see results right away.

This reminded me of so many moments in life when it feels like we're working toward something but not seeing any progress in the beginning. Whether it's a business, a dream, or even personal growth, it's easy to feel discouraged when nothing seems to be happening. Just like that seed, the process doesn't stop just because we can't see it. The roots always grow first, beneath the surface, before anything visible happens. That's why so many people quit too soon. They assume that if they don't see immediate change, nothing is working. In reality, their foundation is only beginning to form.

That avocado seed taught me something valuable: today's choices shape tomorrow's realities. Every small action we take, no matter how insignificant it seems, is planting a seed for the future. The results may not show up right away, and it's better if they don't. In due time, they will. The key is to stay consistent, keep putting in the work, and trust the process. One day, when you least expect it, you'll start seeing the growth you've been waiting for.

Real growth happens behind the scenes in ways you don't notice at first. That realization stuck with me as I watched my avocado seed slowly transform. It taught me one of the biggest lessons in life: just because you don't see immediate progress doesn't mean nothing is happening.

Even with my journey as an author, I didn't see significant growth for many years. In the beginning, hardly anyone read my books. No one knew my name. I put in the effort, but it felt like nothing was really moving forward. For the first few years, I didn't get much recognition, and honestly, there were times I wondered if I was wasting my time. That's when a quiet thought came to mind, one that put everything back into perspective:

With the little I have, I'm planting seeds. Soon, they'll grow into more than enough to sustain my entire life.

I kept writing, promoting, and sharing my work, even when it felt like no one was paying attention. Then, six years later, I started to see the results. People began reaching out, telling me how my words had helped them. More readers started discovering my books. What once felt like small, unnoticed actions had started to turn into something meaningful. It reminded me of that avocado seed. In the beginning, I saw nothing. Beneath the surface, the roots were forming. The foundation was being built, even when I couldn't see it.

At that point, the real excitement began. The stem started growing taller, little by little. It was slow, but I could see progress now. After a while, the seed outgrew the water cup, so I transferred it into a pot filled with soil. I placed it outside, then added fertilizer, made sure it had enough sunlight, and kept watering it regularly. As time passed, the plant kept growing until it reached six feet tall. It was incredible to see how something that started as a single seed had turned into a thriving plant.

That's when I learned that an avocado tree could take up to ten years before it starts producing fruit. That really made me think. Something as small as a seed had the potential to grow into something massive, but only if it had time, care, and patience. Sometimes, the biggest impact comes from the smallest actions. What starts as something tiny, something that seems insignificant at first, can turn into something life-changing if you stay consistent.

Watching that avocado seed grow gave me one of the most valuable life lessons: just because results aren't immediate doesn't mean they aren't on the way. Progress is always happening, even when you can't see it. That's incredible. The time you have right now are where all the possibilities are made. In the present moment, we can change our course, make new decisions, and take actions that shape our future. Focusing on what we can do now opens up opportunities that weren't visible before.

Today's possibilities can heal the past because every positive action we take now can mend old wounds and set us on a new path. For example, if we've made mistakes or regrets, we can learn from them and make better choices today. This act of choosing to do better not only helps us move past the pain but also sets the stage for a brighter future.

Sometimes, the past can stop you. Memories of past failures, disappointments, and regrets can be heavy and overwhelming. They can make us feel stuck, as if we cannot move forward. We must remember that today is a new day. We can use today to make tomorrow possible by taking small steps toward our goals. Every action we take today, no matter how small, is a step away from the past and towards a better future. It's essential to focus on the present, on what we can do now, rather than letting the past dictate our future. By doing so, we can break free from the chains of yesterday and create a new path for ourselves.

Time is a valuable resource, and how we use it significantly impacts our lives. There are moments when we're killing time, and other moments when we feel like we have no time at all. Every second counts in those time crunch moments when you're rushing to get somewhere quickly. Other times, you're stuck in traffic and don't mind because it's your day off, and you can afford to lose a little time. The next day, you could find yourself on that same street, stuck in traffic, but it feels completely different because you're racing the clock.

Time feels different depending on the situation, but it is ultimately about how you manage it.

Time can feel different depending on your day and what you're doing. You might have plenty of time today, but not tomorrow, because of work, family, or other priorities. Have you realized that no one could invent new minutes or hours? We can't add days to our lives. Each one gives us 24 hours, 1440 minutes, 86,400 seconds; no matter how you look at it, no time should be wasted.

Think big with big goals but act small. Work in minutes and hours. Breaking everything down into sections makes everything more manageable, and your brain won't become overwhelmed. When you focus on the seconds, you realize how much you can accomplish in just a short amount of time. Each second adds up, and before you know it, you have made significant progress toward your big goals.

This approach helps you stay focused and prevents you from feeling overwhelmed by the enormity of your tasks. Breaking things down into smaller increments makes everything more manageable. When you look at a big goal, it can feel impossible to achieve. When you break it down into smaller steps, it suddenly becomes much more attainable.

For example, thinking about writing an entire book can be daunting if you want to write a book. If you break it down into writing a page a day, it becomes much more doable. By focusing on the smaller increments, you stay motivated because you can see the progress you are making each day. That steady progress eventually brings your big goals within reach.

YOU CAN NEVER BE TOO YOUNG OR TOO OLD TO BEGIN

No matter where you are in life, every step forward counts and the right moment to start is always available.

When COVID-19 began like a storm in early 2020, it felt like the world crumbled overnight. Businesses shut down, streets turned eerily silent, and every news channel shouted the same message: rising unemployment, jobs disappearing in a flash. It was a time of uncertainty that made everyone wonder, *"What's coming next?"*

I was in my mid-twenties, feeling the weight of both urgent pressure and a sense of helplessness. Amidst all the chaos, one thing burned inside me: a relentless dream to write a book, to make my voice heard. The question was: Could I still make it happen? At the time, I had started writing my first book. I was about twenty pages in, but I felt stuck. Doubts kept creeping in, whispering that maybe I was too young to write something meant for the world to see. I started thinking, *Maybe I should wait until I'm older, more experienced. Maybe then I'll have something worth sharing.*

It was that same old lie I'd been fed growing up, the idea that there's a "right age" for everything: college, jobs, marriage, achievement. Now here I was, mid-pandemic, with a half-written manuscript and dwindling motivation.

One afternoon, I decided I needed some guidance, someone to light a fire under me and remind me why I started in the first place. That's when I called my friend Ethos Creed, host of the Creed Podcast, and fellow author. Creed and I had always been like-minded. He was working on his book and podcast while I was trying to write mine. It felt good to know someone else was in the same boat, navigating the storm. So, I drove over to his apartment for a quick meeting.

Creed lived in a small but cozy apartment. It wasn't anything fancy, just a few simple pieces of furniture, a stack of books on the coffee table, and a motivational poster on the wall that read, *"Just get it done."* It was the perfect environment for the kind of conversation I needed. I stepped inside, feeling both nervous and hopeful. Creed wasn't the kind of guy to sugarcoat things, but I knew he genuinely wanted the best for me.

I sat down on his worn leather couch, sinking into the cushions as the weight of my uncertainty settled around me. Creed sat across from me in a small armchair, just a few feet away. He had a serious look on his face, like he could sense the discouragement I was carrying.

"So, what's going on, Jon?" he asked, leaning forward with genuine interest. I swallowed the lump in my throat and let it all out, including the doubts, the fear of failure, and the constant feeling that maybe I was starting too soon. That maybe I should wait until I was older.

Creed listened quietly, nodding every now and then. When I was done talking, he leaned back in his chair and looked me straight in the eye.

"Jon, you could finish this book in two weeks if you really wanted to," he said, his words hitting me like a bolt of lightning. "There are tens of thousands of seconds in just a few weeks, and every second counts. If you use those seconds intentionally, you can get anything done."

His words were simple, but they carried a weight that I couldn't ignore. The room seemed to shift. I felt a surge of energy, as if a switch had been flipped. He kept going, his voice steady and confident. "You've got to stop letting age define your timeline. You have all the time you need right now. Don't wait until you're forty or sixty to begin. Start now and let the experience come as you go."

I felt a spark ignite. It was like someone had flipped a switch, turning the darkness into light. The way Creed spoke, the way he believed in the power of those seconds, made everything seem possible. "You can do this," he repeated. "Don't let the culture you grew up in hold you back. You don't need permission to pursue your dream. Just do it."

As he spoke, I could feel the atmosphere change. What started as a discouraging, heavy conversation suddenly felt light, hopeful. It was like the weight had lifted off my shoulders. I even joked about finishing the book when I was forty or sixty, but Creed wasn't having it.

"No," he insisted. "You can get it done in a few weeks." I left Creed's place that day with a new sense of determination. It was like a fire had been lit under me, and I wasn't going to let it burn out. After that, I didn't reach out to him for nearly a month. No texts, no calls, no updates. There was only silence between us. I was in the zone, fully locked in and completely focused on finishing my book.

Then, about a month later, I finally called.

"Hey," I said, trying to keep my voice steady, "I finished the book." There was a pause on the other end of the line, and then Creed's voice came back, filled with disbelief.

"No way," he said. "Are you serious?"

I could hear the surprise. Creed was used to giving advice that people rarely took seriously, but this time was different. I had done it.

"Most people say 'cool' or 'awesome' when I give advice," he said, "but they never actually act on it."

This time was different. I had taken those tens of thousands of seconds, one by one, and turned them into something real, something tangible.

In one of our podcast interviews on YouTube, recorded in January 2023, Creed and I talked about that pivotal conversation. He admitted he never expected me to take his advice so literally. That conversation with Creed changed my life. It wasn't just about finishing one book; it was about realizing that I didn't have to wait for the "right" age to do something different. As long as I was old enough to take responsibility for my own decisions, I was old enough to achieve anything, and I did it. Three years had passed, and I found myself writing my fourth book, and the journey had been nothing short of incredible. Creed and I still work together as we push each other to grow in our endeavors each year.

Looking back, I've realized something powerful: if you start young, you can build credibility early. You don't have to wait until you're older or more experienced to do something significant. You can accumulate that experience along the way. If you keep waiting for the perfect time, the right age, or just a little more experience, you might wake up one day and wonder how so much time slipped away, unused.

This whole journey reminded me of Jeremiah in the Bible. In the very first chapter, when God called Jeremiah to prophesy to a nation, his response was, "I'm too young." God told him, "Don't say, 'I am too young.' You must go to everyone I send you to and say whatever I command you." (Jeremiah 1:7)

It wasn't about age. It was about obedience. It was about showing up and doing what you were called to do. In Jeremiah's time, only the older, more experienced people were considered fit to speak. God was stepping outside of culture norms, choosing someone others wouldn't have—He still does today. That's what Creed and I came to understand: starting early isn't just okay, it's wise. When you begin now, you gain wisdom along the way. You grow into the person you were always meant to become.

Any day could be your last. All you really have is now. Don't let anyone dictate when you should start, because they don't know how much time you have left. You could be young, you could be old, but that doesn't matter. What matters is taking action *today*, right now. Don't wait for the "right" moment, because it may never come. Just start. Thirty or forty years from now, you'll be grateful that you did.

Creed and I still talk about that day. We keep working hard and showing up with the same hustle we believed in back then. We still believe that as long as there's breath in your lungs, you have a chance to do something great. I owe Creed big time for waking me up that day, and for showing me that age is just a number, and that all you need is a little faith and a whole lot of hustle.

FINAL THOUGHTS
Small Steps Still Move You Forward

Sometimes, the biggest challenges require the smallest steps.

→ The present moment is where change begins, and possibilities open up.

→ Every small action you take today can help heal the past and shape a better future.

→ Mistakes and regrets don't define you; your choices now do.

→ Don't let past failures hold you back; you can always choose a new path.

→ You're never too young or too old to start.

→ Every step forward, no matter how small, still counts.

PRUNING DEAD BRANCHES

"Do not be misled: bad company corrupts good character."

—1 CORINTHIANS 15:33

SOMETIMES, IT'S necessary to make sacrifices by letting go of those who aren't there to support you, because eventually they can become dead branches. You are the living tree, and pruning those dead branches is imperative. If you don't eliminate them, they can infect the surrounding healthy branches of your life and slowly cause the entire tree to wither and die. Even the people closest to you, cherished friends or family members, can impede your progress. Making the difficult decision to part ways with them may be essential to achieving your dreams and reaching your full potential.

The message is clear: don't let the fear of being too young or inexperienced hold you back. Your age or experience level isn't a barrier; it's a starting point. Let it fuel your drive instead of holding you back. Even I've had people watch my progress from the sidelines as I began my journey as an author. Some came out of the woodwork with remarks like, *"You know, you're working too hard,"* or *"You are too young and inexperienced to write a book."* I've even had people close to me advising against this path altogether, saying becoming an author takes years of experience.

In a way, they weren't wrong, because over the last five years, I've *have* accumulated lots of experience. Back then, it felt like a constant wave of doubt, especially from those I thought would support me. When I shared my dream of seeing my books on bookstore shelves one day, some laughed and said, *"You think too much. That won't happen."* Of course, I was in the early stages of writing, so it brought me down.

Do you know what? They were wrong.

Five years later, my books are now sold in multiple Barnes & Noble locations. I proved to myself, and to them, that the dream was possible. Here's a piece of advice I'd give: work in silence. No one needs to know what you are up to. They cannot critique you if they don't know what you're doing. Let them see your results, but talk less. As Solomon wisely put it, "Even fools are considered wise if they keep silent, and discerning if they hold their tongue." (Proverbs 17:28)

Let your success do the talking. Remember, time is not on your side, it won't wait for you to feel ready or confident. The longer you wait, the more opportunities you miss. So, take the first step today. Choose to start now, and you will be amazed at how far you can go. Focusing too much on the future without taking action today wastes energy. As Billy Graham once said, *"Indecision is a decision,"* and not choosing is a choice not to try.

Do not let age or fear of inexperience stop you. Jeremiah's story proves that even the young can be called for great purposes. Starting young gives you an early advantage and builds valuable experience.

Sometimes, those dead branches aren't just bad habits or old ways of thinking; they're the absence of the right people. Not having a strong community is like a dead branch that slowly spreads, weakening the whole tree. Without the right relationships, you end up carrying everything alone. Over time, that isolation can drain the life out of you. It reminds me of something I experienced years ago.

It was sometime in 2013, back when I worked at a Subway restaurant in Oro Valley, Arizona. The store was located on Lambert and La Cañada, and at that point, I had been working there since I was eighteen, going on about seven years. One of my coworkers, Christina, was an assistant manager. She was around thirty-five at the time, a hard worker, but on this particular day, she was not having it. She was just burnt out, frustrated, and on edge.

We had a business meeting to attend at another Subway store about four miles away. It was me, Christina, her aunt, and our manager Mike, all in the mix. We closed up the restaurant for a few hours, locked the doors, and piled into a Chevy Equinox. It was one of those required meetings where all the Subway employees from different stores would get together to discuss upselling strategies, things like avocado and bacon add-ons. The franchise owner, Les White, was hosting it, and there was an annual sales competition tied to it. Whoever's store sold the most add-ons throughout the year would get a big bonus.

So, off we went. Even before we left the restaurant, I could tell Christina was checked out. She had been glued to her phone all day, constantly scrolling and texting. Her son was stationed in Japan with the Air Force, and she was distressed beyond belief about something going on over there. Also, her husband had been in prison for seven years, and for some reason, the prison did not grant her access to see him for the longest time, and that just made everything worse.

She was anxious, overwhelmed, and not present. She tried to keep her composure, but you could feel the tension radiating off her. As we drove, things were quiet. The hum of the engine sounded steady, the occasional chime of a text notification went off from Christina's phone, and a few murmurs about the meeting were exchanged. Then, just like that, we pulled up to a stoplight. To the right, nestled in a little plaza, was a smoke shop called Sticky's Smoke Shop. Christina saw that smoke shop immediately.

"Pull over!" she snapped, suddenly coming to life. "Mike, I need you to stop at that smoke shop. I have to light up. I need it! Just for a second!" Her voice was sharp, urgent. She was in the backseat next to me, leaning forward, practically gripping the front seats. Mike was driving. He didn't flinch.

"No," he said firmly. "You're three years sober. We're not doing this."

She wasn't having it. "Come on, please! I just—I can't do this today. I need a pack. Just a pack. One cigarette. I need to breathe!"

She was panicking now, almost gasping for air. It was like the distress, the anxiety, and the addiction had all merged into this massive force that took over her mind. She wasn't thinking about her sobriety anymore. She was just thinking about relief. That smoke shop—just a few feet away—was screaming her name.

"Mike, the light's still red! You still have time! Just turn in really quick! Come on, before it changes!" Her aunt jumped in. "No, Christina. We're not letting you throw three years away."

I stayed quiet. I didn't know what to say. She was unraveling, and I didn't want to be the next person she snapped at. It was extremely tense. It felt like those few minutes lasted an eternity. She was yelling, pleading, her voice rising with every second.

Then, the light turned green.

Mike didn't hesitate. He drove forward. Christina lost it.

"NO! NO! You should've pulled over! You don't understand!" She kept going, yelling, cursing, accusing him of not caring about her.

She wasn't wearing her seatbelt, shifting around in frustration. The tension in the car was unbearable, but Mike just kept driving. He didn't say anything. He just drove. Minute by minute, we got farther from that smoke shop. The first few moments were the hardest, she was still screaming, still angry. Something happened as we created distance. The further we went, the more the intensity started to fade.

She was still upset but not as explosive. By the time we got to the Subway store where the meeting was being held, she was still visibly distressed, but the immediate desperation had dulled. We went into the meeting, talked about sales, listened to strategies, and did the usual. After about two hours, we got back into the car to drive home.

Christina was quiet this time, with no more yelling, no more pleading, just stillness as we were a few minutes away from our store and she finally spoke.

"Hey," she said, almost hesitant. "I just...I just want to say thank you. I know I was losing it back there. I wasn't thinking. I'm glad you didn't pull over. I wasn't thinking about my sobriety at all. I almost lost everything because of that."

Mike just nodded. "We got you."

She exhaled. "Three years sober…I almost threw that away. You guys didn't let me. So…thanks."

I kept thinking about how all it took was creating distance. At first, on our way to the meeting, everything felt brutal. She was screaming and the atmosphere was tense. After that first outburst, the tension eased a little. By the time we were miles away from that smoke shop, she was breathing again.

It made me realize something. That first moment, where you make the decision to go the other way, is the hardest. It's like stepping out of glue. It's sticky, it holds you down, it doesn't want to let you go. If you just take one step away, even if you're not sure how, even if your mind is screaming at you to stay, that single step makes the next step just a little bit easier.

It's a compounding effect. The first moment is sheer force, going against the gravitational pull of addiction, stress, or bad decisions. Then the second moment comes, and it's slightly more manageable. Then the third moment. Before you know it, you're miles away from the thing that almost consumed you.

James Clear, the best-selling author of *Atomic Habits,* once said, *"Move towards the next thing, not away from the last thing."* That's exactly what happened here. We didn't pull over because we weren't just moving away from the smoke shop; we were moving toward the meeting, toward maintaining her sobriety, toward something better. That shift in direction made all the difference.

When we returned to our Subway restaurant, everything was normal again. Christina was calm. The crisis had passed. In the end, that single decision—to just keep moving forward—saved her three years of sobriety. At the time, it didn't feel like an investment. It felt like a struggle, like something she just had to get through. Every difficult moment, every time she had to fight against old habits, every time she wanted to give in but didn't, it all felt like an uphill battle with no end in sight. It was frustrating, exhausting, and at times, it seemed impossible.

What she didn't realize then was that every single one of those moments was a deposit into her future. Every time she chose to keep going, to not turn back, to push through the discomfort, she was investing in the person she would become. She wasn't just surviving those moments; she was building something. She was creating a life that, one day, she would wake up to and realize was worth all of it.

That's exactly what happened.

Now, looking back, she sees it differently. What once felt like suffering now feels like a steppingstone. What once felt like rejection now feels like redirection. What once seemed like the hardest thing she'd ever had to endure was shaping the future she's now living.

She didn't know it then, but she was making choices her future self would thank her for. Every moment she resisted temptation, every time she walked away instead of falling back into old patterns, every time she chose growth over comfort, it all added up.

Now, she's living in the result of those decisions. A life she never thought she'd have. A peace she never thought she'd experience. A sense of freedom and self-respect that once felt so far away. If she could go back and talk to the version of herself who was struggling, who was fighting through those tough moments, she'd tell her one thing: keep going. Because every hard choice, every moment of perseverance, every second of discomfort is worth it. She is so, so thankful she never gave up.

THE THREE-SHIFT RULE

The Three-Shift Rule is something I came up with through personal hardships that helped me build and keep strong resistance, and I thought, what better way to share it with you. To make difficult moments easier for your mind to handle during heated situations is shifting your focus, your environment, and your perspective, one step at a time. Breaking free from addiction, or any bad habit, isn't just about resisting. It's about shifting.

Moments have power, but only if you move through them intentionally. The hardest part of any craving isn't the craving itself; it's what your mind does with it. Your mind will try to convince you to stay where you are, to give in, to believe the lie that you can't escape it. I've learned something: if I shift my environment, my focus, and my mindset, I can break the cycle.

That's what the Three-Shift Rule is all about. Instead of trying to fight the craving head-on, you move through it: physically, mentally, and spiritually. This rule gives you a mental framework, so you're not stuck wondering when the struggles will end. Most people secretly give up because they don't know how long they need to endure before the next breakthrough. There's no plan they can grip and hold onto.

SHIFT #1: MOVE AND SPEAK LIFE

The first shift is all about movement. It's about taking that *first step*, that *first action,* even when it feels impossible. Let me be real with you: it *will* initially feel impossible.

Your mind is going to resist. Your cravings will try to hold you back. Everything inside you will want to stay right where you are. This is the moment you *cannot let your mind take over.* This is the moment where you take control. It starts with something simple: *just move.*

When cravings hit, when temptation rises, when your mind starts pulling you back into old patterns, the first thing you need to do is *physically move to a different location.* It could be another room, outside for a walk, or even just standing up. The key is to *change your environment.* Why? Because movement creates momentum.

The hardest part of breaking free from a craving or destructive thought patterns is getting started. Once you move, even just a little bit, your brain starts catching up. You start maneuvering out of that place. If your craving feels like it's holding you in place, here's a trick that works every time:

Count down.

Out loud, say: "5, 4, 3, 2, 1..."

Then *move.*

There's something about counting down that sends a signal to your brain that it's go time. It stops overthinking in its tracks. It eliminates hesitation and *you take action* instead of sitting there, stuck in your own thoughts.

Mel Robbins, a best-selling author of *The 5 Second Rule,* mentions that counting down helps your mind gain traction and take small initiatives. This happens by engaging the prefrontal cortex, the part of your brain that helps you focus and make decisions, making it easier to take that first step.

Funny enough, this trick isn't just for battling cravings. It works for getting out of bed in the morning. It works for starting a task on which you've been procrastinating. There's power in counting down and immediately taking action.

Now, moving isn't enough on its own. You also need to *speak life* over yourself. Choose a verse from the Bible and speak it out loud. In fact, it's even better if you take one verse and meditate on it throughout the day. One of the best ways to understand how meditation works, is by watching how a cow digests its food. A cow has one stomach made up of four compartments: the rumen, the reticulum, the omasum, and the abomasum. Each compartment plays a role in breaking down the same portion of food slowly, patiently, and thoroughly. Meditation works the same way. You begin by *reading* the Word of God and letting it settle in. You *pray* through it, reflect on it, *sing* it, and *talk* about it with your friends. Each step draws it deeper into your heart until it becomes part of how you live and respond. That is how the Word of God becomes your greatest weapon against the enemy. The Word of God is living and active, and it will fight for you if you surrender your will to the Lord.

Your words shape your reality. What you say out loud has power. When you're battling addiction, temptation, or any kind of struggle, your mind will try to convince you that you're weak, that you're stuck, that you can't win. So, what do you do?

You counter it with truth, not just in your head, but by *speaking it out loud.* There's something effective about your own ears hearing your own voice declare truth. It's different from just thinking positively. When you physically say something, your brain starts believing it.

So, say it out loud:

"I am free."

"I am strong."

"I am a new creation in Christ."

"I have made it this far, and I'm going even further."

Even if you don't feel it, *say it anyway*. What you say will start shaping what you believe. What you believe will shape what you do. The reason this shift is so important isn't just because it gets you moving or because it gets you speaking life. It's because it teaches you the *power of choice*.

Addiction, temptation, and cravings often make you feel like you don't have a choice, as though you're powerless; but you're not. By counting down from five and then physically moving, you're practicing the power of making a decision. By speaking truth over yourself, you're reinforcing that power. You're *taking back control*.

See, when cravings hit, they try to create a blind spot; they try to make you forget how far you've come. When you shift into movement and declaration, you create a different blind spot, one that blocks the cravings instead. Instead of being blinded by temptation, you are *surrounded by truth*. That truth is this: you are free, you are strong, and you are fearfully and wonderfully made. That means God himself intentionally crafted you with a rare design. His hands are skillful and eternal, filled with purpose. The same purpose in His hands is now written into your life.

Proverbs 18:21 says, *"The tongue has the power of life and death."*

Think about that for a second—life and death. What you say out loud either builds you up or tears you down. It either gives you strength or weakens you. It either pushes you forward or holds you back.

So, when you open your mouth, make sure you're *feeding your spirit with life*. Because words aren't just sounds; they're *seeds*. Whatever you plant in your mind and heart is what will grow. If you constantly say, *"I can't do this. I'll never be free. This is too hard,"* then guess what? Those words remain active behind the scenes, much like an app running in the background on your phone.

Many people brush them off, thinking they didn't mean anything, and they move on with their day as though nothing went wrong. That single word you once thought was harmless keeps working in the background of your mind. It begins solidifying and building walls of false identity, which the Bible describes as false arguments:

"We use God's mighty weapons, not worldly weapons, to knock down the strongholds of human reasoning and destroy false arguments." (2 Corinthians 10:4-5, NLT)

One day, you'll notice those walls, and by then, they'll already have started gaining territory over your mind. You'll believe it, and your actions will follow.

If you say, *"I am strong, I have self-control, and God has set me free,"* your mind starts believing it and your body follows.

Every time you move, speak life, and make a conscious choice to push past cravings, you are building your future self. You are laying bricks for the person you are becoming. Sobriety is about more than avoiding something; it's about becoming someone. Every time you choose to move, *shift,* or speak life, you create a future where you are stronger, freer, and more in control than ever before.

So don't let your mind take over. Don't let cravings control your choices.

Take the first step.
Move.
Speak life.
Keep going.

SHIFT #2: GET AROUND THE RIGHT PEOPLE

If there's one thing that will *make or break* your journey to freedom, it's this: the people you choose to surround yourself with will either pull you forward or hold you back. Cravings thrive in isolation and around bad company. When you're alone, your thoughts begin to take control, influencing how you feel and what you do. It starts whispering lies:

"No one will know."

"It's just this once."

"You're already struggling, so what's the point?"

If you stay in isolation, those thoughts only grow louder. That's why the second shift is simple but powerful—*get around the right people.*

The Power of the Right People

When you surround yourself with the right people, such as those who encourage you, speak life over you, and set the kind of example you want to follow, you start becoming like them. You start thinking, talking, and acting differently.

Why? Because *environment shapes behavior.*

Think about it: if you spend time together with people who are always negative, always complaining, and always focused on the past, it won't be long before you start thinking the same way. If you get around people who are focused on growth, faith, and taking action, then suddenly, their mindset starts rubbing off on you. That's exactly what you need before cravings begin.

When you surround yourself with people who are uplifting, they help you become someone greater than your struggles. Even if you're not talking to anyone, just being in a place where people are active, productive, and engaged can shift your mindset. If you do have someone you can talk to, even better.

If you can't physically be around people, then pick up the phone and call a friend, a mentor, or someone who reminds you of the truth. It doesn't even have to be a deep conversation. Just hearing another voice can be enough to break the cycle of isolation and snap you out of a craving. Temptations aren't just physical. They're *mental and spiritual.* The more you sit alone with your thoughts, the stronger they get. So don't give them that power; reach out, make a call, step outside, go somewhere, and do something. You were never meant to fight this battle alone. From the very beginning, *God designed you for community.*

The Bible says in Ecclesiastes 4:9-10, *"Two are better than one... If either of them falls down, one can help the other up."*

Isolation is the enemy's greatest weapon because when you're alone, you're vulnerable. When you have people around you, you're reminded that you are part of something bigger than your cravings and past struggles.

What defines you is who you choose to be today. One of the most powerful choices you can make is *who you surround yourself with.*

Who You're Around Shapes Who You Become

Have you ever experienced a time when you realized you had started thinking and behaving like someone you've been around often, almost without noticing it? It's because your *environment shapes you.* If you're always around people who are pushing you forward, making wise choices, and living with purpose, then over time, you start to absorb that mindset. The opposite is true, too. If you're surrounded by people who are negative, unmotivated, or caught in destructive habits, you'll eventually pick up on those patterns as well. That's why getting around the right people is a game-changer. When you're struggling, don't just sit in it alone.

This is another way you *exercise the power of choice.* When you're in the middle of a craving, your mind wants to keep you stuck. It wants to isolate you, to make you feel like you're alone in the fight. You always have a choice. You can choose to sit in that craving, or you can reach out, move, and get around the right people who want what's best for you. You don't have to do it alone. You weren't meant to do it alone.

So, make the shift. Step into the right community. Get around the right people. When you do, you'll start to see that your cravings don't control you. God helps you overcome it. Every time you choose to get around positive people, you're reminded that you are stronger than your cravings.

SHIFT #3: LET GRATITUDE TAKE OVER

This final shift is where everything changes. The pull of physical urges that once felt overpowering begins to fade away.

Up until this point, you have taken intentional actions. You've moved to a different location, you have spoken life over yourself, and you have gotten around the right people. Now, it's time to go one step further. In this shift, you replace the *blind spot* that cravings create with something far stronger: *gratitude.* Instead of allowing physical urges to distort your perception and make you feel as if you haven't made any progress, you choose to look back, reflect, and appreciate how far you've already come. This simple yet powerful shift allows you to remove the false sense of urgency that cravings create, replacing it with a mindset of strength, peace, and appreciation.

One of the most dangerous aspects of cravings is that they don't just *pull you toward temptation;* they also block your ability to see your progress. When a temptation rises, it can feel all-consuming, as if nothing else matters, and it may seem as though the battle you've been fighting has been completely erased. It creates a blind spot: one that makes you forget how long you've been sober, how many times you have resisted, and how much strength you have already developed.

Your progress is real, and nothing can take that away. The moment you stop and choose gratitude, you begin to regain peace in your life. You start to see your sobriety for what it truly is, not just something you are fighting to maintain, but something valuable that you have built over time.

Instead of feeling like you are just trying to "hold on" to your progress, you begin to cherish it, protect it, and appreciate it for the life-changing victory that it is. Something incredible begins happen: the craving that once felt overwhelming begins to shrink, and your *perspective shifts completely.*

THE PURPOSE OF THESE THREE SHIFTS

The goal of these three shifts is to transform your mind because ninety-nine percent of the battle is fought in your thoughts. The mind doesn't like change, often keeping you in old habits and patterns, but that's exactly why taking physical action is so important. By moving, speaking life, and surrounding yourself with the right people, you are training your mind to think differently, even before the desire fully passes.

Learning to manage your mind is one of the best ways to love the Lord your God with the mind He has given you. When you prioritize Him in your life, it becomes easier to manage your thoughts, because your mind begins to revolve around Him.

This third shift, which is allowing gratitude to take over, is the one that solidifies everything. It ensures that the progress you've made doesn't fade away the moment you face another challenge. The reason why this step is so critical is because in times of intense temptation or pressure, it is incredibly easy to lose sight of how far you have come. When you are in a difficult situation, your mind tends to focus only on what is happening right now, forgetting about all of the victories that have led up to this point.

That's why choosing gratitude is not just helpful. It's necessary.

The Bible gives us a clear guide on how to combat anxiety, temptation, and times of struggle through gratitude.

"Do not be anxious about anything, but in every situation, by prayer and petition, with thanksgiving, present your requests to God. The peace of God, which surpasses all understanding, will guard your hearts and your minds in Christ Jesus." (Philippians 4:6-7)

Gratitude is not just a positive thought or a temporary feeling of thankfulness; it is a spiritual weapon that invites divine peace into your life. When you choose to be grateful, you are not just shifting your perspective; you are aligning yourself with truth and allowing God's peace to protect your heart and mind. This is one of the most powerful ways to safeguard your sobriety because it keeps you grounded in who He is. It quiets the lie that tries to convince you that you're weak, and instead, it reminds you of how strong you are.

The more you practice gratitude, the more you begin to see temptations for what they truly are: temporary and insignificant. Each time you overcome a craving, you are reinforcing a new mindset, a new reality, and a new version of yourself, one that is no longer controlled by temptation, but rather, is guided by strength, wisdom, and self-control.

By focusing on what you are grateful for, you are not just resisting cravings. You are actively *shaping a new mental framework,* one that prioritizes your growth, healing, and future over temporary urges. This is why gratitude is such a powerful tool: it transforms your cravings from something that feels overwhelming into something that becomes smaller, weaker, and ultimately, irrelevant.

As this shift becomes part of your daily routine, something remarkable happens. You start to become overprotective of your sobriety. No longer do you see it as something fragile, something that you're barely holding onto. Instead, you see it as something precious and worth guarding at all costs. You recognize how much work you have put into this journey, and you refuse to let a fleeting craving take that away.

You see your sobriety as a victory that you have fought for, prayed for, and built with your own choices and actions. You realize that the strength you have developed is not something you want to trade for a moment of weakness. This is what makes gratitude so powerful: it shifts your mindset from fear of losing progress to fiercely protecting what you have built. It removes the illusion that cravings have power over you and instead reminds you that Jesus is in control.

At the beginning of this journey, temptations often felt overpowering. They seemed to have control over your thoughts, actions, and emotions. As you moved through these three shifts, something changed. You shifted your way forward when you felt stuck. You spoke life when your mind tried to speak doubt. You got around the right people when isolation tried to keep you trapped. Now, you choose gratitude: the final step that seals your victory. Next time temptations come, remind yourself of the bigger picture:

You are not fighting *for* freedom. You are fighting *from* freedom.

You are not struggling to stay sober. You are *protecting* your sobriety.

You are not weak. You just have a *strength out of balance*, and you're realigning it.

Every time you invite gratitude in, you make your freedom even more unshakable.

The reason I say you're fighting *from* freedom and not *for* freedom, as I mentioned earlier, is because Jesus Christ won the victory when He took the punishment that was meant for you. When you surrender your entire life to the Lord daily, you will no longer die in your sins. What He did on the cross is the reason freedom is already available. When you turn from your sinful nature, repent, and accept His salvation every day, you begin to live from the freedom He already gave you. You are not striving for it. You are walking in the result of it.

The world often tells you to chase freedom, love, and happiness as though it's something far away. In Christ, those things already belong to you. The word "world" refers to the *order of influence* of an evil system that pulls people away from God. Gratitude is a gift from God that helps you resist that influence and stay rooted in what has always been true.

PUTTING THE THREE SHIFTS INTO DAILY PRACTICE

The real power of these three shifts: Move and Speak Life, Get Around the Right People, and Let Gratitude Take Over—comes from using them daily. Just knowing about them isn't enough. You must make them part of your life, one day at a time. That's really the key: it's simply about taking it one day at a time. You must fully lean into it, putting the weight of your focus and effort behind it.

Your entire life is made up of days, and the only one you ever really have is today. Yesterday is already gone and tomorrow hasn't happened yet. In fact, tomorrow can't happen until you first face today. That's why what you do right now matters more than anything else. If you make the choice to put these three shifts into practice each day, even in small ways, you'll start to build momentum. You'll train your mind to think differently, and over time, it will become more natural.

This isn't something that will transform you overnight, and it's not supposed to. Real change doesn't happen instantly. It happens gradually, steadily because it's your new lifestyle.

Think of it this way: slow is smooth, and smooth is fast. This phrase is commonly used in military training, where staying focused and moving with control leads to better results.

If you focus on just taking it one day at a time, without worrying about the big picture all at once, you'll start to see results. You'll become a better person: not just physically, but mentally and spiritually, too. Before you know it, these shifts won't feel like something you have to force yourself to do. They'll just be part of who you are.

WHY THIS WORKS

Temptations will keep trying to pull you back when you're trying to move forward, but moments in motion are powerful. The minute you begin shifting your location, focus, and your mindset, you break the pattern that keeps pulling you back into the same temptations. I know this because I've lived it. Every time I've chosen to shift, even in small ways, I built something better for my future. Every moment of resistance is a chance to invest in your future, and someday your future self will thank you.

FINAL THOUGHTS
Shift, Move, and Speak Life

Get rid of the wrong people: prune the dead branches so you can grow stronger.

→ Letting go makes space for real growth and new strength.

→ The Three-Shift Rule helps you move through hard moments: shift your focus, environment, and perspective.

→ When temptation hits, move first, change your environment to break the cycle.

→ Count down: "5, 4, 3, 2, 1…" and take action, this creates momentum.

→ Speak scripture over your life because the Word of God is living and active. What you say shapes how you see yourself.

→ You don't have to stay stuck; start small, shift one step at a time, and freedom will follow.

A LONELY DREAM

Don't wait. The time will never be just right.

- NAPOLEON HILL

WHEN I was twenty-five, I thought of writing a book, becoming an author, and selling books worldwide. Some critics told me I was too young to achieve such big things, but I persisted. It wasn't about how much I knew or my limitations; it was about seizing the opportunity in front of me. That's all that mattered. I knew that as I got older, my experience would accumulate.

As you may already know by now, my ex-girlfriend broke up with me in April 2019, and the very next day, I suddenly had a passion for writing. The reason I had this passion was because the breakup made me realize how even painful experiences can lead to growth, wisdom, and something worth putting on paper. No one in my family had ever become an author. At that point, I was the first to do it; it was a lonely road. It was confusing, but I stayed persistent and dreamt big because I had a big imagination.

There was a lot of speculation from some people around me. Most people do not know how to see beyond what meets the eye. All they saw was me trying to write a book, thinking I was a wannabe or something. I kept going and moving forward. I believed in my vision even when others couldn't see it. I spent hours writing, revising, and learning about the publishing industry daily. I researched how to self-publish, how to market my book, and how to reach readers worldwide. It was a steep learning curve, but I was determined to make my dream a reality.

The critics' voices were loud, but my passion was louder. I remember sitting in my small Oro Valley apartment surrounded by notes and drafts. The nights were long, and the road ahead was tough, but I didn't give up. I knew I could achieve my goal if I kept working hard and stayed focused. My ex-girlfriend's departure was painful, but it catalyzed my journey. I channeled all my emotions into my writing. The heartbreak fueled my creativity, and I poured my soul into my book. It was a story that needed to be told, and I was determined to tell it.

As the months passed, my manuscript took shape. I faced numerous rejections from publishers and agents, but each rejection made me more determined. I believed in my book, and I knew it was worth fighting for. Self-doubt crept in many times, but I reminded myself why I started. It wasn't about proving the critics wrong but fulfilling my dream.

I reached out to other authors and joined writing groups. Their support and advice were invaluable. I learned that persistence was key and that progress took time. Every successful author has faced obstacles, and I was no different. I embraced the challenges, knowing they were part of the journey. It is important to understand that every good thing in life takes time. Much like cooking, great meals require more time than microwavable foods.

After months of hard work, my book was ready for publication. I self-published it and began marketing it online. I used social media to reach potential readers and connected with book bloggers for reviews. Slowly but surely, my book gained traction. People started buying and reading it, and the feedback was positive. Seeing my book in readers' hands was an indescribable feeling. It made all the hard work worth it. My persistence paid off, and my dream was slowly becoming a reality. I continued to promote my book, doing book signings and events to reach more readers. My confidence grew, and so did my audience.

Now, I am a published author. I am on the third segment of my book signing tour across the entire Phoenix valley during the summer of 2024 as I write this manuscript. I am humbled and proud to say that Barnes & Noble stores are placing orders of my hardcover and softcover books. It's incredible to walk into a bookstore and see my book displayed. All the doubts and criticisms have faded away. I proved to myself that I could do it.

Looking back, I realize it wasn't just about writing a book. It was about believing in God and in the vision He has given me. It was about taking a chance and not letting fear or criticism hold me back. My journey taught me the importance of persistence and the power of following your dreams, no matter how impossible they may seem.

To anyone who feels too young or inexperienced to chase their dreams, I say this: start now. Don't wait for the perfect moment because it may never come. Every moment you spend idling is a moment lost. Take the first step, no matter how small, and keep moving forward. The road may be lonely and confusing but stay persistent. Trust in the Lord and He will guide you. Critics will always be there, but their words don't define you. What matters is your belief in God and His plan for you. Embrace the challenges and learn from them. Every obstacle is an opportunity to grow and become stronger.

Remember the story of Jeremiah from the Bible. He was appointed a prophet at a young age and felt inadequate, but God told him not to say he was too young. Jeremiah trusted in his calling and went on to do great things. Age is just a number, and inexperience is temporary. What matters to God is your willingness to take action and seize the opportunities in front of you.

In the end, your journey is yours alone. Others may not understand or support you, but that's okay. Keep your eyes on your goal and stay true to your path. Your dreams are worth pursuing, and you have the power to make them a reality. When I look around, I see most people following a path that's been set for generations. This path, familiar and steady, usually starts with going to college, getting a solid education, then finding a job with a steady paycheck. They buy a house, make payments, and work for a boss who sets their income. This routine includes plans for retirement, and everything seems so well-structured and predictable. It's a road that's been followed for decades, maybe even hundreds of years.

When you have a God-given dream of your own, suppose you want to carve out a unique path, it feels different. You stand out. Sometimes, God sets you apart. He brings people into your life who understand, support, and encourage you to keep going. He also may remove people who don't share or understand this vision, and that can make the journey feel lonely.

You may feel like you're walking a solitary road, and there are moments when it's tough. It's not easy breaking away from what everyone else does and pursuing something that might not come with the same guarantees, structure, or familiarity. When you stay focused on what's in front of you right now and stay consistent, then you're creating a foundation for the future. Being in the moment, putting in the work daily, is how you build toward your dreams. It's how you can turn "someday" into reality. While it may differ from what others are used to or expect, that's okay. Oftentimes the road less traveled is the one that leads you to where you are meant to be.

So, I remind myself daily that if I focus on today, on the opportunities right here, I can make tomorrow look the way I dream it to be. It's a journey that takes patience, consistency, and a lot of faith. I know that every step I take, even when it's hard, is leading me somewhere worth going.

IF YOU FEEL GOD HAS PLACED SOMETHING IN YOUR HEART, PURSUE IT

So, if you have a vision, go after it with everything you have. Don't let fear or doubt hold you back. Be persistent, be resilient, and most importantly, believe in the promises the Lord has in store for you, because He knows the right path for your life better than you do.

The journey won't be easy, but it will be worth it. Over time, through the development of experience and knowledge, you will grow in value. Not just because of what you've achieved, but because of what you've endured and learned along the way. Your dreams are within reach. All you must do is take the first step and keep moving forward. Start now, and you will be amazed at what you can achieve. In most cases, especially when uncertainty clouds your path and you're not sure what the next step is, the best thing you can do is simply step out the door. Opportunities often present themselves spontaneously when you move forward, and that simple act of showing up has been one of the most valuable rules I've learned.

The most important thing is this: fear regret more than failure. The reason why is because time is non-refundable. There are no reset buttons. That's why time is so valuable. Even the wealthiest people in the world spend fortunes just to find time with their families and friends.

Looking back, I am grateful for every challenge and criticism. They shaped me into the person I am today. The critics, in their own way, helped shape my motives and pushed me to clarify why I was doing what I was doing. Whether they realized it or not, my doubters were my biggest fans because they watched me closely when I thought no one was looking. They helped me understand the importance of time and how crucial it is to fulfill the plans that the Lord has for my life. No one else can walk out what God has called me to do. I know I can't do it without the help of the Holy Spirit. I am proud of my journey and excited for what the future holds. It all started with a vision and the decision to take action, despite the odds.

THERE IS NO PERFECT TIME. ACT NOW.

I still remember vividly when my sister Ruth and I planned a spontaneous trip to Scottsdale, as we often do, to visit some stores in the Fashion Square Mall and explore the area. Ruth, a perfume expert with a large variety of niche perfumes in her collection, was excited to introduce me to some new fragrances at Neiman Marcus. The highlight of our trip was testing out perfumes and colognes, which I found both intriguing and enlightening.

As we walked into Neiman Marcus, the elegant atmosphere and sophisticated scents filled the air, making me eager to dive into the world of fragrances. Ruth guided me to the perfume section, her eyes sparkling with enthusiasm.

"You have to try White Gardenia Petals by Illuminum," she said, handing me a sleek bottle. "It's the perfume that Kate Middleton, Princess of Wales, wore on her wedding day to Prince William. It's a delicate and elegant floral scent."

Her voice was brimming with anticipation. I was fascinated by this fun fact and excited to experience the fragrance that held such historical significance. As I inhaled the scent, I was immediately struck by its elegance and delicacy. The floral notes were subtle yet captivating, and I could understand why it was chosen for such a momentous occasion.

Ruth, being the expert she is, didn't stop there. She had me try several other niche perfumes, each with a unique and enchanting aroma. However, after a very short time—about five minutes—my ability to distinguish between the different fragrances started to diminish. Everything began to smell the same. It was as if my senses had been overwhelmed, and I could no longer appreciate the distinct qualities of each perfume.

Sensing my frustration, one of the store associates approached me with a cup of coffee beans. "Here, smell these," she suggested. "It will help neutralize the previous scents." I took a whiff of the coffee beans, and it was like hitting a reset button for my nose. Suddenly, I could discern the unique characteristics of each fragrance once again.

That experience showed me as a powerful metaphor for the mind. Just as even the most classic and elegant fragrances can become dull to our senses after repeated exposure, dwelling on a brilliant thought or profound idea for too long can cause it to lose its impact. When you first conceive a goal, a plan, or a vision, it often feels fresh, exciting, and full of potential. However, if you overthink it without taking action, the initial enthusiasm can fade, and the idea may begin to seem less significant.

This phenomenon is known as analysis paralysis, where overthinking an idea or situation leads to inaction or a loss of enthusiasm. It's a common trap that many people fall into, especially when they share their dreams and thoughts with others and receive feedback that causes them to second-guess themselves. The initial excitement wanes, and what was once a profound, incomparable idea begins to appear dull and insignificant.

I realized that while it's important to seriously consider an idea, especially if it involves taking notes and planning, there comes a point where you must take action. Lingering too long in hesitation can cause you to lose sight of how brilliant your idea is. Just like how my ability to appreciate exquisite perfumes faded after prolonged exposure, the same can happen to our thoughts and ideas when we don't act on them.

To avoid this trap, you need to balance contemplation with action. Yes, plan and think things through the steps, but don't let your mind overrun you to the point of stagnation. Take decisive steps. Start building momentum. Even keeping your dreams private until they're well underway can help preserve your enthusiasm and keep outside opinions from dampening your spirit.

The lesson I learned that day in Neiman Marcus with Ruth wasn't just about the fascinating world of niche perfumes. It was about the importance of acting on our ideas before they lose their luster. Like the majestic scent of an expensive cologne, even brilliant ideas can fade if you don't move on them. It all starts with a decision, and choosing not to decide is still a decision. That indecision is dangerous. I know people who claim they "just have trouble getting started." Truthfully, they don't have an issue. They have a choice they're refusing to make.

If you feel lost and unsure of your life path, your answer is simple: get moving. Move in any direction. Go for a walk. Take a swim. Make *any* move. Sometimes God plants ideas in your mind once you're already in motion. So, walk out the door every morning and just move. Ask the Holy Spirit for guidance. Seek first the Kingdom of Heaven. Then move. God can steer you, but you need to start the car.

Now, maybe you're thinking, "Well, Jon, God has me in the waiting season. Maybe I need to be still." What will help you understand is that even though Moses and the Israelites were in the wilderness, they were still moving, and to them it may have seemed like waiting. They were walking. They were going somewhere. So, move. Your time is right now. If you still don't know what to do with your life, find someone who is hard to love and serve them. That's where God begins to work on your heart. It's almost like a solo version of military service. Serve someone difficult. Love them. Let God work in you through that. As you serve, He'll begin to show you the next step. It starts with one thing: move.

Take that leap of faith. Your mind is very powerful, but sometimes it can work against you. That's why simple thinking often works best. Keep it simple and just start. Time is not refundable, and it doesn't wait.

WAITING COULD HOLD YOU BACK

Acting now opens doors that hesitation keeps closed. Take the first step today and see where it leads.

We make choices all the time, even when we don't realize it. When it comes to the big decisions, the ones that could shape our future, we often handle them differently. Sometimes, we hesitate, hoping for the "perfect" moment, or waiting until we feel "ready." What some may not know is that not making a decision is a decision in itself. It's a choice to stay exactly where you are, which often leads to missed opportunities.

Making a choice now is crucial because too often, we waste energy worrying about what tomorrow will bring or planning for the future without taking the appropriate steps today. I've experienced this myself. There were times I kept thinking about the future, trying to get everything "just right" before taking action, only to end up with nothing to show for it. It's easy to keep putting things off, telling ourselves we're waiting for the right time, but honestly, that moment doesn't always come. If we're not careful, indecision starts to control our lives.

When we don't choose, we're actively choosing not to try. This kind of hesitation can be one of the biggest obstacles to success. As Billy Graham once said, *"Indecision is itself a choice."* That thought really resonates with me because it's a reminder that not acting is still an action, and it's usually not one that leads us forward. People often feel they're either too young to go after their dreams or too old to start fresh. I've seen this in myself and others. That kind of thinking can keep us from tapping into our full potential. It's vital to start now regardless of your age.

My favorite Bible story, one that I tend to share frequently, is about the prophet Jeremiah. He was called by God to be a prophet while he was still very young, even though he felt far too inexperienced to handle such a big task. When God revealed Jeremiah's calling, Jeremiah responded with doubt: *"I do not know how to speak; I am too young."* God's response was direct and simple: *"Do not say, 'I am too young.' You must go to everyone I send you to and say whatever*

I command you." Then God touched Jeremiah's mouth and reassured him, *"I have put my words in your mouth."*

This story is a reminder that it's less about your age and more about your willingness to act. Jeremiah could have allowed his fears to keep him from his calling but instead, he chose to trust and move forward. When he chose to obey the Lord's command, he became one of history's most significant prophets.

Whether you're starting young or are much older and have only now found yourself reading this book, know that it's never too late to begin planning and taking action toward what you feel called to pursue. When you start early, you're not only building experience but also resilience and adaptability. Still, taking that leap isn't always easy, is it? Even later in your years, when you are advanced in age, taking initiative and starting now holds far greater value than the thought that tells you it's too late.

The fear of failure looms large for many of us, me included. It's tempting to think that failure means we're not cut out for something, but I've come to believe that failure is part of the process, not the end of it.

Thomas Edison, the inventor of the lightbulb, said it best, *"I have not failed. I've just found 10,000 ways that won't work."* His persistence is a perfect example of how embracing failure can lead to something world-changing. If Edison had waited for the perfect condition, or let fear stop him, we might not have had the electric lightbulb today.

So, why is it so important to act now? The reason is because every moment you spend waiting is a moment lost. Life is full of opportunities, but you have to be willing to seize them, even if it means stepping into the unknown. Waiting for the "right" time is often just another form of procrastination. Let's be honest, procrastination is a thief. It steals tomorrow's opportunities one delayed decision at a time.

Don't let the fear of being "too young" or "too old" hold you back. Time won't wait, but you can make the most of it by choosing to act today.

WHERE'S YOUR ENERGY GOING?

I remember back in the summer of 2013, I was, in all honesty, a bit of a mess. My room was chaotic. Clothes were scattered around, papers were piled up on my desk, and random things were just lying everywhere. It wasn't just my room that felt disorganized; my mind was just as cluttered. I looked around one day and thought, *this isn't how I want to live.* I didn't want my life to feel this messy, so I made a decision right then. *I'm going to change this. I'm going to start now.* I decided to start small, focusing on cleaning my space as a way to clear my mind, too.

At first, it was simply about getting my room in order. I didn't even have a car at that time. I realized that if I couldn't keep my room and desk clean, then any new responsibility, like owning a car, would likely become just as chaotic. So, I began with the basics. I organized my desk, sorted through my belongings, and tossed out things that weren't serving me. Each time I put something in its place, I felt like I was organizing a part of my mind as well. As my room became less chaotic, so did my thoughts. I noticed a shift happening, as if each small step towards tidiness was clearing out mental clutter.

Keeping my space organized became a routine that changed more than just my surroundings. I started making my bed every morning, cleaning my desk every night, and paying attention to those little habits that kept my environment clear and peaceful. This simple act of taking care of my space taught me discipline and consistency. It gave me a sense of control that I hadn't felt before. As I developed this routine, I found myself naturally focusing more on things that mattered. The small things I did daily began to make a real difference in my life. It wasn't just about a tidy room; it was about setting up a life that reflected my goals and values.

When I eventually got my first car, a 2004 Honda Civic, I carried this mindset with me. I kept my car as clean and organized as I could. I took time to clean the seats, the steering wheel, and even the little crevices. It might seem small, but it was important to me. I didn't want my car to become another source of chaos in my life. I wanted it to reflect the order I was working hard to create. The discipline I had built through simple habits like cleaning and organizing was starting to spill over into other areas of my life.

Slowly working on these little tasks had a bigger impact than I could have imagined. It helped me filter my mind, making me eager to focus my energy on things that truly mattered. I began to realize the importance of the things I spent my mental energy on, like the people I surrounded myself with, the food I chose to eat, and the personal growth I wanted to pursue. Doing something as simple as keeping my surroundings clean sparked a deeper desire to better myself as a person. I found myself being more aware of what I watched, what I listened to, and who I associated with. The more I focused on these little positive habits, the more I wanted to invest in things that added value to my life.

As time went on, I noticed that my interests started to shift. I wanted to be around people who uplifted me, who shared my values and goals. I became selective about the energy I allowed into my life. This wasn't just about a tidy space anymore; it was about creating a healthy mental environment, one that encouraged me to grow and improve. I began questioning the content I consumed and the conversations I engaged in. Instead of just passively letting things influence me, I took charge. I began to fill my life with things that aligned with the person I wanted to become.

So, think about how you're really spending your time. Are you caught up in family gossip? Watching too much TV, or playing endless video games? Maybe you're just going through the week without any plan. Are you spending time with people who aren't growing or getting caught up in useless chatter or jokes that don't add any value to your life? These things might seem small, but they can really hold you back from moving forward, or from doing what God might have planned for you.

Your brain uses energy just to function, whether it's processing information or making decisions. The more you fill it with distractions and things that don't help you grow, the less capacity you have to focus on priorities. If you want to make something meaningful out of your time, these little choices add up. I know I used to fall into these same habits by letting time slip by on things that weren't helping me grow. Once I started engaging with each moment fully, I began to see real changes.

It's all about choosing where you put your energy. Every hour you spend on distractions or unhelpful people is time you could be investing in something much better, like your goals, your relationships, or your future. So, ask yourself: Are the things you're spending time on helping you get closer to where you want to be? Make every moment count and use your brain's energy to fuel your growth and become the person you're meant to be.

You must change how you think. Disciplining yourself is the first step toward that. Catch the words you say. For example, if you say, "I don't have time," catch yourself and say, "I do have time." If you want more time in your day, get even busier. Words are what fuel and empower your mind, either powerfully or negatively. Fill up your schedule to the max, fill up your calendars, and try to get busier than ever before. That's how you will be hungry to find more time than you thought you didn't have. You can say, "I will create time. I will find a way. I will find time," because ultimately, you make time for things you care about.

FINAL THOUGHTS
Start Now, Don't Overthink It

There is no perfect time. Act now.

→ Overthinking leads to delays, so don't let your mind talk you out of progress.

→ Some planning is wise, but waiting too long without action slows momentum.

→ Even small steps, like jotting down notes, move you forward.

→ Think briefly, then take action. Don't get stuck in analysis.

→ Surround yourself with a growth-minded culture and healthy mindset.

→ Remember, you don't have to accept everyone's opinion, protect your mental space.

→ Pay attention to where your energy is going. Small daily choices shape your future.

EFFICIENT TIME WITH GOD

"Be still, and know that I am God."

— PSALM 46:10

ULTIMATELY, GOD is the creator of time, so placing Him first in the morning makes you more effective in your thinking. The letter of the Apostle Paul to the Philippian church wrote that making your requests known to God and prioritizing Him will guard your heart, and most importantly, your mind. Not just from sin (although that is often the focus of Paul's message), but also from the worries and troubles of life. Prioritizing God frees your mind, allowing you to focus more on the things that are right in front of you.

Paul had much to say about the mind. In fact, most of his teaching is about protecting your mind from the devil and allowing the

Holy Spirit to take the lead. Your mind is the most important device you have. It can either make or break your life. So, ask yourself: what are you focusing on that's preventing you from focusing on a simple task in front of you and taking it one step at a time? Is it worry, financial issues, spiritual problems, or family affairs?

The Holy Spirit's role in your life is to lead you into all truth, to comfort you, and to help you with every detail of your life. By setting aside time in the morning to be in the Word and spend time with the Holy Spirit, your mind becomes protected. That way, when you head to work or wherever you go, your mind will be alert and clear, focused on whatever you need to accomplish that day.

Starting your day with God sets the tone for everything that follows. When you wake up, the first thing you should do is spend a few moments in prayer and reading the Bible. This practice centers your thoughts on God and His will for your day. You'll find that your mind feels more at peace, and you can handle challenges with a calm and focused demeanor. The Holy Spirit works within you, providing guidance and strength, making even the most difficult tasks seem manageable. When you make time for God in the morning, you're inviting Him into every part of your day. Your relationship with Him grows stronger, and you become more attuned to His voice. You start to recognize His presence in all aspects of your life, whether at work, with your family, or while running errands. That constant awareness helps you stay grounded and less likely to be overwhelmed by the distresses of daily life.

As Philippians 4:6-7 reminds us, *"Do not be anxious about anything, but in every situation, by prayer and petition, with thanksgiving, present your requests to God. And the peace of God, which transcends all understanding, will guard your hearts and your minds in Christ Jesus."*

This verse is a powerful reminder that we do not have to carry our burdens alone.

When we prioritize our time with God, we allow His peace to fill our hearts and minds, protecting us from anxiety and worry. Another important aspect of starting your day with God is that it helps you to focus on what matters. In today's fast-paced world, it is easy to get caught up in the hustle and bustle and forget about the things that are most important. When you spend time with God, you are reminded of His love and His plans for you. That perspective helps you to prioritize your tasks and focus on what's important, rather than getting bogged down by trivial matters.

Spending time with God in the morning also helps you to develop a habit of gratitude. When you start your day by thanking God for His blessings, you set a positive tone for everything that follows. This attitude of gratitude can help you to see the good in every situation, even when things don't go as planned. It also helps you to become more mindful of how God is working in your life, which can strengthen your faith and trust in Him.

Beyond the spiritual benefits, starting your day with God brings practical benefits, too. When your mind is clear and focused, you're more productive and efficient in your work. You make better decisions and think more creatively. This can lead to greater progress in your work and deeper fulfillment in your personal life.

A STRONG START

Spending time in God's presence renews your mind and refreshes your spirit, grounding you in peace and purpose. Like a battery recharged, you're empowered to face the day with grace and confidence, fully aligned with His guidance. The Holy Spirit plays a crucial role in this process. As the third person of the Trinity, the Holy Spirit is our helper and guide. He gives us wisdom and discernment, helping us navigate the challenges of life. When we spend time with God in the morning, we are inviting the Holy Spirit to be an active participant in our day. That means you do not need to live life alone. This allows us to be more in tune with His guidance and more open to His leading.

One of the key teachings of the Apostle Paul is the importance of renewing our minds. In Romans 12:2, he writes, *"Do not conform to the pattern of this world, but be transformed by the renewing of your mind. Then you will be able to test and approve what God's will is: His good, pleasing and perfect will."* This verse highlights the importance of aligning our thoughts with God's thoughts. When we start our day with God, we are taking an important step in this process of renewal. We choose to focus on His truth and His promises rather than the lies and distractions of the world.

Making time for God in the morning is one of the best things you can do for your spiritual, mental, and emotional well-being. It sets the tone for the rest of the day, helping you to stay focused, calm, and productive. It strengthens your relationship with God and allows the Holy Spirit to work more effectively in your life. It helps you to prioritize what is important and develop an attitude of gratitude. Most importantly, it protects your mind from the worries and distresses of life, allowing you to focus on the task at hand and take things one step at a time.

So, what is stopping you from making this a priority in your life? Is it worry, financial issues, spiritual problems, or family affairs? Whatever it is, know that God is ready and willing to help you. All you need to do is make the time to invite Him into your day. You are running on borrowed time. Every single day, every moment, is time that ultimately belongs to God. So, make it meaningful, because how you use it is a form of worship. Whether it's for your family, church, or business, whatever God has placed in your hands is for His glory. That's why renewing your mind in Christ is so important. Consider the time that you've been given and understand how sacred it is. Everything we do, in the time we have, is ultimately for Him.

JOSEPH'S STORY:
The Power of Putting God First

Joseph's life is a powerful reminder that when we put God first, everything else, including success, wisdom, and provision follows, as seen in his journey from slavery to a position of high command.

Joseph's story is one of those powerful examples that show what it means to keep faith, even when things look completely hopeless. Here's a guy who was sold into slavery by his own brothers. He ended up in Egypt, working as a slave for Potiphar, an officer of Pharaoh. Now, Joseph could have easily become bitter, angry, and given up on any hope for his life, but he didn't. He chose to keep trusting God and to stay faithful, even in the middle of what looked like a total mess.

When you're facing hardships, do you find it easy to keep faith, or is it a struggle? Joseph's story reminds us that it's possible to keep going, no matter what's thrown our way. His life shows us that it's not about what happens to us, but about how we respond. He didn't let his circumstances define him. Instead, he let his faith in God guide him through each tough situation. God was with him, blessing him in everything he did. Even Potiphar, his boss, noticed something different about Joseph, because everything he touched seemed to succeed. Potiphar put Joseph in charge of his entire household. Imagine that: a slave being given control over everything! That alone speaks volumes about Joseph's character, but more importantly, it shows what can happen when God's presence is with you.

It wasn't all smooth sailing from there. Joseph's life didn't suddenly get easy once he was promoted. In fact, not long after he became overseer, he was falsely accused by Potiphar's wife and thrown into prison. Just like that, everything he had worked for was taken away.

In moments like that, it's easy to feel abandoned, or to question why things happen the way they do. When setbacks hit, do you ever wonder if God is still there? Or if He has a plan through it all?

For Joseph, the answer was to keep going. He didn't let prison crush his spirit. He continued to trust God and served in whatever ways he could. The prison warden noticed his faithfulness and, just like before, Joseph was given a position of responsibility, this time by overseeing all the prisoners. This kind of faithfulness, even in a dark place, is something we can all learn from. Joseph's story challenges us to ask, *"How can I remain faithful and serve, even when I don't understand what's going on?"*

FINDING PURPOSE IN SERVICE

One of the most amazing turning points in Joseph's story is when he was asked to interpret dreams for two of Pharaoh's officials while he was still in prison. Joseph didn't have to help them, because he could have stayed focused on his own problems. He listened to the cupbearer and baker's dreams and offered interpretations, trusting that God would give him wisdom.

Sometimes, helping others can become a blessing for us, even when it seems inconvenient. Have you noticed that stepping out to serve others often brings unexpected rewards? Joseph's act of kindness ended up changing his life. Two years later, when Pharaoh needed someone to interpret his dreams, the cupbearer remembered Joseph's gift and mentioned him to Pharaoh.

Joseph was brought out of prison and given the chance to interpret Pharaoh's dreams, which predicted seven years of abundance followed by seven years of famine. Joseph stayed faithful and trusted God's guidance, he not only interpreted the dreams but also provided a plan to save Egypt from disaster.

Joseph's story is packed with lessons, especially about keeping God first. When we put God at the center of our lives, we invite His presence and guidance into everything we do. His life shows us that when we honor God with our time, our actions, and our choices, He blesses us in ways we couldn't have imagined. Trusting God means making real, daily commitment to follow Him, keep Him first, and rely on Him even when it's hard.

What would it look like to keep God at the center of your life?

Think about it: Joseph didn't let his circumstances hold him back. He didn't let bitterness or anger take over. Imagine if he had given up after being thrown into prison, his story would've turned out completely different. He kept God first; he rose above every challenge and ended up changing not only his life but the lives of countless others.

Today, a lot of people are searching for hope and success, whether in their careers, their relationships, or their personal goals. True success isn't about money, status, or fame. It's about living a life that honors God. When we keep God first, our idea of success changes. It becomes less about what we can get and more about what we can give, how we can serve, and how we can live according to God's purpose for us.

How do you define success, and is that definition aligned with what God wants for your life?

SEEKING FIRST THE KINGDOM

The Bible says, *"Seek first the kingdom of God and His righteousness, and all these things will be added to you"* (Matthew 6:33). This verse really captures what Joseph's story is all about. When we prioritize God, everything else begins to fall into place. It doesn't mean life will be easy or free from problems, but it does mean that we can trust God to guide us and bless us along the way.

Are there areas in your life where you could put God first and trust Him with the outcome?

Like Joseph, we can experience God's favor by making the effort to put Him first. That might mean starting our day with prayer, making choices that honor Him, or staying faithful even when things are tough. By doing that, we're setting ourselves up for blessings and purpose beyond anything we could arrange on our own.

Joseph's journey is a reminder that faithfulness and perseverance go hand in hand. When we're faithful to God, even in the small things, He is faithful to us. Joseph didn't know how things would turn out, but he trusted God with each step. He kept going, even when he didn't have all the answers. He accomplished things that were beyond his own abilities.

PRAYER HELPS CARRY THE HEAVY LOAD

I first met Tami on April 13, 2024, at a book signing in Arizona. She stopped by my table late in the afternoon, and though our initial exchange was brief, it left an impression on me. Tami introduced herself as the owner of The Wet Clam food truck business and mentioned how much she admired my journey as an author. There was something about her demeanor, a quiet heaviness that made it seem as though she was carrying the weight of the world on her shoulders. Before leaving, she asked if I'd be open to grabbing coffee the next day. I agreed, not realizing how much her story would resonate with me.

When we met the following morning, Tami opened up about the challenges she was facing. Her food truck business, which she had worked tirelessly to build, was struggling to stay afloat. On top of that, she was dealing with personal financial issues and a deep sense of spiritual unrest.

She shared that not long ago, her best friend was murdered right in her own home, and she had been dealing with numerous court appearances ever since. She had also gone through several major surgeries, adding to everything she was already carrying. Her adulthood had been shaped by deep loss, as both of her parents had passed away, leaving her to face life's challenges on her own.

As she spoke, her voice wavered between tears and urgency, and I felt an immediate pull to be there for her in any way I could.

"Everything just feels chaotic," she said, stirring her coffee absentmindedly. "I wake up every day feeling like I'm already behind, and no matter what I do, nothing seems to change."

She went on to share how she had been juggling countless obligations, including running her business, managing her household, and trying to maintain her faith. The stress was unrelenting, and it was starting to take a toll on her health and well-being.

"I'm doing everything I can, but it feels like I'm drowning," she admitted. Yet, amid all the hardship, there was one thing she had clung to: prayer.

"I don't even know how to explain it," Tami said. "It's not like my problems just disappear, but there's something about praying that helps me stay grounded. It gives me a deep, lasting peace that keeps me going."

As Tami spoke, I could see how much her connection to God meant to her. Despite everything falling apart around her, she held on to her faith like a lifeline. Each morning, she set aside time to pray, read her Bible, and seek guidance from God.

"It's not always easy," she confessed, "but it's the only thing that gives me the strength to handle everything I have on my plate."

Her words reminded me of Philippians 4:6-7: *"Do not be anxious about anything, but in every situation, by prayer and petition, with thanksgiving, present your requests to God. And the peace of God, which transcends all understanding, will guard your hearts and your minds in Christ Jesus."*

Tami was living proof of that promise. Her circumstances hadn't magically changed, but her mind was at peace, and that peace allowed her to navigate her challenges with clarity and strength. Over the weeks that followed, Tami and I stayed in touch. She would often update me on her progress, sharing both her victories and setbacks. Though life didn't suddenly become easy, she was learning to manage her many obligations in a way that felt sustainable. Prayer, she explained, had become her anchor.

"It's what keeps me balanced," she said. "I still have a lot on my plate, but I don't feel as overwhelmed as I used to."

Tami began to approach her days differently. Instead of rushing into the chaos, she started each morning by centering herself in God's presence. That time of prayer and reflection helped her focus, giving her the clarity she needed to prioritize her tasks. Slowly but surely, things began to improve. Her food truck started attracting more customers, and she found creative ways to cut costs and increase profits. More than anything, she found the strength to keep going, even when things got tough.

"There's something about handing everything over to God," she told me. "It's like letting go of this enormous weight I've been carrying. I don't have to have all the answers because I know He's in control."

Listening to Tami, I couldn't help but think about how often we try to handle everything on our own. We juggle endless responsibilities, thinking we have to do it all ourselves, and then wonder why we feel so drained. What if we took a step back? What if, like Tami, we made time to connect with God and invite Him into our struggles?

The Bible reminds us in Jeremiah 29:12-13: *"Then you will call on me and come and pray to me, and I will listen to you. You will seek me and find me when you seek me with all your heart."* Tami sought God with her whole heart, and in doing so, she found a peace that surpassed understanding. That peace didn't erase her problems, but it gave her the strength to face them.

One of the things that stood out to me most about Tami's story was how her mindset had shifted. She no longer felt paralyzed by stress or overwhelmed by her obligations. Instead, she approached each day with a sense of purpose and trust.

"It's like my perspective has changed," she said. "I'm still busy, and there's still a lot to do, but I feel equipped to handle it now."

Her story shows how staying connected to the One who gives us strength can carry us through and help us keep going. When you align your plans with God's will, you're not just relying on your own abilities. You're tapping into a power far greater than yourself.

Tami often described prayer as a way of "resetting" her mind each morning. "It's like stepping into a calm space before the day starts," she explained. "Even if the rest of the day is chaotic, I carry that peace with me. It changes everything."

That peace, she said, allowed her to juggle her many responsibilities without feeling consumed by them. It gave her clarity to make better decisions and the assurance that she wasn't facing her challenges alone. Her story shows how life can start to change when someone decides to put God first.

"There's just something about knowing God is in your corner," she said. "It makes all the difference."

Romans 12:2 says, *"Do not conform to the pattern of this world, but be transformed by the renewing of your mind. Then you will be able to test and approve what God's will is—His good, pleasing and perfect will."*

For Tami, that renewal began with prayer. It was in those quiet moments with God that she found the strength and peace to navigate her busy life.

So, how do you start your day? Do you dive headfirst into the busyness of life, or do you take a moment to connect with God?

Whether you're juggling work, family, or personal challenges, remember that you don't have to carry it all alone. Take a moment to pray and see how it transforms your day. You might just find, like Tami did, that peace of mind makes all the difference.

TOO BUSY FOR WHAT MATTERED MOST

I remember so many times, especially back in 2018, when life felt like a constant cycle of work, exhaustion, and trying to keep up with everything. That year, I was working two busy jobs, dating a girl, and just trying to stay afloat. My full-time job was at The Views Golf Club in Oro Valley, Arizona, a beautiful eighteen-hole golf course, surrounded by a retirement community, with some of the best landscaping I'd ever seen. The entire course was so well-maintained, designed with incredible attention to detail. Everything from the greens to the fairways felt perfectly constructed.

It was cool when I first learned that The Views Golf Club had recently received an award, not long before I started working there. Thanks to its exceptional maintenance team, it had been recognized for having some of the best fairways, approaches, and greens. One of my main responsibilities was cutting new hole locations on the greens each morning, an important task that kept the course in top condition and provided variety for golfers.

To do this, I used a specialized hole cutter, a heavy, hollow metal tool with handlebars. I would press it into the green and rotate it to cut a clean section of turf, then pull it out to leave a fresh hole. The removed turf was placed in the previous hole to help the green recover. After cutting the new hole, I'd insert the cup, carefully leveling it with the surface. If it sat too high or too low, it could affect the way the ball rolled across the green surface, making putts unpredictable. The location of the hole changed daily based on skill levels. The front of the green (red area) was for beginners, the middle (white) for intermediate players, and the back (blue) for advanced golfers. Rotating hole placements helped preserve the greens and added variety for returning players.

Doing that job before sunrise required precision, even in low visibility. A properly placed hole made a significant difference in the quality of play. Golfers appreciated the effort behind the scenes to make every round smooth and enjoyable. While it was a peaceful place for visitors, for me, it was where my day began. When I say began, I mean early. I'd wake up at 4:00 in the morning, barely awake, and get ready for my shift. From 4:30 a.m. to 2:30 p.m., I was at the course cutting holes, maintaining carts, and handling a variety of tasks. It was exhausting. That wasn't even the hardest part. As soon as I clocked out, I wasn't heading home to rest.

By 3:30 p.m., I was already driving across town to work another shift at Subway, from 4:00 p.m. to 11:00 p.m. I worked five days a week, closing the store, mopping floors, restocking, and handling late-night customers. By the time I got home, it was close to midnight, I barely had time to eat or unwind before getting up and doing it all over again. For a year and a half, that was my routine. Nonstop work. Barely any sleep. No real time to process anything. I was constantly moving, constantly exhausted, constantly trying to catch up with life. I thought I didn't have time for the things that mattered. Most mornings, I'd wake up, grab my phone, check my messages, and immediately start thinking about everything I had to do that day. I'd rush through my morning routine, barely have time to eat, and then be out the door. My mind was already full before I even stepped outside.

When I started my day that way, it didn't take much to throw me off. If someone cut me off in traffic, it irritated me. If a customer at Subway was rude, it stuck with me. If something unexpected happened, I had no mental energy to handle it. It felt like my entire day was running me instead of me running my day. Eventually, I realized the error of my ways.

I was starting my days on the wrong foundation.

START YOUR DAY WITH THE BIG THINGS FIRST

Have you ever noticed how starting your day with the small, easy tasks can make it almost impossible to fit in the important ones later. It's much like filling a large glass cup with sand first before trying to add large cubes, which won't fit properly. You might not have known, but the order in which you start your day matters. There's a natural rhythm to the way you go about your day and following that order can make things easier on your mind and help keep your mental health in check.

Filling a cup with sand before the large cubes doesn't allow everything to fit. The sand takes up all the space, and no matter how much you shake the cup, those big cubes just won't fit. If you put the large cubes in first and then pour the sand afterward, it seeps perfectly into the small areas in between. Every square inch of the cup gets filled, no wasted space and no air gaps, because of the order it was filled.

Now imagine the opposite: if I filled the glass cup with hectic "sand" first, such as distractions, distress, and worries, that would be the end of my day. Everything would be packed in, leaving no space for your most important priorities. That's precisely what was happening to me. I was letting the little things like worries, distractions, and busyness fill up all the space. There was no room left for the things that was necessary.

Jesus said in Matthew 6:34, *"Do not worry about tomorrow, for tomorrow will worry about itself. Each day has enough trouble of its own."* That verse is simple but powerful. Every day brings its own worries. There will always be things to stress about, like work, responsibilities, and unexpected challenges. If we don't set the right foundation first, those things will take over.

I realized I needed to switch things up. Instead of waking up and filling my mind with pressing obligations, I needed to start with God. Even if it was just five or ten minutes, making Him my priority was essential to me. So, I made a change. Before checking my phone and rushing into my day, I prayed for a few minutes. Some mornings, I'd read a quick Bible verse, nothing long, just something to center my thoughts. Other times, I'd sit in silence and just breathe, letting myself be still before the day's craziness started. I began to notice something. On the days I started with God, everything else felt lighter. I still had the same workload, long shifts, and responsibilities, but my mindset was different. I wasn't as easily irritated. The things that used to stress me out didn't affect me as much. I felt more at peace, more focused, and more patient because I had already made sure to put the big things first.

Just like those big cubes in the glass, I put God in first, and everything else fit around Him. The sand, which represents the daily responsibilities, eustress, and distractions, still came, but it didn't overwhelm me. It just settled into place.

That's the power of starting your day with a big, loving God.

The best part is that it doesn't have to be complicated or time-consuming to start your day with God. You don't need to spend an hour in deep Bible study every morning (though if you can, that's great). Even a five-minute prayer, or a moment of stillness, can completely shift your day. If you're feeling overwhelmed, like your day controls you instead of the other way around, I challenge you: start your day with God. Pause, pray, thank Him for the day, and meditate on His Word; doing this can realign your heart, shift the atmosphere around you, and make the challenges ahead feel lighter. I promise, it makes a difference. When you put the right things in place, everything else will fit exactly where it's supposed to.

WHY PRIORITIZING GOD CAN PROTECT YOUR MENTAL HEALTH AND WELL-BEING

A study from Harvard T.H Chan School of Public Health found that people who prioritize their spiritual lives and seek meaning beyond themselves tend to have better mental health and overall well-being. They are more resilient in the face of eustress and challenges. This aligns with the biblical principle of seeking first the Kingdom of God. When you focus on God and His purposes, you are better equipped to handle life's difficulties and find true success.

Only the Lord can guard your mind from the worries and distresses of this life. Ultimately, your life is a spiritual experience. Though you live on earth, you are a spiritual being living in a temporary human body that is running out of time.

Time is not going to wait for you. In fact, if you become indecisive, time will eventually make the decision for you. So why not start it off with the Lord in the morning? By doing this, you set the tone for the rest of your day. It doesn't take long to spend time with the Creator of the universe. Simply talk to Him, read His Word, and see what He wants to speak to you through it. It's that simple. Before you know it, thirty minutes have flown by.

I've seen the difference between people who prioritize time with the Lord and those who don't. Those who do often walk around with a glow on their faces and joy in their hearts. The hope of their Savior fuels them during the day. Those who don't manage their lives often carry the weight and worries of life on their shoulders, draining their energy.

How wonderful it is to know that your life is covered by the blood of Jesus and that you've been made right with God. That joy alone brings peace into your mind and heart. You walk with a sense of purpose, especially in your workplace, and it's a beautiful thing.

Think of the entire universe. It's incredibly complex, and yet it operates smoothly. Don't you want the same God who controls the universe to take charge of your busy schedule? I do. After all, God is an expert. Trusting Him in everything gives me a deep sense of peace. No human mind can begin to imagine the complexity of two hundred billion galaxies that spin in our universe, each with hundreds of millions of stars. Yet, God numbers every star by name.

That's why it's my joy to surrender my entire life to the Lord who made it all, giving Him my mind, heart, soul, and strength. It saves me time when I am carefree during a major problem. I can stay calm during a major problem because I know the same God who controls the universe is also in charge of my mind and daily schedule.

There were times I felt completely weighed down by worries about the future. I had dreams of starting a family and building a new career, but focusing too much on what lay ahead robbed me of what I could have experienced in that moment. The enemy stole my peace, and I felt burdened every day. The key is to focus on today. Prepare for your future using today. Plan for tomorrow by being intentional with today. If you're always weighed down by what's coming next, you'll miss the opportunity to be present with the day you are given.

Today is all you have. It's the only gift you have to work with. Don't let the enemy rob you of your day and your peace. Life is busy, and we have much to do, but when you allow God to be the Lord over your time, when you surrender to Him what belongs to Him (your time), you'll experience peace like never before. Becoming serious about the things of God by studying His Word and spending time in prayer protects you from losing your peace. People who don't keep God first often become overwhelmed by life and what's happening around the globe. They become distressed, weighed down, and distracted. They lose time by worrying.

You can save time by spending time with the Lord. It takes time to save time. Protecting your peace in God will ultimately save you from the outside noise, like bills, pressures, and other kinds of distractions. When you spend time with God, you stay focused and grounded. You stop wasting time, and you start walking with purpose, on purpose.

HOW BRANDON STAYS STRONG THROUGH LIFE'S CHALLENGES

I remember the time when I met my friend Brandon. It was at Black Rock Coffee in April 2023. He walked in while I was standing in line on a Sunday morning, rushing to grab a coffee before heading to church. Brandon was behind me with his family, and I casually mentioned my newly released book to him. He seemed genuinely interested, so I offered to share it with him.

We started talking about the book, which was about my father, Viorel, and how he escaped Romania's communist regime in 1989. Our conversation was brief but left a strong first impression. We touched on topics like faith, freedom, resilience, and something about that moment stuck with me. A week later, I was back at the same coffee shop, again rushing to get my coffee before church. Brandon walked in, and to my surprise, he had my book with him, the one he had purchased after our first conversation. That simple moment of recognition and connection turned into a friendship. Over time, we started talking more, and I learned that Brandon had served as a motorcycle police officer before retiring. A few months later, we began running a bi-weekly Bible study together.

One year later, during a Radiant Men's dinner event that Brandon invited me to, we found ourselves sitting in the courtyard, enjoying the outdoor game activities with some friends. As we chatted, Brandon turned to me and said, "Jon, I've been feeling spiritually drained because of my busy work schedule. It's really weighing me down."

His words made me realize how much our spiritual walk with the Lord influences the course of our lives, our days, our weeks, and even our years. Brandon explained how missing church due to his hectic work schedule often left him feeling disconnected and exhausted. On the other hand, when he would find time to attend church and spend time in fellowship with other believers, his spirit and mind would recharge.

"It's a spiritual condition," Brandon said. I could see that he was right. When he goes to church and spends time with God, he feels empowered. When he skips it, he feels drained. It's a reminder of how much we all need that time of spiritual renewal. For Brandon, it's not just about going through the motions of attending church; it's about being spiritually filled so he can face life's challenges with peace and purpose.

FELLOWSHIP MAKES A DIFFERENCE

We meet for coffee almost every Tuesday morning now. It's nothing fancy. I grab a coffee and sit across the table from him. We talk about everyday things, like work, family, life in general. Brandon is the kind of friend who is blunt and sharply focused about everything, a mindset shaped by his years as a police officer. Being sharp and focused helped him on the road to protect himself, and that training taught him to stay attentive to his surroundings and intentional in every situation.

What I've noticed during these meetings is how much the power of association matters in life. Being around like-minded people who share your values and faith can change everything. Brandon has found that being equally yoked with me and some other friends has been a game-changer. He's told me how much it means to him to feel known and cared for by us. That sense of belonging, the feeling of being part of something bigger than yourself, is special and divine.

It's that deep inner feeling in your soul that reminds you there's more to life than just going to work, paying bills, and going home. When you surround yourself with the right people, it gives you a sense of purpose. You feel like you're contributing to something real and that's a feeling money can't buy.

Brandon cares deeply about the spiritual fellowship that goes beyond friendship. Knowing he's investing in something eternal gives him a real sense of peace and belonging. It's not just about today; it's about knowing that one day, we'll all be in heaven with the Lord because we've invested in our spiritual lives.

There's something powerful about being known by others. When you're surrounded by people who genuinely care about you, it fills a deep need within your soul. Without that connection, life can feel lonely, even depressing. When it's just you—or worse, the wrong people—in your life, it's easy to feel like no one cares about you. That's why fellowship is so important. It's not just about hanging out; it's about building relationships that uplift and encourage you.

A JOY THAT COMES FROM FELLOWSHIP

Brandon often talks about how his perspective on life has changed since he started prioritizing fellowship and his spiritual life. He's more focused, more joyful, and more at peace. He sees his life with new clarity, focused more on God's greater plan than daily routines or work.

There's something incredibly fulfilling about knowing that your life is about more than just you. When we invest in fellowship, we're reminded that we're part of God's bigger plan. We're not just living for ourselves, but we're living for Him and for each other. That's what gives life meaning and purpose. That realization has brought Brandon joy and hope. He knows that his time spent with friends, in prayer, and in fellowship is making an eternal impact. That's something we can all strive for. Life is busy, but when we make time for God and for each other, we discover a peace and fulfillment that can't be found anywhere else.

START YOUR DAY WITH GOD'S PEACE

When you put God first, everything else falls into place, bringing clarity, purpose, and strength to handle life's challenges. It's often hard to remind ourselves that today is all we have. Yesterday is gone and tomorrow hasn't arrived yet. It's just a possibility. Today, this very moment, is the only gift we have to work with. When we make ourselves available to God's voice, we honor Him in ways that ripple into every other area of our lives. By choosing to spend time with Him and placing our worries in His hands, we protect our peace. We become intentional with our time, saving it from being consumed by distractions and distress.

You may be thinking, *"If I don't worry about my problems, then who will? Who's going to handle all the things I need to figure out?"*

God doesn't ask us to worry; He asks us to trust Him. The Apostle Paul reminds us in Philippians 4:6-7, *"Do not be anxious about anything, but in every situation, by prayer and petition, with thanksgiving, present your requests to God. The peace of God, which transcends all understanding, will guard your hearts and your minds in Christ Jesus."* This verse is not just a suggestion, but it's a promise.

When we give our worries to God by means of being thankful, He replaces them with peace that doesn't make sense in the natural world. It's like letting go of a heavy weight that we were never meant to carry in the first place.

When you pray and let God take over your mind, it's more than just a spiritual exercise in many ways, it's a profound act of relief. You're handing over what you were never designed to manage alone. You see, the future is not yours to bear. The Bible tells us in Matthew 6:34, *"Therefore do not worry about tomorrow, for tomorrow will worry about itself. Each day has enough trouble of its own."*

That doesn't mean we shouldn't plan or prepare for the future. It means we are called to work in the now. When you use today intentionally, you're building a future without letting the weight of "what-ifs" paralyze you.

By prioritizing God, we tap into a strength and wisdom that are beyond our own abilities. The Holy Spirit, given to us as a gift from the Father, becomes our guide and partner in every detail of our lives. When you wake up in the morning and spend time with God, by reading His Word, praying, and inviting Him into your day, then you're aligning yourself with His perfect will. You're letting the Creator of time show you how to use it most effectively.

Think about that for a moment. The God who spoke the universe into existence cares enough about you to help you manage your schedule. Isn't that incredible?

The Bible tells us in Proverbs 3:5-6, *"Trust in the Lord with all your heart and lean not on your own understanding; in all your ways submit to Him, and He will make your paths straight."* When we prioritize time with God, He clears our minds and gives us wisdom. He doesn't just make us feel better, but He equips us to do better. He shows us what tasks to prioritize, how to balance our responsibilities, and even how to multitask with efficiency and grace.

Life is busy, and we all know it all too well. Between work, family, church, and personal goals, it can feel like there aren't enough hours in the day. When you spend time with God first, you'll notice something remarkable: you accomplish more. Your mind is clearer, your energy is focused, and you're less likely to waste time on things that don't matter. It's like starting your day with a full battery, and that energy sustains you through whatever challenges come your way.

I've seen this firsthand. When I rush into my day without spending time with God, everything feels harder. Problems seem bigger, stress feels heavier, and I'm more prone to making mistakes. When I take just thirty minutes in the morning to pray and read the Bible, the difference is undeniable. My challenges may not disappear, but I face them with a sense of peace and clarity. I'm reminded that I'm not walking through life alone because God is with me, guiding me, and working behind the scenes in ways I can't always see.

Let me ask you this: what would happen if you gave your first moments of the day to God? Instead of scrolling through your phone, turning on the news, or diving straight into work, what if you spent that time in prayer? What if you opened the Bible and asked God to speak to you through His Word?

It doesn't have to be complicated. A simple conversation with God by inviting Him into your day can make all the difference. Think of it this way: the same God who keeps the universe in perfect order, who knows the names of every star in the sky, is offering to help you manage your time and responsibilities. Why wouldn't you take Him up on that?

Psalm 147:4 says, *"He determines the number of the stars and calls them each by name."* If God can handle the complexities of the universe, surely, He can handle the details of your life.

There's something deeply powerful about starting your day with prayer. It's like recalibrating your heart and mind to focus on what truly matters. When you talk to God about your concerns, you're acknowledging that He's in control, and not you. There's a peace that comes from knowing you don't have to have all the answers. God is already at work behind the scenes, orchestrating things for your good. Romans 8:28 assures us, *"We know that in all things God works for the good of those who love Him, who have been called according to His purpose."*

When we prioritize God, it's not just about what we gain, but it's about who we become. We become people of peace, people of purpose, and people who reflect God's love in everything we do. That peace allows us to handle life's challenges with grace. It helps us to be more present with our families, more productive at work, and more intentional with our time. It shifts our perspective from *"I have to do this all on my own"* to *"God is with me, and He will help me."* Isn't that what we all want? To feel empowered, focused, and at peace? To know that our lives are important to God, and that we're not just running in circles? When you keep God first, you're using your time with purpose. You're choosing to live a life that honors Him and reflects His goodness to the world.

So, let's make today count. Let's give our worries to God and trust Him to handle them. Let's spend time in His Word and invite Him into every detail of our lives. Let's keep Him first, knowing that when we do, everything else will fall into place.

FINAL THOUGHTS
Peace Begins With God

Time with the Lord clears your mind for efficiency.

- → Spending time with God brings peace, clarity, and focus for your day.

- → Make Jesus your first priority. He created time and helps life flow better.

- → Starting your morning with prayer and thanksgiving guards your heart and mind.

- → Today is the only moment you can work with, so honor God by making it count.

- → Trust God with your worries instead of trying to carry them alone.

- → God doesn't ask you to worry. He asks you to trust.

- → His peace will carry you through what your own strength can't.

ONE CONVERSATION AT A TIME

"There are 'friends' who destroy each other, but a real friend sticks closer than a brother."

- PROVERBS 18:24 (NLT)

I REMEMBER back in 2022, sometime around winter, I was out making a delivery to a few businesses in the Surprise, Arizona, area. At the time, there were many new developments going on, like coffee shops, restaurants, and little boutique stores, all popping up in this one area. Interestingly enough, the city of Surprise was considered the eighth fastest-growing city in the country. I didn't think much of it, just another growing part of town. There was one building in particular that got my attention.

It was this new coffee shop called Black Rock Coffee Bar, I wasn't familiar with it at first. In fact, I didn't even know what kind of place it was going to be. Honestly, I thought it was some kind of private cafe owned by that big investment company BlackRock, like a place they built just for their employees. Which sounds ridiculous now, but that's really what I assumed at the time. Twice a week, like clockwork, I found myself stopping by to deliver what appeared to be paperwork, registers, furniture, and little things that would help get this place up and running. That's all it was to me at the time, just another stop, much like all the other buildings I delivered to.

Little did I know, though, that this place was about to become something much more than just another spot on my delivery route. A few months later, once the coffee shop officially opened, I found myself walking through its doors, not as a delivery guy, but as a customer. I figured, why not? After all, I had been delivering to this place for months. I mean, if you think about it, I kind of helped build the place in a way. So, on my day off, I decided to stop by and check it out.

The moment I walked in, I noticed something. To my left, sitting at one of the tables, was an older gentleman. He had a cup of ice and a Pop-Tart, the kind they sell at the shop. As soon as I stepped in, while wearing a navy-blue Air Force Veteran cap, he looked up at me and said, "Hey, good morning."

I said "hey" back, grabbed my coffee, waved at him as I left, and went about my day. Didn't think much of it. Then, the next time I came back, he was there again, sitting in the same spot. Then again, the time after that. It became a routine twice a week, I'd stop in for coffee, and every time, I'd see him sitting in the same spot. Eventually, after about two weeks of this, I figured, why not sit down and talk?

His name was Roy Hurly Lukens, a United States veteran, an eighty-three-year-old man, just a kind, simple man. The kind of guy who doesn't try too hard, doesn't force anything, just real, genuine, and easy to talk to. Before I knew it, I found myself in a full conversation with him, learning about his time in the military, his background as an entrepreneur, and just his experiences in life.

It was funny because, as an author and entrepreneur myself, we had more in common than I expected. The conversation just flowed, no effort, no awkwardness, just two people talking and sharing stories. I didn't realize it at the time, but this simple, casual conversation was about to lead me to something even greater. Roy mentioned a Bible study that he was part of and said it took place at the Black Rock Coffee Bar every other Tuesday at 8:00 p.m. He invited me to join. The group was called "Tuesday Night Tombs," an older men's Bible study. It was for men 65 years and older, and they invited me to join to bring a younger perspective into the conversation.

I've always had a deep passion for preparing myself to become a pastor. It's something that's been on my heart for a long time. So, when Roy invited me to that Bible study, it felt like more than just an invitation. It felt intentional, like something bigger was at play. I accepted his invitation and went. Let me tell you, that one small connection led to something incredible.

Through Roy, I met new people. I found a community of like-minded individuals, people who were passionate about faith, about growth, about real, meaningful conversations. Only later did I realize Roy had already connected with Brandon, who was also part of the same Bible study. I found it inspiring to see Roy unite great men, and it all started with a simple "good morning" at a coffee shop.

It's often the small conversations and unplanned encounters we overlook that leave the deepest mark. Sometimes, those are the moments that change everything.

LEADING THE TUESDAY NIGHT TOMBS BIBLE STUDY

Over the next few weeks, the Bible study became a core part of my routine. Twice a month, I sat in that circle, surrounded by men who had lived through more than I could imagine. Men who had walked through hardships, victories, and long roads of faith.

Brandon began to notice something about me. He saw the way I engaged in the Bible study, the way I was passionate about Scripture, the way I loved to lead, and one day, he approached me with an idea.

"Hey, I've been thinking," he said, "would you be interested in leading this Bible study?"

"Yes, I would absolutely love to," I replied. Leading men of God had been on my heart for a long time, but the opportunity never presented itself, and the path wasn't clear. This invitation felt like the right place to begin.

By late 2024, I was leading the Tuesday Night Tombs Bible study at Black Rock Coffee, crafting seven-week series focused on topics like the Fruit of the Spirit, breaking down Scripture, and guiding discussions.

The power of one small connection is something I think back on often, like how one conversation turned into a Bible study, how one introduction became a friendship, and how one simple moment in a coffee shop turned into something that changed my life. That's the power of purposeful connections; they don't happen by accident.

They happen one small, intentional moment at a time. When you have the right people around you, such as individuals who build you up, challenge you, and walk alongside you in faith and in life, everything begins to change.

Even as an introvert, even as someone naturally quiet and reserved, I've come to see the beauty in selecting the right people. At the end of the day, life is just better with the right people, starting with one small connection at a time.

CHERISHING SMALL STEPS:
How Growth Happens Little by Little

When I first started leading the Tuesday Night Tombs Bible study at Black Rock Coffee, I wasn't necessarily good at speaking; it was quite difficult. I wasn't projecting my voice loudly enough, and because the coffee shop usually played loud music in the background, it made things even harder. We often asked the barista to turn it down a little.

So, I had to adjust how I led the study by speaking up. After about a month, I learned how to project my voice, speak with confidence, and engage with people in a way that made them feel seen. It didn't happen overnight. Every time I showed up to lead the study, one small improvement happened at a time. It wasn't something I just stepped into and was immediately good at, but I cherished the small steps, the little changes that made a difference.

I remember one of the first things that Brandon pointed out. There were only about four people attending that first Bible study, but he noticed something that I wasn't aware of. After the study, Brandon pulled me aside and said, "Hey, you're doing a great job, and I can tell the difference. You're learning, and you're growing. Just a suggestion, based on something I noticed earlier, that you only looked toward the front and the right side of the table the entire time. Try panning to the left too, so that everyone feels like they're a part of the conversation."

That might seem like a small thing, but it mattered. Little by little, week after week, I started making those adjustments. I became more aware of how I engaged the group. I worked on projecting my voice so that it could rise above the background noise. I noticed that I was slowly getting better.

SLOW GROWTH, BUT REAL GROWTH

I've always known that God called me to be a pastor, that He had something special for me. If I'm being honest, for most of my life, I never had the opportunity to lead. I've been a part of many mega-churches, especially during my time at Bible college in Tucson at Zion City Church. I was part of big events, national conventions, and countless Bible studies; I never led them.

The main reason might be that I had a speech impediment growing up. I used to stutter a lot, and because of that, I struggled to engage in conversations. Even maintaining a simple discussion was difficult.

AN UNFORGETTABLE GAME NIGHT

There was one night back in 2015, around the time I first started going to Zion City Church, when I was invited to a game night. I was still trying to find a sense of community, to figure out where I fit in. A group of guys invited me, and I figured, why not? Maybe this was my chance to finally connect. I didn't really know what to expect, but I showed up hoping for a fun, easygoing night. The pizza, the games, and the casual conversation all made it seem like a fun, easygoing night. I didn't expect anything complication, just a chance to relax and maybe connect with a few people. I didn't anticipate how loud, energetic, and socially overwhelming the night would be.

From the moment I walked in, I could tell these guys were wired for social energy. They weren't just talkative; they thrived in group settings, jumping from one conversation to another without missing a beat. They could react in real-time, joke freely, and speak without hesitation. I was the only introvert there. It felt like a nightmare.

We were in a living room, playing Mario Party on a GameCube, and the room was electric. Every time something happened in the game, whether someone won a round, lost a turn, or got knocked out of the lead, the guys were shouting, jumping, throwing their hands in the air, laughing like it was a stadium crowd, and there I was sitting there watching it all unfold. I wanted to join in. I wanted to feel as comfortable as they did. I wanted to laugh, talk, and throw in a joke without overthinking. I felt completely out of sync, as though I was buffering while everyone else was moving in real time.

Every time I thought of something to say, the words wouldn't come out fast enough. By the time I came up with the words, the conversation had already moved on, or someone else had already filled the silence. It kept happening. The more it happened, the more I shut down. I wasn't just quiet; I felt completely invisible.

As I sat there, something crept in, a mix of panic and isolation, like I was trapped in my own head with no way out. My hands were sweating, my heart was pounding, and my mind was racing. I kept telling myself to relax, enjoy the moment, and stop overthinking. No matter how hard I tried, I looked around the room, and wondered: Why does this have to be so difficult for me? Deep inside, I was very frustrated. I was mad. I knew that this wasn't just a one-time thing. It was something I had dealt with my entire life. I had prayed about it, begged God to make it easier for me to connect with people, and yet, there I was. Feeling like a complete outsider in what was supposed to be my community.

So, I asked the same question I'd asked so many times before: Why? Why does something as simple as joining a conversation feel impossible? Why do I have to fight for something that comes so naturally to others? I didn't get an answer that night. All I knew in that moment was I had never felt lonelier in a room full of people. Unfortunately, because of that, I didn't get many opportunities to lead a Bible study group. I wasn't asked to preach in my twenties, and I wasn't invited to give Sunday morning announcements. It's a hard reality, but it's true.

Now, God is allowing me to step into my calling. The most beautiful part was it didn't happen on a big stage. I didn't suddenly find myself leading a massive congregation or preaching to thousands of people. It started at a coffee shop, in a simple moment that marked a quiet beginning. That's what I've come to realize, that God often works in the small things.

There's a verse in the Bible that says, *"Do not despise these small beginnings, for the Lord rejoices to see the work begin"* (Zechariah 4:10). I think that's exactly what He's doing in my life.

SMALL STEPS LEAD TO BIG CHANGE

Looking back, it's incredible to see how small, consistent steps lead to real growth. Every week, I got just a little better. My voice became stronger. My pacing improved. I spoke more clearly. The stutter that I used to struggle with wasn't noticeable anymore. I even asked them. I remember saying, *"Are you sure you don't notice me stuttering?"* They told me, *"No, you sound natural. You're clear. The only thing was your voice projection, but you've improved so much."*

Week after week, it was the little things that made a difference. At first, I was only leading the Bible study. Over time, I was given more responsibility, and now I also manage the Bible study's social media and marketing. It's funny because digital marketing is something I've been trying to improve at, and now I have a chance to practice. I've started creating compelling videos, using different platforms to promote the study on Instagram, and helping to grow our reach. All of this happened one small step at a time.

THE BEAUTY OF SMALL GROWTH

I'll be honest: I'm not always a big fan of slow progress. Sometimes I wish things moved faster. I wish I could just step into something big right away. That's not how God is working in my life. He's teaching me to cherish the small steps, to appreciate the little improvements, to trust the process.

Maybe that's exactly what I need, because the smallest seed often becomes the biggest tree. I believe that those who experience small and slow growth often develop the deepest faith. As much as I might want things to happen faster, I'm grateful for this journey. I'm thankful for every small moment, every bit of progress, every piece of constructive criticism that's helping me grow into the person God is shaping me to be. I'll keep going, taking it one small step at a time.

UNPACKING UNCERTAINTY

What you thought was against you was designed for you. There are things I know now that I wish I had understood years ago. They would have made certain struggles easier to face and certain challenges less overwhelming. That's the thing about life; sometimes we don't see the purpose in what we're going through until much later, when the weight has lifted, the lessons are clearer, and the pain has settled into wisdom.

Looking back, I can see that the struggles I faced, both big and small, weren't just random obstacles meant to slow me down. They were preparation for something greater, something I couldn't yet see in the moment. Difficulties in life come in all shapes and sizes. Some people face massive challenges, like losing a loved one, battling deep anxiety, or wrestling with direction. Others face smaller, persistent battles, that may seem insignificant to outsiders but feel like impossible mountains in the moment. I've had my share of both. Some challenges felt monumental and made me question everything. Others were quiet, everyday struggles that still managed to weigh me down.

What I didn't realize at the time was that every one of those experiences, whether major setbacks or subtle frustrations, were shaping me, refining me, and preparing me for something more. There are seasons when life doesn't seem to make sense. The path feels blocked, and no matter how hard you push, you keep running into resistance. It's easy to assume you're not meant to move forward, that certain things just aren't for you. I've come to believe that many obstacles we face aren't walls meant to keep us out; they are steppingstones designed to strengthen us for what's ahead.

We often think we're waiting on God to move, but sometimes, He's waiting on us to be ready. What seems like delay is often preparation. He's allowing the struggle to mold you for something you can't yet see. There is always more happening than we can see with our physical eyes. There are things being put in place that we won't understand until later. It's in those in-between moments, when the struggle feels meaningless, when the effort feels wasted, that we must remind ourselves: nothing is random. Every hardship has a purpose.

Many of us sense something greater on the horizon. It's hard to explain, but you can feel it approaching, even if you don't know what it is. Often times, that feeling comes with resistance. Unexpected setbacks show up. Challenges you weren't prepared for seem to pop up out of nowhere. It's easy to think those things are distractions. What if they're part of the process? What if they're the very things that are strengthening you for the next season?

I've had to learn this lesson the hard way. I've struggled with feelings of inadequacy. For years, I felt like I was standing in front of a massive wall, too high to climb and too solid to break through. What I didn't see then was that the very wall I thought was blocking me was becoming a ramp, a launchpad into a new path. What once felt like a barrier was transforming into a pathway.

That's why I keep going. That's why I don't despise the slow process; I embrace it. One day, the future version of me will look back and say, *"I'm glad you didn't give up. I'm grateful you were intentional. Thank you for pushing through, even when it felt pointless."* That's what keeps me moving forward, because it's the awareness that the things I do today aren't just about today. Tomorrow doesn't exist yet, yesterday is already gone, and most of today hasn't even happened.

The future is shaped in this very moment, right now, not in days or hours, but in minutes and seconds, in the small unnoticed choices we continue to make. That's the beauty of it, because we have the power to shape the future. Not in some distant, vague way, but in this exact moment, in how we spend our time, in how we invest in ourselves, our dreams, our faith, and our relationships. Every decision adds up, and every moment builds toward something greater.

Eventually, those small steps, those everyday choices, will become something bigger than we ever imagined. That's the life God designed for us: a life of purpose, growth, and constant transformation. It's a life where we don't wait for things to happen, but of stepping forward, intentionally, into what's ahead.

CONCLUSION

There is something about life that we often overlook, not because we don't care, but because we've been conditioned to see things only in the way they've always been presented to us. We grow up believing that each day consists of twenty-four hours, that there are a set number of days in a week, months in a year, and that time moves forward in a structured, predictable way. The truth is that time is not just about the hours on a clock: it's about the moments you choose to own.

Life isn't lived in days; it's lived in small, intentional choices that accumulate over time and shape the future before it even arrives. Once you start seeing it that way, everything changes. You don't just have twenty-four hours in a day, you have countless *moments,* countless opportunities.

People tend to focus on the big picture, always looking ahead to some far-off vision of success, fulfillment, or happiness. The reality is your future is not built in the future. It's built *right now,* in the smallest of moments, in the simple choices you make today. What you decide to do with ten minutes could change the course of your entire life. It could be the difference between progress and stagnation, clarity and confusion, momentum and hesitation. When you truly grasp the power of a moment, you stop seeing time as something that just passes you by, and you start seeing it as something you *can create with*.

Your future isn't standing still and waiting for you to catch up; it's already moving with you, responding to every step you take. Every small decision, every moment of effort, every simple step you take is weaving together the life you're going to live tomorrow. So, when you wake up in the morning, don't just see another day ahead, see the *countless chances* you have to build something meaningful. It doesn't always have to be a massive step forward and it doesn't have to be groundbreaking. It just has to be intentional. That's where transformation happens, not in some distant future, not when circumstances become perfect or obstacles are removed, but right now, in this moment.

Too many people wait for the "right time" to start living fully, but the right time has always been now. It's easy to get caught up in the idea of transformation, to romanticize change and dream big. Real transformation begins when you learn to be present with the moments in front of you. Seeing them for what they are: building blocks, stepping stones, foundations. If you focus only on the destination, you'll miss the significance of the journey. If you embrace the journey, the destination will take care of itself.

Yes, there will be challenges. There will be setbacks and disappointments that make you question whether you're on the right path. That's not a sign to turn back, it's proof you're moving forward. Challenges belong to the process and help shape the path forward. Disappointments are part of the process and offer a chance to adjust your perspective while continuing with resilience.

Many people set out believing that if they're on the right path, everything should unfold effortlessly. That's not how great things are built. If you want fulfillment, expect the *obstacles*. Prepare for the resistance. I hope you can recognize that your purposeful struggles are shaping you, slowly breaking you into a better fit for what's ahead.

Longevity in any pursuit, whether personal, professional, or spiritual, comes from understanding that difficulty isn't failure. It's a sign that you're building something worthwhile. So, if you find yourself feeling stuck, discouraged, or uncertain about what's next, don't underestimate the power of the small choices in front of you. Don't wait around for clarity or motivation, and don't let the big picture overwhelm you. Take action, fuel your own drive, and focus on what's within your control right now.

Your life is not happening in some distant tomorrow. It's happening now. What you do with this moment matters more than you realize because it's leading you toward the future you were made for. That Future is not far off because it's already unfolding one moment at a time, so live and own your moment. Everything you've ever hoped for, everything you've ever envisioned for your life, begins the moment you choose to own it, build with it, and step into it.

NOTES AND RELIABLE SOURCES

An article published in *Psychology Today* by Leigh W. Jerome, Ph.D., on November 18, 2024, shows how worry can pull your focus away from the present moment. People with high levels of anxiety often focus on negative things, which makes it hard to enjoy what's happening now.

Worry keeps your thoughts locked on what *could* go wrong in the future, instead of allowing you to be at peace and enjoy today. It robs you of your present peace, and that's exactly what the enemy, the adversary, the devil wants. He wants to steal your peace. God wants you to have peace of mind.

How Worry Affects Focus:

- Anxiety makes you pay more attention to threats or negative things.
- This makes it hard to concentrate on what's happening right now.
- Instead of being present, you're stuck thinking about future problems.

Impact on Peace of Mind:

- Constant worrying means you're always preparing for the worst.
- This can prevent you from enjoying positive moments today.
- You miss out on being at peace because your mind is focused on potential future issues.

Why This Matters:

- Focusing on the future all the time can make you feel unsettled.
- It creates a cycle where you're always anxious about what's next.
- To find peace, it's important to break this cycle and focus on the present.

Worry robs you of the ability to be *in the moment*. It keeps you focused on potential future problems, making it hard to relax and enjoy life as it happens. This insight supports the idea that being worried can prevent you from experiencing peace and contentment today, aligning with the belief that the devil wants to steal your peace, but God desires you to have a peaceful mind and heart.

In the New Testament, the Greek term for "worry" is **merimnáō**, which comes from **merízō**, meaning "to *divide*," and **nous**, meaning "*mind*." This suggests that worry creates a divided mind, pulling thoughts in different directions and leading to distraction, anxiety, and mental unrest. This aligns with Jesus' words in Matthew 6:25-34, where He teaches not to worry about tomorrow, as it adds nothing to our lives.

In the Hebrew Bible, the word for anxiety or worry is **de'agah**, meaning distress or apprehension. Proverbs 12:25 states, "Anxiety in a man's heart weighs him down, but a good word makes him glad." This reflects how worry is often tied to fear and uncertainty.

Both biblical languages emphasize that worry is not just a fleeting thought; it is a state of mental division, a force that steals focus and peace.

A GIFT FOR YOU

While writing this book, a process that took me nearly two long years, I spent a great deal of time researching the Bible, searching for scriptures that would not only support the ideas in these pages but also bring guidance and encouragement to those who read them. Throughout the process, God continually downloaded new ideas into my heart and mind, often in unexpected moments: sometimes in the middle of the day, other times during quiet reflection, or even while I was working and going about my daily routine.

Through these revelations, I discovered incredible, profound scriptures that deeply inspired me and helped shape the message of this book. Many of these verses are not directly mentioned in the chapters you've just read, but they are just as powerful, and I've included them here as a gift for you. This collection of passages is meant to stay with you long after you've turned the final page. These scriptures that can serve as a foundation for living in the moment, making the most of today, and trusting God through every step of your journey.

I pray they encourage and strengthen you, just as they have strengthened me.

Scriptures on How Today Shapes Tomorrow
- *Galatians 6:7-9 – "Do not be deceived: God cannot be mocked. A man reaps what he sows."*

- *Proverbs 16:3 – "Commit your work to the Lord, and your plans will be established."*
- *Proverbs 24:27 – "Prepare your work outside; get everything ready for yourself in the field, and after that build your house."*
- *Psalm 90:12 – "Teach us to number our days, that we may gain a heart of wisdom."*
- *Ephesians 5:15-16 – "Look carefully then how you walk, not as unwise but as wise, making the best use of the time, because the days are evil."*
- *Matthew 6:34 – "Therefore do not worry about tomorrow, for tomorrow will worry about itself. Each day has enough trouble of its own."*
- *Luke 16:10 – "Whoever is faithful in very little is also faithful in much."*
- *2 Corinthians 9:6 – "Whoever sows sparingly will also reap sparingly, and whoever sows generously will also reap generously."*
- *Ecclesiastes 11:6 – "Sow your seed in the morning, and at evening let your hands not be idle, for you do not know which will succeed."*
- *James 4:13-15 – "You do not know what tomorrow will bring... Instead, you should say, 'If the Lord wills, we will live and do this or that.'"*

Scriptures on Small Moments and Their Impact

These verses highlight how small choices, small moments, and seemingly insignificant actions build a meaningful life.

- *Zechariah 4:10 – "Do not despise these small beginnings, for the Lord rejoices to see the work begin."*

- *Proverbs 6:6-8 – "Go to the ant, you sluggard; consider its ways and be wise! It has no commander, no overseer or ruler, yet it stores its provisions in summer and gathers its food at harvest."*
- *Matthew 13:31-32 – "The kingdom of heaven is like a mustard seed... the smallest of all seeds, yet when it grows, it is the largest of garden plants."*
- *1 Kings 19:11-12 – "The Lord was not in the wind, the earthquake, or the fire, but in a still small voice."*
- *Mark 12:41-44 – The story of the widow's two small coins—small in amount but great in significance.*
- *Ecclesiastes 3:1 – "For everything, there is a season, and a time for every purpose under heaven."*
- *Luke 21:1-4 – "This poor widow has put in more than all the others..." (The power of small sacrifices.)*
- *Matthew 25:21 – "Well done, good and faithful servant. You have been faithful over a little; I will set you over much."*
- *John 6:9-11 – "There is a boy here who has five barley loaves and two fish, but what are they for so many?" (Jesus multiplies what seems insignificant.)*
- *Proverbs 10:4 – "Lazy hands make for poverty, but diligent hands bring wealth."*

Scriptures on Handling Expectations, Disappointments, and Obstacles

These passages teach how to expect challenges instead of assuming only good things, so you can persevere with wisdom and endurance.

- *John 16:33 – "In this world, you will have trouble. But take heart! I have overcome the world."*

- *James 1:2-4 – "Consider it pure joy, my brothers and sisters, whenever you face trials of many kinds, because you know that the testing of your faith produces perseverance."*
- *1 Peter 4:12-13 – "Beloved, do not be surprised at the fiery trial when it comes upon you to test you, as though something strange were happening to you."*
- *Romans 5:3-5 – "We rejoice in our sufferings, knowing that suffering produces endurance, and endurance produces character, and character produces hope."*
- *Ecclesiastes 7:14 – "When times are good, be happy; but when times are bad, consider: God has made the one as well as the other."*
- *Proverbs 3:5-6 – "Trust in the Lord with all your heart and lean not on your own understanding; in all your ways submit to him, and he will make your paths straight."*
- *2 Corinthians 4:16-18 – "So we do not lose heart. Though our outer self is wasting away, our inner self is being renewed day by day."*
- *Matthew 7:24-27 – The wise man built his house on the rock, expecting storms to come, while the foolish man built on sand.*
- *Psalm 34:18-19 – "The Lord is close to the brokenhearted and saves those who are crushed in spirit."*
- *Isaiah 41:10 – "Do not fear, for I am with you; do not be dismayed, for I am your God."*

RECOMMENDED READINGS FOR FURTHER STUDY

I've been a slow reader for most of my life, and to be honest, it's still something I struggle with. Sometimes when I read out loud, I lose my breath, or I get tongue-tied. If I'm not careful, I even start to feel lightheaded because I can't always control my breathing. There are moments when I lose track of words, when my eyes move faster than my mind can process, or when I have to reread something just to fully understand it.

Reading has never been easy for me, but I've learned that it's not about speed or how well you read; it's about what you take from it. Books have helped me grow, think more deeply, and sharpen my mind, even when the process felt slow. So, I encourage everyone to read more, not to be faster or better, but to be inspired, informed, and strengthened in way you might not expect.

 If I can do it, so can you.

For those who want to go deeper into these topics, here are some books that align with the principles in this book.

Recommended Reading

- *The Ruthless Elimination of Hurry*—John Mark Comer
- *The Time Paradox*—Philip Zimbardo
- *Atomic Habits*—James Clear
- *The Compound Effect*—Darren Hardy
- *The Obstacle Is the Way*—Ryan Holiday
- *The Purpose Driven Life*—Rick Warren
- *The Holy Spirit*—John Bevere
- *The 10X Rule*—Grant Cardone

LINKS TO RELIABLE SOURCES

- https://hearttreasure.net/prayer-is-the-way-to-restore-peace/

This link supports page 48 on how prayer helps you have a peace of mind

- https://www.theverge.com/2015/5/14/8605597/elon-musk-discusses-spacex-tesla-near-bankruptcy?

This link supports page 106, discussing Elon Musk's major decision to choose between saving SpaceX or Tesla

- https://www.shamashalidina.com/blog/ellen-langer?

This link supports page 42 with Dr, Ellen Langer, talking about mindfulness.

- https://news.stanford.edu/stories/2009/08/multitask-research-study-082409?

This link supports page 44, a study from Stanford University on multitasking

- https://www.sciencedirect.com/science/article/abs/pii/S0005796720302138

This link supports page 73 with Behaviour Research and Therapy on worrying

- https://www.breath-body-mind.com/richard-brown-md?

This link supports page 80 with Dr. Richard P. Brown regarding breathing

Dr. Patricia's co-authored book chapter description supports page 81 on proper breathing

Dr. Patricia Gerbarg's co-authored book, The Healing Power of the Breath, includes a powerful chapter, chapter 4, The Winds of Change discusses how breath practices can be customized to address challenges like anxiety, insomnia, depression, and trauma. https://www.amazon.com/Healing-Power-Breath-Techniques-Concentration/dp/1590309022

- https://www.universityofcalifornia.edu/news/bursts-exercise-boost-cognitive-function-ucsb-neuroscientists-find?

This link supports page 101 with the October 17, 2024, study by University of California on short bursts of exercises

- https://jamanetwork.com/journals/jamanetworkopen/fullarticle/2831010?

This link supports page 102 on the March 5, 2025, research from JAMA Network Open regarding memory loss

- https://www.cuimc.columbia.edu/news/even-old-brains-can-make-new-neurons-study-finds

This link supports page 135, research by Columbia University suggesting that doing something new can generate new neural activity.

- https://law.arizona.edu/news/2021/11/partnership-aims-combat-light-pollution-through-development-open-access-database?

This link supports page 146, The University of Arizona astronomy students study the stars at night, requiring the city of Tucson to dim their city nights.

- https://hsph.harvard.edu/news/spirituality-better-health-outcomes-patient-care/?

This Link supports page 204, a study by Harvard T.H Chan School of Public Health. Prioritizing a spiritual live can increase overall well-being and positive mental health

- https://www.psychologytoday.com/us/blog/the-stories-we-tell/202411/how-to-live-in-the-present-moment-and-stop-worrying-so-much?

  This link supports page 221, research in Psychology Today by Leigh W. Jerome, Ph.D., and published on November 18, 2024, shows how worry can pull your focus away from the present moment

- https://www.helpguide.org/mental-health/stress/benefits-of-mindfulness?

  This link supports page 67, a fact from HelpGuide.org, which includes research from Harvard Health, shows that being completely engaged—even during stressful times—can increase mindfulness

- https://www.forbes.com/sites/tonifitzgerald/2024/07/16/study-americans-are-watching-less-and-less-tv-heres-why/?

  This link supports page 61, rising prices are reducing how much time people spend watching TV

- https://www.cnbc.com/2018/06/19/how-elon-musk-founded-zip2-with-his-brother-kimbal.html

  This link supports page 105. CNBC Make It Article mentions Elon Musk slept on his office couch with his brother before expanding his company.

- https://abcnews.go.com/Business/tiktok-china/story?id=108111708#:~:text=More%20noticeable%20differences%20between%20TikTok,Sovereignty%2C%22%20told%20ABC%20News.

Page 65 highlights how China's version of TikTok, called Douyin, focuses on discipline and learning, and this source supports that comparison with how it differs from the U.S. version. Aynne Kokas discusses how China has different laws on how companies target children with social media time limits.

- https://www.queensu.ca/gazette/stories/discovery-thought-worms-opens-window-mind

  This link to Queen's University study supports page 47 when discussing the idea of having around 6,000 thoughts per day.

- https://milehighpsychiatry.com/spring-cleaning-for-your-mind-mental-health-benefits-of-decluttering/#:~:text=Decluttering%20helps%20clear%20mental%20space,You%20a%20Sense%20of%20Accomplishment

  This link by Mile High Psychiatry, supports how decluttering your surroundings can improve mental peace by storing up mental energy and releasing emotional baggage. Page 141

- https://www.verywellmind.com/5-second-rule-for-procrastination-11706675

  This link supports page 175 when talking about The 5 Second Rule book. This speaks on how it engages the prefrontal cortex and helps you take small initiatives.